COMPETING FOR CAESAR

COMPETING FOR CAESAR

RELIGION AND POLITICS IN POSTCOLONIAL ZAMBIA

EDITED BY

CHAMMAH J. KAUNDA

MARJA HINFELAAR

FORTRESS PRESS
MINNEAPOLIS

COMPETING FOR CAESAR
Religion and Politics in Postcolonial Zambia

Cover image: © iStock 2020; Safari inspiration stock photo by momnoi

Cover design: Kristin Miller

Paperback ISBN: 978-1-5064-6151-9

eBook ISBN: 978-1-5064-6152-6

CONTENTS

FOREWORD

Mika Vähäkangas

The relationship between Christianity and politics in Zambia is quite interesting and complex at three levels. First, Christianity, modern statecraft, and politics are intrinsically interwoven since the very beginning. Second, the history and present relationship between Christianity and politics in Africa are complex, contended, and even confusing. Third, Zambia is one of the countries in Africa where these complexities and contestations are most obvious.

The modern state structures and, thereby, modes of political organizations and politics in general are largely a product of the European cultural sphere. This applies also to the basic values undergirding the Western political system despite the seemingly secular and at times even non-religious outlooks. Even the imagined dichotomy between religion and politics is a part of the dialogue between Christian theologies and modern politics. Paradoxically, these intentions to separate religion and politics are expressions of the inevitable intermingling of Christian theological and Western political thoughts. The roots of this thought can be traced to the New Testament (e.g. Matt 22:21), radical Reformation, and the reassessment of the role of religion in politics after the wars of religion.

In modern times, national state has become the standard political unit fueled with its nationalism. The prime models of the concept of nationhood are found in the Bible and likewise, the word *nation* is used in early Bible translations.[1] The narrative of the chosen people,[2] consisting of twelve tribes, yet having the horizontal sense of belonging together to the nation of Israel, is paradigmatic.[3] The Hebrew Bible naturally does not

1 Adrian Hastings, *The Construction of Nationhood: Ethnicity, Religion and Nationalism* (Cambridge: Cambridge University Press, 1997).

2 Anthony D. Smith, *Chosen Peoples: Sacred Sources of National Identity* (Oxford: Oxford University Press, 2003); Hastings, *Construction of Nationhood.*

3 Conor Cruise O'Brien, *God Land: Reflections on Religion and Nationalism* (Lincoln NE: IUniverse, 1999).

contain any modern concept of nationhood, but has served as a source for its formation. The foundational role of the Bible is hardly surprising because the production of literature in national languages was a means of forming the nation.[4] This means that the idea of nationhood already existed but the nation as imagined community was still in the making. The Bible, hymnals, liturgies, and other religious literature dominated the literary scene first. In many cases, after the Bible translation, one could learn to read in one's mother tongue, or a language, or dialect resembling it. Thus, the roots of European national political thought are deep in the Bible. Carl Schmitt goes even so far as to maintain that "all significant concepts of the modern theory of the state are secularized theological concepts not only because of their historical development . . . but also because of their systematic structure."[5]

Colonial powers implemented the modern structures of administration in their colonies—except for citizenship to their subjects. Instead of political subjects, they were treated as colonial subjects. Thus, inasmuch as the colonial powers were democracies, they violated the very core values of their political system. The role of the Christian missions in the colonies could be described as complex complicity. The attitude of the missions and missionaries related to colonial oppressive and exploitative policies and practices varied from full cooperation and support to opposition within the given political framework with different variations of milder critical positions in between. While it was common for missionaries to teach that Christians, or at least ordained ministers or priests, should abstain from politics; yet, a considerable section of early independence leaders were running mission schools, and not government schools, like Kaunda, Nyerere, or Senghor. The mission schools were numerous, but the government schools were producing administrational personnel and therefore more apt to produce leaders.

With independence, the scenario changed. While Christianity was the favored religion in many colonies (with Islam in that position in some, especially French colonies), now it is viewed with suspicion by many among the national elites. Likewise, the former colonial masters shifted their position almost overnight in terms of political representation. Democracy for Africans that they had been opposing so vehemently in the colonies, became a major concern when Communist rule turned threatening. Meanwhile, Christianity was expanding rapidly, which also meant the

---

4 Benedict Anderson, *Imagined Communities: Reflections on the Origin and Spread of Nationalism*, 2nd ed. (London: Verso, 2006); Smith, *Chosen Peoples*; Hastings, *Construction of Nationhood.*

5 Carl Schmitt, *Political Theology: Four Chapters on the Concept of Sovereignty* (Cambridge, MA: MIT Press, 1985), 36.

visible return of religion in African politics. Christianity had actually never been away from politics due to the over-representation of Christian politicians and the same resulted in the interweaving of Christianity and statecraft.

The relationship between Christianity and politics in the nation of Zambia was akin to other major Christian African countries—Christianity that is embedded in the public culture alongside religious pluralism and toleration. After Kenneth Kaunda's regime toying with scientific socialism, President Chiluba's declaration of Zambia as a Christian nation in 1991 was a game changer. This declaration was supported by the Evangelicals and the Pentecostals whereas the Catholic and mainline Protestant churches initially rejected the move and spoke for a pluralist society.[6] Not only the tension between secular or even irreligious politics and Christianity, but also the state of ideological contestations within Christianity between old school apolitical approaches versus liberation theology and traditional pastoral approach versus charismatic healing was seen in the career of Emmanuel Milingo.[7] Additionally, in Zambia, the rise of Pentecostalism in politics has led itself to be contentious among the most visible in Africa.

This book you hold is of immense importance and interest, as all the three levels mentioned above are dealt with in depth. It sheds light on the conundrum of Christianity and politics in present-day Zambia from various spectrums of perspectives, offering detailed analysis from within. Academia has long been occupied with the intermingling of religion and politics; in Islam, it is labeled as Islamism. At the same time, the inherent religious nature of and Christian influence in politics in the West has flown under the radar. Western political structures and cultures have been so hegemonic in political thinking that the normative narrative of secular politics has been the global canon. This has been the case despite the conflicting historical and practical evidences. Several African countries, with Zambia on the fore, make this obvious. Therefore, this book reads not only as a contribution to understanding Zambian or African politics and religion, but also as a contribution to political science in general. Europe, North America, and South America, with their full visibility of religion in politics have a reason to pay attention to Africa with more experience, expertise, and sensitivity on this topic.

---

6 Marja Hinfelaar, "Debating the Secular in Zambia: The Response of the Catholic Church to Scientific Socialism and Christian Nation, 1976–2006," in *Christianity and Public Culture in Africa*, ed. Harri Englund (Athens, OH: Ohio University Press, 2016), 50–66.

7 Gerrie ter Haar, *Spirit of Africa: The Healing Ministry of Archbishop Milingo of Zambia* (London: Hurst, 1992).

ACKNOWLEDGMENTS

Many of the chapters in this volume have their origin in the work presented at the African Association for the Study of Religions (AASR) biennial conference, *Revisiting Religions, Politics, and The State in Africa and African Diaspora*. The conference was held in Lusaka, Zambia, August 1–4, 2018. It was co-sponsored by the International Association for the History of Religions (IAHR) and is recognized as an IAHR Regional Conference. We are grateful to the former president, Prof. Elias Bongmba, the vice president of AASR, Dr. Damaris Seleina Parsitau, and the local organizing committee, of which the editors of this volume Marja Hinfelaar was the chairperson and Chammah J. Kaunda was a member, for allowing us to have our own panel that focused on "Religion and Politics in Zambia."

Chammah J. Kaunda expresses his gratitude to Prof. Soo-Young Kwon, the dean; Prof. Samuel Y. Pang; Prof. Koog-Pyoung Hong, the associate dean; Prof. Young-Gweon You; and Prof. Hyun-Sook Kim, the associate dean, for your constant encouragement. As respected members of Yonsei University, your thoughts carry a lot of significance. I have been truly humbled by your confidence in my intellectual abilities, and promise to continue doing my best always. Thank you for your confidence in me and standing with me.

Additionally, Chammah J. Kaunda is grateful to Yonsei University for the generous grant for 2019 New Faculty Research Seed Funding (March 1, 2019–April 1, 2020) and Yonsei University Future-Leading Research Initiative—New Faculty Grant Program [2020–22–0103].

CONTRIBUTORS

Adriaan van Klinken is an associate professor of Religion and African Studies at the University of Leeds.

Austin Mumba Cheyeka is an associate professor in the Department of Religious Studies at the University of Zambia.

Bernhard Udelhoven is a Catholic priest and a member of the Society of the Missionaries of Africa. He has lived in Zambia since 1989 and he currently works at St. Lawrence Parish, Misisi Compound, Lusaka.

Chammah J. Kaunda is an assistant professor of World Christianity and Theology in the College of Theology/United Graduate School of Theology, Yonsei University, Republic of Korea.

Devison Telen Banda is a lecturer in New Testament and Political Science at Justo Mwale University, Lusaka, Zambia.

Elizabeth Sheridan Sperber is an assistant professor of Political Science at the University of Denver.

Erin Hern is an assistant professor of Political Science at the Maxwell School for Citizenship and Public Affairs at Syracuse University, specializing in African Politics.

Godfrey Msiska is a lecturer and head of Department for School of Theology at Evangelical University, Ndola, Zambia. He is an ordained minister in the Uniting Presbyterian Church in Southern Africa.

Jackie Mapulanga-Hulston is a lecturer in the Faculty of Business and Law at Curtin University, Australia.

Johanneke Kroesbergen-Kamps is a research associate at the University of Pretoria, who taught Sociology and Research Methods at Justo Mwale University in Lusaka, Zambia.

Jonathan Kangwa is registrar at the UCZ University in Zambia who is currently a visiting scholar at Westminster College in Cambridge, United Kingdom.

Joseph Chita is a lecturer in the School of Education, Department of Religious Studies, at the University of Zambia.

Joseph Darius Simukonda is from Zambia who is currently serving as a Congregation Minister at Lubuto UCZ in Ndola/Zambia.

Judith Lubasi Ilubala-Ziwa is a lecturer and former head of the Department of Religious Studies at the University of Zambia (UNZA).

Marja Hinfelaar is the director of Research and Programs at Southern African Institute for Policy and Research (SAIPAR) in Lusaka, Zambia.

Mika Vähäkangas is professor in Mission Studies and Ecumenics at Lund University, Sweden. He has been a lecturer at Makumira University College of Tumaini University, Tanzania, as well as Helsinki University, Finland, and president of the International Association for Mission Studies.

Mutale Mulenga Kaunda is currently a freelance researcher living in South Korea who has published numerous articles and book chapters focusing on the intersection of gender, sexuality, religion, culture, and women's work in Africa.

Nelly Mwale is a special research Fellow and lecturer in the Department of Religious Studies at the University of Zambia in Lusaka, Zambia.

INTRODUCTION: RELIGION AND POLITICS IN POSTCOLONIAL ZAMBIA

Chammah J. Kaunda
Marja Hinfelaar

Scholars have argued that the reason religion and public life have remained inseparable in Africa, Zambia in particular, is because "it is largely through religious ideas that Africans think about the world today."[1] Since the nineteenth century, Zambia has seen major political and societal transformations, from anti-colonial politics that resulted in independence from British colonial imperialism to defeating one of Africa's longest-serving authoritarian presidents, Kenneth Kaunda, who ruled for twenty-seven years, and to ushering in the process of democratization in 1991. In all these political developments, religion has played a vital role and remains visible in postcolonial neocolonial Zambian public life. The Declaration of Zambia as a Christian nation (hereafter, the Declaration) was an affirmation of the significance of religious presence in the public imaginary and its potent political power. However, Christianity's seemingly political guardianship has not only been utilized as a cultural tool for legitimizing state power, but also in promoting an apparent religious hierarchy in which some traditions have positioned themselves as hegemonic by seeking to subordinate minority religious groups, especially those who perceived themselves as architects and protectors of Zambian Christian nationalism.[2]

---

1 Stephen Ellis and Gerrie ter Haar, *Worlds of Power: Religious Thought and Political Practice in Africa* (London: C. Hurst, 2004), 2.

2 Adriaan van Klinken, "Homosexuality, Politics and Pentecostal Nationalism in Zambia," *Studies in World Christianity* 20, no. 3 (2014): 259–281; Adriaan van Klinken, "Pentecostalism, Political Masculinity and Citizenship: The Born-again Male Subject as Key to Zambia's National Redemption," *Journal of Religion in Africa* 46, nos. 2/3 (2016): 129–57.

Thus, the role of religion in Zambian public life has not always been constructive. With all its applauded contribution to the struggle against colonialism and Kaunda's authoritarian rule and the rise of modern democracy,[3] religion has also contributed to endorsing and perpetuating postcolonial autocratic tendencies among Zambian politicians and clandestine denial of human rights for some minority groups.[4] The question most scholars have faced is how religious leaders can emphasize the progressive role of religion beyond self-interest and challenge dominant discourses in which religion is largely associated with conflict, competition, intolerance, social status, and promotion of fundamentalist ideas that legitimize political powers.

This project brings together key scholars, both Zambians and non-Zambians, who have been working on various issues related to religion and public life in Zambia. The bulk of the papers in this volume were presented at the panel under the theme, "Religion and Politics in Zambia," during the African Association for the Study of Religions (AASR) Biennial Conference that took place in Lusaka, Zambia, August 1–4, 2018. In keeping with the panel's aims, this volume explores the interplay between religion and politics in Zambian society and how these religions manage and negotiate their religious identities in public life. It evaluates recent religious dynamics in the nation's political life and considers what constructive role religion could play to promote an alternative political vision that could subvert neocolonialism.

The contributions to this volume explored various questions such as: How do different religions define and are engaged in national politics in Zambia? What is their religious basis for engaging in politics? Can the role of various religious traditions in Zambian politics lead to the emergence of an alternative political vision to neocolonialism? In what ways are religion positively affecting the political orientation of Zambian society? Are there ways in which various religious groups could interact to evolve innovative and inventive ideas for religious and political interaction? How can we define political role of religion in Zambia? What forms of political imaginations are promoted by various religious groups in Zambia? What

3 Chammah J. Kaunda, "'The Altars are Holding the Nation in Captivity': Zambian Pentecostalism, Nationality, and African Religio-Political Heritage," *Religions* 9, no. 5 (2018). http://www.mdpi.com/2077-1444/9/5/145/htm.

4 Paul Gifford, *African Christianity: Its Public Role* (London: Hurst, 1998); Isabel Apawo Phiri, "President Frederick J.T. Chiluba of Zambia: The Christian Nation and Democracy," *Journal of Religion in Africa* 33, no. 4 (2003): 401–428; David M. Gordon, *Invisible Agents: Spirits in a Central African History* (Ohio: Ohio University Press, 2012); Chammah J. Kaunda, *The Nation That Fears God Prospers: A Critique of Zambian Pentecostal Theopolitical Imaginations* (Minneapolis, MN: Fortress Press, 2018).

are some of the political strategies and approaches that various groups deploy in their quest to influence the politics? In what ways do various religious groups act to create political values and morals for promotion of the common good? What are the religious, social, economic, and political factors influencing Zambian religious ideas? How does religion seek to contribute to the process of democratization and political transformation?

Besides being leading voices, the contributors also showcase the breadth and variety of disciplinary backgrounds that enhance our understanding of religion and politics in contemporary globalized society. There are perspectives from history, religious studies, anthropology, sociology, theology, philosophy, political science, and international law. This shows that there have been lively debates on the intersecting systems of religion and politics in Zambia. It also elucidates the interdisciplinary nature of religion and politics. In collating such a wide variety of perspectives, the volume demonstrates the need for intentional inter-and-trans-disciplinary approaches in the study of religion and politics in Zambia.

The volume has included and recognized the fact that for too long, research on religion and politics in Zambia has been dominated by Western scholars. This volume has given an epistemological preference to the voice of Zambian scholars. This is important in the Zambian search for intellectual representation in global society. This clearly acknowledges that production of knowledge is political, value-laden, and interest-based. As an African proverb goes, "Until lions have their own historians, tales of the hunt will always glorify the hunter." Production of knowledge by the powerful sometimes has only worked to reinforce an ever-widening chasm of inequalities and knowledge injustice in contemporary research.[5] We perceive this volume as *insaka*[6]—a Zambian scholar's space of critical and analytical dialogue on issues affecting the nation in which non-Zambian scholars have also a critical role to play in enhancing Zambian scholarship. Therefore, epistemological privilege given to Zambian scholars in this volume refers not only to an ethical commitment to development of Zambian scholarship but also privileging the voice of Zambian scholars. This means non-Zambian allies who have contributed to this volume were either working in collaboration with Zambian scholars or are "already" promoting Zambian scholarship. Thus, the voices of non-Zambian allies in this volume echo the intellectual solidarity that is already existing among Zambian scholars.

5 Chammah J. Kaunda, "On the Road to Emmaus: Together towards Life as Conversation Partner in Missiological Research," *International Review of Mission* 106, no. 1 (June 2017): 34–50.

6 Insaka is a Bemba term that describes a traditional open hut in the middle of the village. It is a place to come together to eat, celebrate, teach, resolve issues, and dialogue on important issues affecting the community.

This volume is divided into three parts. The opening part interrogates, "the Christian nation" as understood in Zambia. In chapter one, Jackie Mapulanga-Hulston argues that almost three decades since Zambia was declared a Christian nation in 1991 by the second republican president, Frederick T.J. Chiluba, the underlying intention of the declaration remains unclear. Mapulanga-Hulston discovers that while politicians have leveraged the declaration for their political mileage, the church has failed to capitalize on, and use the declaration for *collaborative prophetic engagements with the state*. The church remains uninformed on becoming relevant through asking critical questions pertaining to religious affairs in the country, as this is an area that affects their beliefs. The church must redefine its missional praxis in Zambia, as religion too plays a decisive role in the political and social life of the country, particularly with the establishment of the Ministry of Religious Affairs and National Guidance. Chapter two pushes the discussion of the first chapter forward as Nelly Mwale, Joseph Chita, and Austin Cheyeka explore how the formation of the Ministry of National Guidance and Religious Affairs (MNGRA) has set a new tone for church-state relations in contemporary Zambia. Informed by prophetic realism theory, they draw on qualitative data through thematic analysis. Their findings reveal that rather than uniting the churches, the MNGRA contributed to a polarization and compromising the prophetic voice of the church. In other words, the new religious developments that have emerged as a result of the creation of the MNGRA have contributed to unawesome relations between the church and the state in Zambia.

In the third chapter, based on the new religious development in Zambia, Chammah J. Kaunda analyzes various responses of Zambian Pentecostals to the Declaration of the National Day of Prayer and Fasting. Drawing evidence from empirical data, Kaunda establishes that there are several Christians seeking to engage in the Day of Prayer through activism, in order to impact the nation in concrete ways. They are seeking a paradigm shift from empty-talk prayer to a socio-politically engaged prayer that demands an alternative political vision for the nation. Chapter four, another chapter with a similar focus on prayer by Jonathan Kangwa, argues that prayer in Zambia is implicated in the legitimization of political power. Employing anthropological and missiological approaches, he concludes that politicians in Zambia are using prayer to legitimize their political claims and win the support of electorates.

In chapter five, Devison Telen Banda raises concerns on the use of worship spaces as polling stations during political elections. Banda argues that this phenomenon is part of the wider question of how politics and religion relate in Zambia. He notes that such a trend is growing, because of the emerging opinion of some church leaders that usage of worship spaces as polling station is part of giving to "Caesar what belongs to Caesar and to God what belongs to God." Such tendencies however, lead to divided opinions among some followers and fail to distinguish politics from religion. Churches as religious spaces that host elections in this way are deemed politically partisan. The study concludes with a call for maturity toward the practice through propositions that curb extremisms on both sides.

The second part engages Zambian politics as defined by religious worldview in relation to social issues. The opening chapter by Adriaan van Klinken examines the role of religion, specifically Christianity, in the politics of sexuality in postcolonial Zambia. Building on Basile Ndjio's account of sexual politics and postcolonial nationalism in the context of Cameroon, van Klinken applies four strategies distinguished by Ndjio to the Zambian context: the sublimation of procreative and reproductive sexuality; the essentialization and racialization of native Africans' sexuality; the segregation and symbolic "othering" of homosexuals; and the criminalization and demonization of homoeroticism. He observes that these strategies manifest themselves in unique, yet, interrelated ways in the Kaunda era of Zambian humanism and in the era of Christian nationalism since President Chiluba's time. He highlights the considerable influence of Christianity, especially in its pentecostal form, on Zambian politics and nationalism, including on nationalist politics of sexuality and the opposition against sexual minorities.

Chammah J. Kaunda, Nelly Mwale, Mutale Mulenga Kaunda, and Joseph Chita in chapter seven apply a life trajectory approach to analyze the life of the minister of MNGRA, Rev. Godfridah Sumaili, that mirrors the intersection of religion, gender, and politics in contemporary Zambia's public space. The chapter draws insights from a qualitative narrative research in which data were collected through content analysis of representations on religion, gender, and politics in the media. Through the different roles she had played in the corporate world, church, and government as a banker, clergy, and first minister of the Ministry of Religious Affairs and National affairs respectively, it is established that Rev. Sumaili's narrative in the media reveals the pentecostal women's active involvement in politics and raises an ongoing debate on how religion and politics relate in the Zambian context. At the same time, the narrative pointed to relevance of a gendered religion to politics in contemporary Zambia by reflecting how a woman minister's trajectory cemented religion and politics in Zambia.

In chapter eight, Godfrey Msiska analyzes the intersectionality of religion, human rights, and politics in postcolonial Zambia. He argues for constitutional reforms of human rights in the religiously pluralistic Zambia. In this era of sovereign and universalization of human rights, the monopolized unitary religious identity of Christianity on legislation and governance is not justifiable. He underlines that, if religion is true to itself, it should not allow its usage for political gain nor should it seek to assume political power to advance its goals. To do otherwise will set the platform for abuse of human rights.

In chapter nine, Judith Lubasi Ilubala-Ziwa focuses on the interplay of religion, education, and politics amidst conflicting views on the role of religion in Zambian politics. She argues that these social institutions could be complementary, though in some settings they may have antagonistic relationships. In Zambia, religion has been a part of different spheres of life including education and politics. Thus, religion, education, and politics tend to reinforce each other. She proposes a cyclical model relationship of religion-education-politics that focuses on creating a critical mass of people with shared consciousness toward holistic development.

The next two chapters discuss the relationship between witchcraft and politics as appear to be intertwined in Zambian politics. In chapter ten, Bernhard Udelhoven argues that witchcraft can delegitimize political authority in direct ways through political framing; yet more indirectly, where the state, while legitimizing itself through religious discourse, proves incapable of dealing with "witchcraft out of control" that impact on people's day-to-day affairs. In the "Christian Nation," Christianity not only legitimizes the state but is also supposed to keep occult threats at bay. Have state and citizens ever arrived at the ideal of a moral community that has found a common answer to its occult threats? Through analysis of four case studies on witchcraft in a rural community, Udelhoven discovered that the "local community" was pluralistic and did not allow any single discourse to gain a monopoly in dealing with the occult forces. He concludes that "witchcraft out of control" did not delegitimize the state even though the answer to witchcraft was rarely the Christian faith. Similarly, Johanneke Kroesbergen-Kamps in chapter eleven advances the argument to accusations of Satanism against politicians in Zambia. Kroesbergen-Kamps discusses the function of these accusations in the contemporary political debates in the country, and places these accusations in a historical framework. She notes that even in the past, political leaders or chiefs have been rumored to rely on extraordinary spiritual powers. What is new about the current accusations of Satanism is that they are centered on urban worlds of meaning and show a profound disappointment in political affairs.

The third part presents three case studies of how the public church engages with politics in contemporary Zambia. In chapter twelve, Chammah J. Kaunda and Marja Hinfelaar argue that the Declaration has brought identity of politics to the fore, and increased religious competition, and polarization of engagement in Zambian politics, as witnessed in the 2016 elections. Using the Roman Catholic Church and Pentecostalism, Kaunda and Hinfelaar stress that the ever-increasing politicization among churches in Zambian public spheres is part of evolution and intensification in competitive identity of politics in the ongoing religious battle for representation and power.

In chapter thirteen, Elizabeth Sheridan Sperber and Erin Hern affirm the prominence of Pentecostalism in Zambia's public sphere since the late 1980s. They contend that a dearth of reliable data, however, has constrained investigation of the potential influence of these religious movements on political attitudes and participation. They analyze original data from a stratified random sample of 1,500 Zambians collected after Zambia's historic 2011 elections. The findings demonstrate that Zambian Pentecostals reported higher levels of political interest and participation than other Zambian Christians. Pentecostals also shared partisan preferences, which is consistent with scholarship that views Pentecostalism as a politically salient identity linked to party politics. Despite high levels of political engagement, however, Pentecostals were less likely to contact elected officials. This finding accords with ethnographic accounts of pentecostal pastors as political interlocutors for politically mobilized congregations.

In the final chapter, Joseph Darius Simukonda and Jonathan Kangwa employ decolonial public theology to examine the United Church of Zambia's (UCZ) political engagement in Zambia. Based on qualitative method in the generation and analysis of data, Simukonda and Kangwa demonstrate that the UCZ's Christian identity in politics legitimizes political powers. They postulate the need for the UCZ to move toward transformational public engagement—an approach that can empower the church to be a voice of the voiceless by way of exposing systems, structures, policies, institutions, and powers that could deny people the fullness of life.

PART I: INTERROGATING "THE CHRISTIAN NATION"

1

THE DECLARATION OF ZAMBIA AS A CHRISTIAN NATION: POLITICIZATION OF RELIGION OR TRUE COMMITMENT?

Jackie Mapulanga-Hulston

Introduction

Zambia currently has a population of about seventeen million[1] with the majority being Christians belonging to different denominations.[2] The so-called "Christianization" of the country began in the 1880s, when the pioneer Christian missionaries arrived on the African continent. The conversion of the local people to some form of Christianity has since been an important aspect of Zambian life and culture.[3] About thirty years ago, it was estimated that 41 percent of 550 million Africans were Christians. Projections of these numbers in some countries were, for example, in Ghana, more than 60 percent of the nineteen million people were Christians while Zambia had 75 percent of its population identified as Christians. Uganda had at least 78 percent Christians.[4]

With Christianity being the dominant theme at the government and political realm, there is a tendency for the government and the polity in assuming certain religious functions as it has also become a tendency for some religious institutions to assume political functions. This chapter

1 "Zambia Population 2019," accessed March 27, 2019, http://worldpopulationreview.com/countries/zambia-population/.

2 David M. C. Bartlett, "Civil Society and Democracy: A Zambian Case Study," *Journal of Southern African Studies* 26 (2000): 435.

3 Brendan Carmody, "The Nature and Role of Christian Conversion in Zambia," *International Journal for the Study of the Christian Church* 7, no. 2 (2007): 109.

4 See generally, Paul Gifford, *African Christianity: Its Public Role* (Bloomington, IN: Indiana University Press, 1999).

will therefore address the rationale behind the Declaration—the legal and political implications with reference to rights and duties from such a declaration.

Importantly, the chapter questions the significance of the Christian nation Declaration and its legal effect. Before embarking on a discussion of how Christianity has had an impact on the religiopolitical affairs in Zambia, a sort of the development of Christianity in sub-Saharan Africa, and specifically Zambia, will be undertaken.

Development of Christianity on the African Continent and in Zambia

In the twentieth century, European and American missionaries set up missions in Africa and established churches and introduced Christianity to the Africans. Christianity took hold and the expansion of the religion was remarkable.[5] A writer states that this expansion

> unleashed powerful ideological movements that drew much of their energy from the "back to Africa" policy originally adopted by the British government and white abolitionists, and also espoused by Americans.[6]

According to some writers, the eighteenth century saw an evangelical revival that generated extensive spiritual fervor and transformed Christian life throughout Britain and that resulted in religious ideas and philanthropic movements, led to the international exporting of missionaries.[7] This in turn led to Sub-Saharan Africa being referred to as the region where Christianity is growing faster than anywhere in the world.[8] Henry writes,

> Christianity in Africa has resulted in the fastest growing, most controversial, most dynamic, and most schismatic churches in the world. It is safe to say that all Christian communities in Africa (south of the Sahara) are experiencing growth, including Roman Catholic, Protestant, as well as African independent-type churches. This growth has, in fact, surpassed all predictions by colonial missionaries.

---

5 Emmanuel Katongole, "Prospects of Ecclesia in Africa in the Twenty-first Century," Logos: *A Journal of Catholic Thought and Culture* 4, no. 1 (2001): 178–195.

6 Jehu Hanciles, "Back to Africa: White Abolitionists and Black Missionaries," in *African Christianity: An African Story,* ed. U. Kalu (Pretoria: University of Pretoria, 2005), 191.

7 Hanciles, "Back to Africa," in *The New Religions of Africa,* ed. Bennetta W. Jules-Rosette (Norwood, NJ: Ablex Publishing,1979), 194.

8 R. Drew Smith, "Introduction: Christianity and Conflict in Africa," *The Review of Faith & International Affairs* 8, no. 1 (2010): 1.

> Most African societies south of the Sahara would be considered "Christianised" and have had a meaningful penetration of what can be termed Christian influence that at times resembles Christian principles.[9]

As a result of the "Christianization" of the region, it will be found that, particularly in southern Africa, most of the leaders are of the Christian faith. In the case of Zambia, every president since the country gained independence has affirmed their allegiance to Christianity. The rising pentecostal and charismatic influence in the African countries continue to take an increasing pivotal presence in the direction of the religion within the personal and political realms of the nation. Thus, Sanneh notes that while in 1970 there were over seventy-two million Pentecostals or Charismatics, in 2005, the number was as much as 590 million. It is further estimated that by 2025, Pentecostals or Charismatics will number nearly 800 million.[10]

There is a need to briefly examine the evolution and development of religion as this gives us a background for some of the ways in which decisions are made. The term *development* here is defined as implying some kind of directional change in the history of a particular religion, in the present study it is Christianity, whereas "evolution implies comparable directional changes in a number of religious traditions."[11] Christianity, as well as the strong influence of Pentecostalism has had a huge impact on local as well as global politics. The manner in which society is organized and maintained, or the system of governance has tended to be influenced by Christian ideals. This is more apparent with some of the laws, for example, those outlawing homosexuality, which most probably have as the basis the fact that homosexuality is an abhorrent act or sin in the eyes of the Lord.

---

9 Desmond Henry, "Reflections on a Missional Ecclesiology for Africa's Expressions of Christianity through the Tswana Lens," *Verbum et Ecclesia* 37, no. 1 (2016): 1.

10 Lamin O. Sanneh, *Disciples of All Nations: Pillars of World Christianity* (New York: Oxford University, 2008), 275; See also, Alan Anderson, "Pentecostals in Africa: The Shape of Future Christianity?" in *The Charismatic Movement and the Churches*, ed. Viggo Mortenson (Copenhagen: University of Aarhus, 2001): 25–42; Meyer offers an anthropological development of these church movements. Birgit Meyer, "Christianity in Africa: From African Independence to Pentecostal-Charismatic Churches," *Annual Review of Anthropology* 33 (2004): 447–474.

11 Robert N. Bellah, *Religion: Evolution and Development: From the Paleolithic to the Axial Age* (Cambridge, MA: Belknap Press of Harvard University, 2011).

According to Olsen, Zambia "is a country where Christianity infuses every aspect of the culture."[12] Since independence, Christianity is said to have played a large part in bringing legitimacy to Zambia's first government. The country's first leader, President Kenneth David Kaunda, often made reference to his Christian roots, his father having been a preacher.[13] According to Gifford, President Kaunda "used Christian rhetoric to project an image of compassion, uprightness, and integrity, and made political capital from his image as a Christian gentleman."[14]

Over time, churches came to be seen to as agents of political change facilitating a change of government.[15] For instance, after ruling the country for 27 years, President Kaunda was removed from office by the leader of the Movement for Multiparty Democracy, Frederick J.T. Chiluba. President Chiluba was a "born-again Christian" and had the support of the some of the major Christian organizations—namely, the Christian Council of Zambia, the Evangelical Fellowship of Zambia, and the Episcopal Conference of Zambia. Phiri states,

> In accordance with his charismatic beliefs, he did not agree to enter State House until his charismatic friends had performed a cleansing service. A group of fifty Christians from evangelical fellowships went to State House, which had just been vacated by Kaunda. Prayers were said in each room, to chase out evil spirits associated with Eastern religions.[16]

The Chiluba era saw a growth in the relationship between the church and the state. Carmody describes the church–state relations during this period as positive, but also somewhat ambiguous.[17] President Chiluba was a member of the United Church of Zambia and became a born-again Christian in 1981 while he was in prison during the Kaunda rule. He also had connections to charismatic fellowships within the UCZ and to the Northmead Assembly of God.[18]

---

12 Ted Olsen, "One African Nation under God," *Christianity Today* (February 4, 2002), accessed March 27, 2019, https://www.christianitytoday.com/ct/2002/february4/3.36.html.

13 Paul Gifford, "Chiluba's Christian Nation: Christianity as a Factor in Zambian Politics 1991–1996," *Journal of Contemporary Religion* 13, no. 3 (1998): 363.

14 Gifford, "Chiluba's Christian Nation," 363.

15 Paul Gifford, *African Christianity: Its Public Role* (Bloomington: Indiana University Press, 1998), 192–193, 196.

16 Isabel Apawo Phiri, "President Frederick J.T. Chiluba of Zambia: The Christian Nation and Democracy," *Journal of Religion in Africa*, 33 (November 2003): 405.

17 Brendan Carmody, "The Nature and Role of Christian Conversion in Zambia," *International Journal for the Study of the Christian Church* 7, no. 2 (2007): 118.

18 Phiri, "President Frederick J.T. Chiluba of Zambia," 405.

This infusion of Christianity has played and continues to play a major role on the Zambia political sphere and political leaders have been known to make declarations or orders based on Christian beliefs. For example, it did not come as a surprise when the current president, Edgar C Lungu declared a National Day of Prayer. President Lungu declared October 18 of every year to be a public holiday that is to be observed as a Day of National Prayer, Fasting, Repentance, and Reconciliation. This declaration was made in the exercise of the powers as provided in section 3 of the Public Holidays Act.[19] Another example is when former president Michael C. Sata came into power in 2011 and shortly after his inauguration, he made a promise that his government would follow the Ten Commandments and stated, "It is very easy to learn from the commandments how we must behave and conduct ourselves in this society."[20]

As can be seen, there is an interplay between politics and Christianity in Zambia which has been and continues to be an ongoing occurrence. The concern in this chapter is, when declarations are made to uphold Christian ideals and are later included in the laws of the nation without further guidance as to their practical application.

Implications of the Declaration of Zambia as a Christian Nation

On December 29, 1991, just two months after the historic landslide win and coming into office, President Chiluba made a declaration that Zambia was to be a Christian nation.[21] President Chiluba had an anointing service at the Anglican Church of Zambia, where he was instructed by the Anglican Archbishop to be "strong and show yourself a man, keep the

19 Chapter 272 of the Laws of Zambia. The section states: "The Minister shall have power, by statutory notice, from time to time to declare that any day or days shall be observed in Zambia as public holidays in addition to the days mentioned in the Schedule, and any day set apart by virtue of such notice as a public holiday shall be so observed throughout Zambia."

20 Austin Cheyeka, Marja Hinfelaar & Bernhard Udelhoven, "The Changing Face of Zambia's Christianity and its Implications for the Public Sphere: A Case Study of Bauleni Township, Lusaka," *Journal of Southern African Studies* 40, no. 5 (2014): 1031.

21 While some writers state that Zambia was the first country in the sub-continent to make such a declaration, others believe that such a declaration was not the first for the continent and that Liberia was in fact the first African country to make the declaration of a Christian nation. Christian status was declared at the country's creation as a settlement of former slaves, although, according to Jenkins, religion was used to justify the gross corruption of the nation's political elite, and the oppression of the native country people. Philip Jenkins, *The Next Christendom: The Coming of Global Christianity* (New York: Oxford University Press, 2011), 188.

charge of the Lord your God, walk in his ways, keep his statutes, his commandments, his precepts, and his testimonies as it is written in the first and second testaments."[22] Apart from declaring himself as subject to the lordship of Jesus Christ, he proceeded to declare the whole nation as a Christian one. He stated, "On behalf of the nation, I have now entered into a covenant with the living God.... I submit the government and the entire nation of Zambia to the lordship of Jesus Christ."[23] This Declaration was an affirmation that Zambia was a country which recognized the central role of acknowledging God as its supreme deity.

With this background, it is no wonder that one of the first things President Chiluba did was to declare Zambia a Christian nation, though it would allow full religious freedom for all faiths.[24] According to Muwowo and Buitendag,

> President Chiluba believed that, by presidential decree, Zambia could be governed by the principles of God and that God could be officially regarded as the Father of the nation. Through the public pronouncement of such a declaration by then-head of state, the concept of a "Zambian Christian nationhood" was born.[25]

The government then proceeded to amend the Constitution of Zambia to include the phrase that the people of Zambia declare the Republic a Christian nation while upholding the right of every person to enjoy that person's freedom of conscience or religion. Over time, the Christian nation declaration, despite many protests, became the *status quo.* However, some Christians, particularly the Roman Catholic Church, the Christian Council of the Churches in Zambia (CCCZ), and some evangelical groups voiced their concern about the lack of consultations before the declaration was made. The Catholic Church called the Declaration a shameful effort to claim God's approval for whatever policies and programs a particular party puts forward.[26] Pentecostal Christians were however largely satisfied with the Declaration and strongly supported it as they believed that it would bring blessings to the country.

---

22 Paul Gifford, *African Christianity: Its Public Role* (London: Hurst & Company, 1998), 197.

23 Olson, "One African Nation under God."

24 Patrick Johnstone, *Operation World*, 6th ed. (Carlisle: Paternoster Publishing, 2001), 686.

25 Simon Muwowo & Johan Buitendag, "A Scriptural, Theological and Historical Analysis of the Concept of the Zambian Christian Nationhood," *HTS Teologiese Studies/ Theological Studies* 66, no. 1 (2010) art. 327, doi: 10.4102/hts.v66i1.327, 3.

26 Peter Henriot, *Being a Christian in a Christian Nation* (Lusaka: Jesuit Centre for Theological Reflection Press, 1998).

The Declaration of a Christian nation however continues to raise debate and as to the exact legal effect of such a declaration.[27] Phiri writes that many churches denounced President Chiluba's declaration and that when the evangelicals "were provoked to speak out on the Christian nation declaration," this resulted in "an evangelical civil society. Further, that this evangelical civil society continued to grow in confidence and while increasingly being ready to play political roles."[28] According to Chayeka, the Declaration was merely a byproduct of the Pentecostalism which has been sweeping the country for a number of decades.[29] Others like Schoots state that Zambia through the Declaration had become "a nation in which both population and government, including the president, is under full submission to the Lord Jesus Christ. A country that God could use to influence the world in a mighty way."[30]

Examining the Legal Implication and Status of the Declaration

Legal scholars and commentators have questioned the exact legal implications of the Declaration as well as its subsequent inclusion in the Constitution. While the preamble in the Constitution declares Zambia a Christian nation, it also interestingly guarantees a person's freedom of religion. This is a clear contradiction. To compound the confusion, the preamble refers to Zambia as a "multi-religious state," again seemingly contradicting the declaration of the state as a Christian nation. In addition, Article 4(2) declares Zambia a "multi-religious and multi party democratic state." The Christian declaration may also be at odds with Zambia's treaty obligations under the International Covenant for Civil and Political Rights (ICCPR) and the African Charter on People's and Human Rights (ACHR) that guarantee freedom of religion and to which Zambia is a State Party.

Some legal commentators support the Declaration. For example, a Christian lawyer Dr. Beatrice Kamuwanga is reported to have supported the objective of the Declaration in the legal process. She stated that a clause of discretion gave the ruler some room for making an appropriate judgment and was of the view that Declaration was a value standard,

27 Chammah J. Kaunda, "'From Fools for Christ to Fools for Politicians': A Critique of Zambian Pentecostal Theopolitical Imagination," *International Bulletin of Mission Research* 41, no. 4 (2017): 296–311.

28 Phiri, "President Frederick J.T. Chiluba of Zambia," 402.

29 Austin M. Cheyeka, "Zambia, a 'Christian Nation' in Post Movement for Multiparty Democracy (MMD) Era, 2011–2016," *International Journal of Humanities and Social Science* 6, no. 7 (2016): 159–172.

30 Cheyeka, "Zambia"; Refer also, T. Schoots, "Miracles in Zambia: Zambia's Elected Prime Minister is Turning the Nation to God," *Cutting Edge* 9 (1995): 36–37.

rather than a legal one. She further maintained that as all systems operate within a set of values, the choosing of a value system is acceptable and the only thing which needed evaluation were the hallmarks of Christianity if they could provide a set of values for a nation without violating international law.[31] A law professor from the University of Zambia stated that Christianity should be a way of life and not by means of a Declaration. He argued,

> Zambia's subscription to Christianity should be manifest in the way its citizens conduct themselves, and not in the Pharisee-like Christian nation proclamation. Credible Christians, or countries that espouse Christian virtues, do not go around proclaiming it on rooftops. Their Christianness is immediately apparent in the way they carry and conduct themselves. A tiger does not proclaim its "tigerness." "When you see a tiger, you know it is a tiger."[32]

Some commentators maintain that the Declaration by Chiluba was based on his own personal religious conviction and was not made to the people and further that the Declaration ". . . was made to God. It was in a form of a prayer. He was basically saying that I believe in God, and I believe what God has told me to do, and my government will follow."[33] A counter view was that, as it would affect the public, the Declaration should have been democratically discussed rather than it being introduced without any discussion in Parliament or by the government, as would be required in a democratic country. The Declaration could also be viewed as a move by the political leader to confer religious legitimacy on himself. Deacon and Lynch, writing on the concept of neo-Pentecostalism state that neo-pentecostal ideas, rituals, and narratives tend to encourage political events, processes, and relations to be interpreted "through an idiom of spiritual and material world relations that are inherently ambivalent and can heighten a sense of uncertainty regarding relevant forces and appropriate responses' and also that political elites regularly reach out to and are influenced by neo-Pentecostals as they seek to emphasize the legitimacy of their position and policies, and be—or at least be seen to be—good Christians."[34]

Muwowo and Buitendag maintain that a country cannot attain its Christian nationhood by presidential decree, but only by means of

[31] Zambia Law Development Agency Newsletter, September 2005, cited by Muwowo & Buitendag, "Scriptural, Theological and Historical Analysis."

[32] C. Anyangwe, *We should Behave like Christians—Not Proclaim* (Lusaka: Ms Action Aid, 2005), 8.

[33] Phiri, "President Frederick J.T. Chiluba of Zambia," 408.

[34] Gregory Deacon & Gabrielle Lynch, "Allowing Satan in? Moving Toward a Political Economy of Neo-Pentecostalism in Kenya," *Journal of Religion in Africa* 43 (2013): 108.

cultural determination.[35] The authors emphasize the point that religion is something that emanates from the culture of the people and not from a declaration that is made about them. They also state a problem of lack of clarity in the Declaration.

> Without question, the Declaration is unclear both theologically and constitutionally and also with regard to the question of what it means when a political entity such as a nation is declared to be Christian. Certainly, from a dogmatic point of view, one cannot baptise a nation, or even all of the fifteen million or so inhabitants of a nation state, let alone expect that an entire nation should profess the Apostles' Creed. In the same way, neither can a nation perform a liturgical act of Christian worship which, by and large, would manifest a spirit of true Christian nationhood. These are some of the difficult concerns that neither the state nor the churches in Zambia have thought out in a way that might bring clarity and understanding to such a situation.[36]

Religion in a Political Framework and the Politicization of Christianity

To understand the rationale behind the Presidential Declaration, it is necessary to take a closer look at the link between religion and politics. African countries have the tendency to tinker with religion to the extent that it to fits the political realm. Generally, in Africa, religion and politics have historically been linked together and through most or all known pre-colonial African political systems and states, public religious performance is said to have played an important role.[37] This then explains the connection between religion, specifically, Christianity, in countries such as Zambia. Ellis and ter Haar, further state that African political elites do not necessarily use religion to increase their base of popular support but that, in many cases, they also believe that access to the spiritual world is a vital resource in the constant struggle to secure advantage over their political rivals in political in-fighting.[38]

Since the Declaration, there has been a gradual but continued rise in the politicization of Christianity in the country. Both actions were against his definition of democracy as there had been no participation of the people in making final decisions. As already stated, the Catholic Church opposed the Christian nation declaration and stated:

---

35 Muwowo & Buitendag, "Scriptural, Theological and Historical Analysis," 3.

36 Muwowo & Buitendag, "Scriptural, Theological and Historical Analysis," 4.

37 Stephen Ellis & Gerrie ter Haar, "Religion and Politics in Sub-Saharan Africa," *The Journal of Modern African Studies* 36, no. 2 (1998): 187.

38 Ellis & ter Haar, "Religion and Politics," 187.

> The church must endeavor to be seen as independent from political influence and challenge the nation morally as it did so well in the past. In other words, the separation of powers (church/state) must be seen in deed.[39]

Phiri outlines just how this has occurred since the Christian nation declaration.[40] During the Chiluba era, Zambia re-established diplomatic links with Israel, which had been cut by his predecessor, President Kaunda. Diplomatic ties with Muslim countries like Iran and Iraq that had supported Kaunda were severed. Ministers of Religion were appointed as members of the cabinet, and there was an influx of Christian missionaries into Zambia. There was also a rapid increase in the number of charismatic churches or church organizations with some of these being invited by President Chiluba to hold crusades at the government's expense. A Department of Christian Affairs with its own minister was established under the Office of the President. During this period, funds from the presidential support were given primarily to organizations and churches that supported the president. For example, President Chiluba gave Dan Pule, a member of the Chiluba government, K129 million to construct his Dunamis International Church, studio, and offices.[41]

In Christianity, the source of all power lies with God, the Creator. This could be one of the reasons most Zambians were generally not opposed to the Declaration. Most concerns aired revolved around the issue of consultation and discussion. Since the Declaration, the interaction or relationship between the state and the church in Zambia has grown quite strong and church leaders often make statements in reaction to political statements or government policies. The church has been involved in giving advice to political leaders and much of this advice has been taken into account or followed by the various leaders and political parties.[42] The church is definitely not politically disengaged and has a somewhat passive role in governing the nation at all levels. This engagement between the church and the state is not in itself a bad thing. It is stated that state leaders, like most of their constituents, "believe that real power has its roots in the invisible world and that

---

[39] Catholic Commission for Justice and Peace (1998), cited in Phiri, "President Frederick J.T. Chiluba of Zambia," 410.

[40] Phiri, "President Frederick J.T. Chiluba of Zambia," 409.

[41] See Phiri, "President Frederick J.T. Chiluba of Zambia."

[42] Read generally, Austin Cheyeka, Marja Hinfelaar, & Bernhard Udelhoven, "The Changing Face of Zambia's Christianity and its Implications for the Public Sphere: A Case Study of Bauleni Township, Lusaka," *Journal of Southern African Studies* 40, no. 5 (2014): 1031–1045.

therefore the cultivation of spiritual power is vital for their continued political existence."[43]

In Zambia, Christianity and politics have a fairly mutual influence which, to a large extent, forms a relationship that promotes Christianity to take a central role in the political sphere. An example of the danger of merging the two is shown in an interview given in 1995 by then-vice-president, Brigadier General Godfrey Miyanda, who stated, while reaffirming the Declaration,

> Zambia has become the "chosen nation"—the "new Israel." The leaders are anointed; hence nobody has a right to question them or disagree with them. Hence, the view of the opposition is seen as representing evil since they always go against God's chosen leader.[44]

Statements such as these are behind the debates and discussions surrounding the proposals for Constitutional reform in the leading to the current Constitution of Zambia (Amendment) Act, No. 2 of 2016, that included calls for constitutional governance with restraint on presidential powers.[45]

As stated already, in Africa, religious belief operates at every level of society and together with politics, these make up a system in which elements of authority and hierarchy tend to emerge.[46] As such, it will be found that politics and religion are not mutually exclusive as there is a strong connection between politics and piety.

Therefore, there is a lingering need to examine the role of religion in the political and social life of the country, particularly with the establishment of the Ministry of Religious Affairs and National Guidance (MNGRA). This ministry as created on August 28, 2016 by President Lungu and the objective of establishing this ministry was to:

> focus on facilitating the actualization of declaration of the Republic of Zambia as a Christian Nation while upholding individual person's right to freedom of conscience, belief, or religion and the realisation of National Values and Principles as contained in the preamble and

---

43 Ellis & ter Haar, "Religion and Politics," 190.

44 Zambian National Broadcasting Corporation, Interview with Frank Mutubila on "Frank Talk" Programme, ZNBC, August 5, 1995.

45 Muna Ndulo, "Review of the Draft Constitution for the Republic of Zambia," *The Southern African Institute for Policy and Research* (SAIPAR), (June 11, 2012): http://saipar.org/wp-content/uploads/2013/09/Ndulo_Review-of-the-Draft-Constitution-for-the-Republic-of-Zambia.pdf.

46 Ellis & ter Haar, "Religion and Politics," 195.

> Part II Article 8 of the Constitution (Amendment) Act No.2 of 2016 respectively.[47]

According to the ministry, its creation was "necessitated by the need to guide all national undertakings in line with Zambia's Christian identity and facilitate the mainstreaming of national values and principles in the country's programs and projects."[48] However, the mandate of this ministry yet again questions the interplay between religion and politics. The Minister of Religious Affairs stated,

> The mandate of the ministry is to actualise and translate the declaration of Zambia as a Christian nation into practical, workable, and realistic interventions. Therefore, my ministry will provide overall policy and legal framework in all matters pertaining to Zambia as a Christian heritage.[49]

Such a move raises several concerns about the way in which politicians are exercising control over matters that are of a spiritual nature and in the religious realm. It also raises questions about how the religion should be regulated by the government and what sort of regulation it would be. The problem with mixing religion and politics is aptly captured by Ellis and ter Haar—there is general conviction that the possession of great power tempts its holders to immorality or at the very least confronts them with dilemmas that require them to make profound choices concerning good and evil, normally considered the prerogative of gods.[50] After the Declaration, there are further inroads being made in the religious sector by the state that could spell dire consequences for the freedom of religion in the country and especially when a corrupt government is in power. As stated by some scholars, while displays of morality, legitimacy, and authority continue to characterize national and local politics, it is important that analysts interrogate the way in which religion informs the spaces and that which are available to politicians, while being cognizant of ordinary citizens.[51]

---

47 Ministry of Religious Affairs and National Guidance, accessed March 9, 2019, http://www.mrng.gov.zm/.

48 Ministry of Religious Affairs and National Guidance, accessed March 9, 2019, http://www.mrng.gov.zm/.

49 "Ministerial Statement by The Hon. Minister of Religious Affairs and National Guidance, Rev. Sumaili, on the Mushrooming of False Churches and Prophets, and Measures Being Put in Place" (March 21, 2017), accessed June 10, 2020, http://www.parliament.gov.zm/sites/default/files/images/publication_docs/MINISTERIAL%20STATEMENT%20BY%20HON%20SUMAILI.pdf

50 Ellis & ter Haar, "Religion and Politics," 196.

51 Deacon & Lynch, "Allowing Satan in?," 113.

Concluding Remarks

This chapter has examined the link between religion and politics in Africa generally and Zambia specifically. It is clear that there is a need for more studies about this link; so that there is no chance of the integrity of one, namely, religion, will be compromised by political elites. The Declaration of Zambia as a Christian nation on the face of it, seems pretty harmless and a good thing in a country where the majority are Christians. However, there are other implications of such declarations as well. People must ascertain whether there was a motive leading to this Declaration and importantly, its expected impact or force. Most Zambians, especially the common citizens, have never asked what the effect of the Declaration would entail for the country. However, some members of the public did voice some reservations about this Declaration and there were some debates on the issue. In fact, the Mung'omba Constitutional Review Commission (CRC) recommended the removal of the Christian nation Declaration from the Constitution in the draft constitution.[52] Kaunda states that the Constitution appears to suggest that the Zambian people expressed their yearning to surrender the nation to God, when it never started that way.[53] The Declaration and other measures made within the religiopolitical realm by the political leaders must not make inroads into the spiritual realm unless it is to protect people's freedom of religion and any infringements on the right of citizens to worship their Lord according to their beliefs. The statements made by the Minister of Religious Affairs are incompatible with the role of minister.

The church in Zambia has made the most of changing political opportunities. In some churches, politics has taken precedence over spiritual matters. As collective members of civil society, the church has an obligation and a right to question the political elites on matters concerning declarations of a religious nature. It is time that the church begins to engage her organizational structures to support and empower church activities and missions. While they can capitalize on, and make use of opportunities for *collaboration* and *cooperation* with the state and other factors, the integrity of faith and calling should not be compromised. The church in Zambia must be well informed to ask the relevant and critical questions pertaining to religious affairs in the country as this is an area that affects their beliefs. A few churches have raised questions with respect to the

52 See Wila Mung'omba, *Constitution Review Commission Report* (Lusaka: Zambia Education Publishing House, 2005).

53 Chammah J. Kaunda, *The Nation that Fears God Prospers: A Critique of Zambian Pentecostal Theopolitical Imaginations* (Minneapolis, MN: Fortress Press, 2018), 159.

Chiluba Declaration, not in the sense of opposing it, but in terms of going farther in its implementation or significance.

A number of legal scholars have quizzed the legal effect of the Christian nation Declaration. Muwowo and Buitendag surmise the major argument well, that is,

> the declaration of Zambia as a "Christian nation," despite being a unique concept, must be both theologically and ethically sound if, indeed, it is to become more than just a slogan and a single-line entry in the preamble of the country's constitution.[54]

While statements have been made about the Declaration, in reality, it is a mammoth task to educate, enforce, and exemplify at a spectrum of levels or adherence of Christianity in the nation.

[54] Muwowo & Buitendag, "Scriptural, Theological and Historical Analysis."

2

THE MINISTRY OF NATIONAL GUIDANCE AND RELIGIOUS AFFAIRS AND CHURCH-STATE RELATIONS

Nelly Mwale
Joseph Chita
Austin Mumba Cheyeka

INTRODUCTION

On August 29, 2016, the president-elect, Mr. Edgar Chagwa Lungu, mused about creating a ministry of religion at a reception service for a newly elected United Church of Zambia (UCZ) Synod bishop, Rev. Sydney Sichilima, at St. Andrews congregation in Lusaka.[1] This resulted in the creation of Ministry of National Guidance and Religious Affairs (MNGRA). The president's intention illustrated that the declaration of Zambia as a Christian nation remains topical; it is not sterile yet, because just as one is led back in time in search of its origins, so is one enabled to follow its subsequent developments. For example, just days after Chiluba's declaration of Zambia as a Christian nation, pastor Kabila of Future Hope Church in Livingstone urged the government to consider creating a Ministry of Christian Affairs so that the church could have representation both in parliament and cabinet.[2]

The creation of the MNGRA sparked off public debates that attracted media and, yet, its implications for church-state relations escaped the interest of scholars of religion. This was despite the alarm that being a

---

1 Nation Reporter, "Government to Set Up Religious Ministry," *Daily Nation* August 29, 2016, 4.

2 Austin Cheyeka, *The Politics and Christianity of Chilubaism in Zambia 1991–2011* (Ndola: Mission Press, 2014), 93.

ministry with a strong conservative Christian orientation, MNGRA was in danger of falling prey to a pentecostal demo-theocratic (democratic and theocratic) political paradigm that rejects certain human rights, religious pluralism, and knowledge constructions from other religions, which are perceived inferior and, at the same time, a possible tool for social reconstruction and transformation.[3] Therefore, acknowledging the need to generate insights that contribute to a history of Zambia's Christian nationhood, the chapter seeks to make a contribution to knowledge and debate on Zambia's constitutional Christian nationhood by exploring how the new ministry had implications for church-state relations from the perspective of Christian umbrella bodies in Zambia. These include the Zambia Episcopal Conference (ZEC), the Zambia Conference of Catholic Bishops (ZCCB), Council of Churches in Zambia (CCZ), Evangelical Fellowship of Zambia (EFZ), and Independent Churches Organisation of Zambia (ICOZ), and the Bishops Council of Zambia (BCZ).

Officially instituted in 1963, the ZEC (ZCCB) is the administrative body of all Roman Catholic dioceses while the CCZ was established in 1945 as the umbrella body of mainline Protestant churches. The EFZ was officially formed in 1964 to oversee evangelical churches. In 2001, a fourth umbrella body, ICOZ, was formed to bring together charismatic churches, ministries, fellowships, and centers, with the newer pentecostal church umbrella body being the BCZ. Although the chapter concentrates on the period from 2015 to 2017, it situates the discourse of the MNGRA into the broader Christian nationhood discourse in Zambia. We argue that the creation of MNGRA has not only complicated the role of the church in politics as it contributed to divided and compromised voices of the church because the Christian umbrella bodies were polarized, but it also revealed new developments contrary to the view that the declaration of "Zambia as a Christian nation" neither introduced new substantive laws nor established any church.[4]

Methods

The chapter is informed by findings from an interpretive case study, which involved document analysis, interviews, and focus group discussions. The thematic analysis of the print media discourse on the MNGRA covered the period from 2015 to 2017. Focus group discussions and interviews

---

3 Chammah J. Kaunda and Mutale M. Kaunda, "Mobilising Religious Assets for Social Transformation: A Theology of Decolonial Reconstruction Perspective on the Ministry of National Guidance and Religious Affairs (MNGRA) in Zambia," *Religions* 9, no. 6 (2018): 176.

4 Paul Freston, *Evangelicals and Politics in Asia, Africa and Latin* America (Cambridge: Cambridge University Press, 2001), 154.

with purposively chosen Christian church leaders and laypersons were also conducted to consolidate what emerged from the media. Prophetic realism theory helped to interpret how the formation of the ministry had shaped church-state relations in Zambia. Prophetic realism theory as expounded by Fowler (1987) is an extension of Niebuhr's writings (1952) on Christian realism.[5] Suffice to note that Christian realism is a political theology in the Christian tradition whose key political concepts are balance of power and political responsibility. With the term prophetic borrowed from the biblical Old Testament (prophets spoke against the evils in the society), prophetic realism theory became a lens in our study because of its quest to address a balanced approach (in this case in the relationship between the church and the state), and thus avoids the danger of extremes. Prophetic realism theory as a strategy in the spirit of biblical prophets refuses to let people ignore the oppression and injustices that the society produces and condemns by seeking to raise awareness of the structural and personal evils that distract society.[6] It further points to practical and concrete terms of what changes are needed for the society to be in the light of the word of God. This theory was valuable because of its balanced and critical role in society as we sought to understand what would become of the church in the context of the MNGRA as an arm of the state.

The Ministry of National Guidance and Religious Affairs

Whether the president had been persuaded by Pentecostals or not to come up with the ministry that would oversee the affairs of the church in relation to the state—creating a link between the Church and the state[7]—revealed that African Christianity remains enchanted[8] and as such African Indigenous Religion remains influential in people's reasoning and church-state relations. In Zambia, like many African countries, there is no sharp separation between religion and politics as is the case in many Western countries.[9]

---

5 Robin Lovin, *An Introduction to Reinhold Niebuhr and Christian Realism* (Cambridge: Cambridge University Press, 1995), 1–32.

6 See Chammah J. Kaunda, "'The Altars are Holding the Nation in Captivity': Zambian Pentecostalism, Nationality, and African Religio-Political Heritage." *Religions* 9, no. 5 (2018): 145; Chammah J. Kaunda, *The Nation that Fears God Prospers: A Critique of Zambian Pentecostal Theopolitical Imaginations* (Minneapolis, MN: Fortress Press, 2018), 37.

7 Nation Reporter, "Government to Set Up Religious Ministry," 2.

8 Paul Gifford, *Christianity, Development and Democracy in Africa* (London: Hurst & Company, 2015), 329.

9 Gerrie Ter Haar, *Spirit of Africa: The Healing Ministry of Archbishop Milingo of Zambia* (London: Hurst, 1992), 200–201.

The MNGRA was situated in the country's wider Christian nationhood because Lungu replayed Chiluba's declaration of Zambia as a Christian nation and re-invigorated it. The creation of the ministry was a build-up of events since 2015 and as far back as 1991.[10] The build-up of events included the rise to power of Lungu when President Michael Sata who had been elected president in 2011 died. Under the Zambian law then, the death of a sitting president required a new presidential election to take place within 90 days, and consequently a special poll was organized on January 20, 2015, in which Lungu won.

A short and insubstantial biography of Lungu by Anthony Mukwita (2016) does not reveal much about the new president's religion. His family is reported to be staunch Baptists though Lungu converted from the United Church of Zambia and his wife, Esther, from the Roman Catholic Church.[11] Lungu reconfigured the Christian nation fervor in 2015 when he made the Declaration part of his campaign message. In doing so, not only did he mobilize voters, but also created pentecostal clienteles who perceived him as a defender of the Declaration of Zambia as a Christian nation and probably Lungu and Pentecostals intended mutual benefits in such a move. Upon becoming the president in 2015, he created a chapel at the State house with Bishop Peter Ndhlovu of the Bible Gospel Church in Africa (BIGOCA) as some sort of chaplain.[12] This confirmed the assertion that the symbol of national political power in the pentecostal imagination is the State house which is perceived as the seat of authority and ultimately a national altar.[13]

The announcement of MNGRA raised expectations especially in the pentecostal fraternity. It seems that Lungu had worked out what to underpin his campaign message in the by-election of 2015 and the general elections in 2016.[14] The declaration of Zambia as a Christian nation was idyllic. While he was interim president after President Michael Sata's death in office in 2016, Lungu positioned himself as a born-again Christian and began making public appearances in various church services, as a result winning the favor of the majority of Pentecostal Christians.[15] During his

---

10 Rev. Pukuta Mwanza, personal communication, June 12, 2017.

11 Antony Mukwita, *Edgar Lungu, Against All Odds: Zambia's President Edgar Chagwa Lungu's Rough Journey to State House* (Milton Keynes: Patridge, 2017), 94.

12 Rev. Mwanza, personal communication, June 12, 2017.

13 Kaunda, "Altars are Holding the Nation," 145.

14 Andrew Mukoma, "Zambia Shall Remain Christian Nation—Government." *Daily Nation*, June 24, 2017.

15 Chammah J. Kaunda and Mutale M. Kaunda, "'An Announcement of a New Spiritual Dispensation.' Pentecostalism and Nationalisation of Prayer in Zambia," *Journal of Theology for Southern Africa* 161 (2018): 71–88; Mutale M. Kaunda

campaign, pictures of Lungu in church or with clergy were constantly posted on social media, all depicting him reading the Bible or in prayer.[16]

Thus, before the start of the 2016 general elections, he told his supporters during a campaign-planning meeting at his home:

> Let me remind my colleagues in government and the ruling party (PF) that the period before the elections is very short. We must, therefore, work very hard in the remaining eighteen months to retain the confidence of the Zambian People . . .. God has been gracious to Zambia, and we pledge to honor him by adhering to Christian virtues. Zambia shall remain a Christian nation tolerant of other religions.[17]

Inevitably, the whole saga of MNGRA is quite rightly best understood in the wider context of the two elections after the death of Sata and the electioneering that witnessed appeals to Christianity by politicians. Lungu won the presidential by-election of January 20, 2015, and in due course of the year he declared a "National Day of Prayer, Fasting, and Reconciliation" that would be held on October 18 of every year.

> I felt, we, as a nation, as a people, were drifting away from the face of God by incessantly insulting each other, attacking each other, and so on . . .. It is a personal decision based on faith, and I will not respond to it politically. Those that do not want to pray, please leave us alone with our God.[18]

One consequence of the proclamation of the day of prayer, reconciliation, and fasting is that it galvanized political big men[19] and women into political action of supporting Lungu. It led to the formation of an organization named "Christians for Lungu" (C4L) by Dr Liya Mutale with a pledge to help Lungu's party to win the August 15, 2016 general elections.[20] After the 2016 general elections, the MNGRA was established and Godfridah Sumaili, a pentecostal pastor was appointed as the first minister.

---

and Chammah J. Kaunda. "Pentecostalism, Female Spirit-Filled Politicians, and Populism in Zambia," *International Review of Mission* 107, no. 1 (2018): 23–32.

16 Chammah J. Kaunda, "Christianising Edgar Chagwa Lungu: The Christian Nation, Social Media Presidential Photography and 2016 Election Campaign," *Stellenbosch Theological Journal* 4, no. 1 (2018): 215–245.

17 Mukwita, *Journey to State House*, 85.

18 Mukwita, *Journey to State House*, 125.

19 John F. McCauley, "Africa's New Big Man Rule? Pentecostalism and Patronage in Ghana." *African Affairs* 112, no. 446 (2012): 1–21.

20 Austin Cheyeka, "Zambia, a 'Christian Nation' in Post Movement for Multiparty Democracy (MMD) Era, 2011–2016," *International Journal of Humanities and Social Science* 6 (2016): 168.

Functions of the Ministry of National Guidance and Religious Affairs

The mandate for the ministry, as it turned out did not, after all, require a think-tank because events in the country provided what issues to address through policy and legislation. In a focus group discussion, comprising eight pastors and two lay persons from different denominations of mainline churches as well as Pentecostals, despite mixed feelings about the ministry, there was consensus on the need for it to guide the nation and churches, to regulate churches, and to check on pastors and evangelists, a scenario that confirmed prophetic realism's call for balance of power. The focus group was concerned about what they termed as "cults" in the country[21] that they hoped the MNGRA would address.

One vexing problem that the public wants to deal with decisively is that of false prophets who extort money from gullible Christians who seek healing and prosperity. They have to give false prophets money before they are prayed for. The Permanent Secretary for Central Province, Mr. Chanda Kabwe in his complaint about false prophets, said, "The most saddening thing is that these prophets and apostles have turned the church into a money-spinning venture. If anybody wants to see the prophet or apostle, he or she has to pay."[22]

> At our economic front, we have been moaning about Zambia being a dumping ground for foreign goods and services, but I bet, Zambia has become an even much bigger dumping ground for foreign gods and religions in the whole of Southern Africa. Honourable Minister Sumaili, please do not wait until our women are made to eat grass before you can intervene.[23]

Chilufya's statement not only showed the enormity of the problem, but also a direct reference to what had happened in South Africa where a pentecostal pastor asked his congregants to eat grass to grow in their pentecostal faith.[24] It has long been established that pentecostal pastors in the name of prophets or apostles have become African traditional diviners of the twenty-first century. Pentecostalism in Zambia has seized both the indigenous and contemporary Zambian cultures' anthropocentric focus. It has thrived on the fertile ground of Zambian indigenous cosmologies by appropriating notions of salvation within the framework of

21 Focus Group Discussion, February 24, 2017.

22 Rogers Kalero, "Central Province PS Warns Fake Prophets, Apostles," *Daily Nation*, May 8, 2017, 5.

23 Mukuka Chilufya, "Religious Fanatics Should not be Entertained," *Zambia Daily Mail*, May 26, 2017, 6.

24 Tankiso Makhetha, "Religious Body Findings Slammed," *The Star*, July 12, 2017, 2.

their inherently religious and anthropocentric cosmology.[25] Pentecostal spiritual leaders have not utterly blamed demons for the problems facing Zambia but progressively begun to over-spiritualize societal problems and failed to point out visible structures that precipitate abuse in the country. Immorality as the cause of problems does not include grand corruption in the higher echelons of power.

While the public had their own expectations of what would be the mandate of the MNGRA, from the ministerial statement read out in Parliament on March 21, 2017, the mandate was arguably vague in nature: "The mandate of the ministry is to actualise and translate the declaration of Zambia as a Christian nation into practical, workable, and realistic interventions. Therefore, the ministry will provide overall policy and legal framework in all matters pertaining to Zambia as a Christian heritage."[26] The actualization of Zambia's Declaration as a Christian nation would be done through interdenominational dialogue, national guidance, national values, principles, and ethics, public religious celebrations, preservation of Christian and religious sites, and religious affairs.[27]

What the minister had failed to tell Parliament was how things like national guidance, national values, principles, and ethics were going to be enforced. In the final analysis, the minister's statements were organized by a concern about proliferation of churches under leaders who are exploiting the favorable environment of religious freedom by engaging in strange practices that put some people at such risk as hood-winking them into believing that they will obtain power or strength by sleeping [having sex] with a virgin, too much emphasis on material wealth, emphasis on acts or miracles rather than the word of God, and false and misleading messages such as stopping HIV and AIDS patients from taking medication.[28]

Upon scrutiny, the MNGRA aims to bring sanity among pentecostal churches in Zambia and to police them. This, however, was not the idea of Lungu when he formed this ministry. "I do not want to see this ministry policing religious organizations and exert pressure on churches. Churches should be left alone. The Ministry needs legal structures and statutes

25 Teddy C. Sakupapa, "Christianity in Zambia," in *Anthology of African Christianity*, ed. Isabel Apawo Phiri, Dietrich Werner, Chammah J. Kaunda, and Kennedy Owino (Oxford: Regnum Books International, 2016), 761.

26 Ministerial Statement by the Honorable Minister of Religious Affairs and National Guidance, Rev. Sumaili, on the Mushrooming of False Churches and Prophets, and Measures Being Put in place, March 21, 2017.

27 Ministerial Statement, March 21, 2017.

28 Ministerial Statement, March 21, 2017; C. Malambo, "Extortionist 'Men of God' Have No Space in Zambia—Government," *Daily Nation*, May 8, 2017, 3; Catherine Mumba, "Immorality Abominable—Sumaili," *Zambia Daily Mail*, June 10, 2017, 3.

first."[29] The MNGRA, perhaps the praying department of the Patriotic Front government, has yet to find its feet and become relevant to the well-being of Zambians and therefore a factor for church-state relations.

MNGRA and Church-State Relations

The broad implications of the MNGRA revolved around strengthening and weakening church-state relations.

Strengthened Church-State Relations

From inception, some Christian mother bodies particularly the Evangelicals were excited with the creation of the new ministry because of how it was perceived as having a bearing on church-state relations. For example, welcoming the president's intimation first and foremost, EFZ executive director Rev. Pukuta Mwanza said that the creation of a ministry would promote Christian values and give more meaning to the Declaration of Zambia as a Christian nation. He argued: "Religion plays a huge role in the daily affairs of our country and so, it is only befitting that we have a government arm responsible for that."[30] In expectation of whatever would come with the ministry, Rev. Mwanza appealed to the president-elect to put in place a thorough consultative process in order to set up a structure for the proposed ministry.[31] These sentiments confirmed our earlier argument that the ministry was seen as an avenue to bring the church closer to the state, hence deemed as a pointer to sound relations by the EFZ.

Similarly, the Pentecostal Fellowship of Zambia's (PFZ) executive director Naison Nyonyo described the president's announcement as long overdue because the church was a big institution that required representation.[32] This reflected the understanding that the ministry would enhance the church-state relations if the church got represented in the structures of the state. Perhaps, it was in the light of this that the ministry was an opportunity for the clergy to contribute to national development.

> The church must utilize the Ministry to contribute to national development, it gives the clergy the opportunity to work with government for the benefit of the Zambian people.[33]

Apostle Nicolas Mwanangombe of New Word Church in Kamanga compound of Lusaka hoped the relations between the church and the

29 Rev. Mwanza, personal communication, June 12, 2017.

30 Steven Mvula & Nancy Siame, "Religion Ministry Praised," *Zambia Daily Mail*, August 30, 2016, 2.

31 Mvula and Siame, "Religious Ministry Praised."

32 Mvula and Siame, "Religious Ministry Praised."

33 Anne Zulu, "Clergy Should Guide Nation," *Daily Nation*, November 9, 2017, 7.

state would be strengthened by the ministry's curbing of "fake men of God" and tackling the mushrooming of unregistered churches, as some men were taking advantage of people who were in need of salvation by swindling, abusing, defiling, or raping them and others being abused, defiled, or raped.[34] These sentiments pointed to the ministry as the moral eye of society, and in the words of prophetic realism, the voice that seeks to raise awareness of the structural and personal evils that destroy society.

The association of the ministry with the creation of moral community reveals how Lungu (2015–2017) synthesized Kenneth Kaunda's Zambian Humanism, Frederick Chiluba's Christian nation, Michael Sata's populism, and his own style of leadership. The idea of the state providing national moral guidance that was embedded in Zambian Humanism has been appropriated in the MNGRA. According to Kaunda's Humanism, the moral and spiritual development (of the citizen) must also be part and parcel of the party and government (i.e., the state) program.[35] From Chiluba's Christian nation, Lungu becomes not only the custodian of the declaration of Zambia as a Christian nation but, most importantly, he intercedes to God on behalf of the people through the MNGRA. On Michael Sata's populism, Lungu rides on the former's reputation as a hard worker and a troubleshooter who had declared that he would rule the country on the basis of the Ten Commandments and the Social Teaching of the Roman Catholic Church to which he belonged. If Lungu is also influenced by the African traditional worldview, which he is perhaps, then this synthesis is also mixed with ingredients from the indigenous political repertoire, which might explain the assumptions that by bringing the church into the structures of the state, the relationship between these entities would be strengthened.

The MNGRA's association which strengthened church-state relations in the country by stopping churches operating illegally by means of registering with the Registrar of Societies was an indication that there was public concern over the upsurge of pentecostal churches and swift spread of their doctrines. Ultimately, this demonstrated the complex understanding of religion and politics, especially the fact that politics in Zambia cannot be fully be understood without taking its religious dimension into account.[36]

34 Nation Reporter, "Government to Set up Religious Ministry"; Adeodatus Matafwali, "Religious Affairs, Ministry Welcome," *Daily Nation* October 6, 2016, 8.

35 Kenneth D. Kaunda, *Humanism in Zambia and a Guide to its Implementation, Pt II* (Lusaka: Division of National Guidance, 1974), 119.

36 Naomi Haynes, "Why Can't a Pastor be President of 'Christian Nation?': Mapping the Diverse Political Theologies of Zambia's Pentecostals," Unpublished typescript, 2016.

Weakened Church-State Relations

Some sentiments that pointed to how the ministry would weaken church-state relations were also raised, which reflected the complexities of how religion and politics were understood. By and large, the church umbrella bodies were polarized with the creation of the new ministry, hence the MNGRA was perceived to have weakened church-state relations. If the new ministry is yet another product of the Declaration of Zambia as a Christian nation on December 29, 1991, the polarization of the church umbrella bodies cannot be detached from the manner they reacted to that Declaration in comparison to the reaction to the creation of the MNGRA. Quite evidently, there was unity of purpose, the spirit of ecumenism, and serious dialogue among the three church mother bodies (CCZ, EFZ, and ZCCB) in responding to the Declaration, and the Press Statement on January 16, 1992. Thus, the position of church leaders was clear: Zambia was to be a Christian nation not in pronouncement, but in deeds. On the MNGRA, however, there was utter polarization.

Munshya wa Munshya was apt in his analysis of what had not happened but ought to have taken place in the context of the MNGRA.

> It is important that the churches in Zambia show some level of unity on their theological interpretation of the implications of the state's involvement in religious affairs. The CCZ and ZCCB should extend their ecumenical hospitality to Pentecostals so that Pentecostals can see the importance of maintaining a theological praxis that maintains a distance between the state and the church . . .. All church leaders in Zambia from the EFZ, ZCCB, and the CCZ should come together and show some ecumenical hospitality that listens to each other and dialogues with each other to ensure that the church does not lose its critical prophetic voice to call the temporal leaders to accountability. Pentecostals should adopt the position taken by ZCCB and CCZ for the church to be the conscience of the society.[37]

This invitation to the church umbrella bodies to work together was a glaring evidence of the polarization of the church umbrella bodies. The ecumenical spirit of the past years before multiparty politics and the Declaration is a religious nostalgic heritage, analogous to a paradise lost. The church has never been as divided as it is since the Declaration and subsequent developments thereafter; lately the creation of the MNGRA has widened the division.

The most unfortunate thing to have ever happened is that the Catholic Church that is known for setting the tone of church-state relationship

37 Munshya wa Munshya, "In God's Name: President Lungu, the Church and the New Ministry of Religious Affairs," *Daily Nation*, 2016, 9.

seems to have abandoned that role and does not initiate dialogue with other church umbrella bodies to make public statements. The current scenario is that, on the one hand, ZCCB occasionally makes a joint statement with CCZ and, on the other hand, EFZ makes its own public statement while ICOZ makes statements that are solicited by the media houses, and that are sympathetic to the ruling party.

The MNGRA was also seen to be a formula for weakening the church-state relations by way of attracting the clergy to be fully engaged in politics and abandoning their prophetic roles as the Old Testament prophets. For example, prophets, pastors, and bishops supporting the creation of the MNGRA were advised:

> I see prophets, pastors, and bishops abandoning the work of God and flocking into politics. Zambia will face hardship for abandoning the Lord our God. These men of God are supposed to denounce the injustice that is happening in our country, Zambia. People are being denied justice; it's written in the Bible that the truth will set you free. So, let justice prevail in our land, then, we can say Zambia is a Christian nation. Men of God, do not be lovers of money but stand for the truth because you are the messengers of God. Stay away from politics.[38]

Some of these pentecostal leaders vie for political office and/or cozy relations with political authorities. When a church helps to establish a new government, religious leaders often expect some kind of recognition of their authority, perhaps even a share in government.[39] As the church began to be part of government, the balance of power and political responsibility were threatened.

The Division within the Christian Mother Bodies over MNGRA

While the PFZ, BCZ, ICOZ, and EFZ brought out voices that suggested that the MNGRA would strengthen church-state relations, the ZCCB and CCZ asked searching questions about the relevance of the MNGRA at a time when the country was going through serious economic challenges. For example, the ZCCB and the CCZ released a press statement to register reasons against the creation of the new ministry. Their concerns were that the ministry had the potential to compromise the current church-state relationship as the state would begin to react favorably only to Christian denominations or religious groups that are supportive to the government. They were also concerned that the creation of a dedicated religious

38 Concerned Citizen, "Prophets, Pastors, Bishops Rush for Money," *Daily Nation*, September 12, 2016, 8.

39 Philip Jenkins, *The Next Christendom: The Coming of the Global Christianity*, 3rd ed. (New York: Oxford University Press, 2011), 186.

cabinet ministry was not at all a priority for a government that was struggling with uncontrollable debt and overblown expenditure as this was not going to help fiscal discipline. The major fear of ZCCB and ZCC is that: "Submission to the 'Christian state' can easily turn into a willful refusal to acknowledge the flaws of that regime, and to connive at official corruption and [even] violence."[40]

It is for this reason that Munshya wa Munshya has been fiercely critical of Pentecostals' reluctance to confront social and political causes of poverty in Zambia. He further argues that pentecostal pulpits teach that it is God's will to be rich, but fail to prophetically denounce political corruption.[41] At the root of the problem, we argue, is a lack of political theology although Munshya wa Munshya has argued that there is a pentecostal theology that lies dormant in Zambia. The question is, when will it surface and is there a cohort of pentecostal clergy with sound theological education to articulate it? Pentecostals in Africa see their role as engaging the political world from the spiritual realm[42] such that the growth of Pentecostalism in Zambia is essentially attributable to "health and wealth" teaching rather than a desire for social justice.[43]

Conclusion

In the period between 2015 and 2017, Lungu reconfigured the Christian nation fervor in Zambia to the extent that most Pentecostals and Charismatic born-again Christians have come to regard him as the custodian and defender of the Declaration so that Zambia remains a Christian nation. The creation of the MNGRA raised debates on the implications of the ministry on church-state relations. Therefore, this chapter has demonstrated that the discourse on the MNGRA with regard to what the ministry entailed for church-state relations revealed excitement on the one hand (EFZ, ICOZ, BCZ), and anxieties on the other (ZCCB and CCF). While the ministry was viewed to strengthen the relationship between the church and state by providing opportunities for promoting national morals, unity, and governance among others, some voices were still worried that the ministry would tone down the relationship especially as the church became part of government, a reality that mirrored a lack of consensus on the role of religion in politics and vice versa. We have therefore

40 Jenkins, *The Coming of the Global Christianity,* 188.

41 Munshya wa Munshya, "On Faith and Politics: Towards a Pentecostal Political Praxis in Zambia," *Daily Nation*, October 30, 2015, 11.

42 Jody Fleming, "African Pentecostalism and Social Action," in *Pentecostal Theology in Africa*, ed. Clifton R. Clarke (Eugene, OR: Pickwick Publications, 2014), 174–192.

43 Paul Gifford, *African Christianity: Its Public Role* (Bloomington: Indian University Press, 1998), 34–38.

argued from the perspective of prophetic realism, that the creation of MNGRA eventually has complicated the role of the church in politics resulting in a divided and compromised voice of the church. Because the Christian umbrella bodies were polarized, the ministry was largely perceived as a praying department of the Patriotic Front government that was yet to find its feet and become relevant to the well-being of Zambians.

3

THE NATIONALIZATION OF PRAYER AND PRAYERIZATION OF THE NATION

Chammah J. Kaunda

Introduction

This chapter delineates nationalization of prayer as the means by which prayer is utilized as a religio-cultural tool to articulate and enact political interests within the public spheres through state initiatives.[1] It seeks to interrogate how the National Day of Prayer and Fasting (hereafter, Day of Prayer) discourses are shrouded in a religio-nationalistic character that blurs the distinction between religion and politics. This results in sacralization of the reigning political system and elevates it beyond human critique. They operate as powerful religiopolitical instruments that are harnessed and deployed by particular social classes and religious groups to advance their religious and nationalistic interests. As such, most Zambian politicians are increasingly seeking to leverage the influence of Christians, especially Pentecostal-charismatics, to create an elite system of control conforming to pentecostal informed ideo-theologies about the ultimate source of power and authority. In the context of the Day of Prayer, the president of Zambia, Edgar Chagwa Lungu, appears to have a preferential option for Pentecostalism, even in the method of prayers. This is a direct development from the second republican President Frederick Chiluba's Declaration of Zambia as a Christian nation (hereafter, the Declaration) in which he excluded mainstream churches and non-Christian faith communities in favor of Pentecostalism.[2] In keeping

1 Jayeel Cornelio, "The Nationalisation of Religion: Youth and Soka Gakkai in Singapore," *Social Compass* (2018):1–17.

2 Chammah J. Kaunda, "The Day of Prayer and its Potential for Engendering Public Ecclesiology Ecumenism in Zambia," *Religions* 9, no. 12 (2018): 393.

with this orientation, first, the chapter begins by evaluating how scholars from various disciplines have engaged the notion of prayer in relation to sociopolitical transformation. Second, it presents the missio-political approach used to analyze data gathered on the pentecostal response to the Day of Prayer. The third section outlines the historical background to the call for the Day of Prayer. The final section investigates responses and contestations to the Day of Prayer within pentecostal communities.

On Prayer and Sociopolitical Transformation

Existing literature shows that Pentecostals interpret public spheres as terrains of contestation between good and evil. Richard Burgess argues that given the African pentecostal preoccupation with spiritual warfare "and restricted access to the corridors of power, there is an inner logic to pentecostal preferences for prayer as the principal tool for political engagement, which belies the movement's acquiescent image."[3] However, not all Pentecostals have limited access to political power, as they relate differently to national politics in various African countries. In some countries, such as Zambia, Pentecostals have enjoyed access to the corridors of political power, starting with Chiluba in the 1990s, and their influence has re-emerged with the current president. Despite this access to power, most Pentecostals would still argue that prayer is an indispensable aspect of their political action.[4] The challenge many scholars face is how to measure the impact of prayer on national politics. Some, such as Ruth Marshall,[5] Stephen Ellis, and Gerrie ter Haar,[6] argue that spiritual warfare contributes to social transformation in some African countries. However, she cautions against essentialism as there are some charismatic political activists who have articulated socially informed pentecostal theologies of liberation.[7] In

3 Richard Burgess, "Pentecostals and Political Culture in Sub-Sahara Africa: Nigeria, Zambia, and Kenya as Case Studies," in *Global Pentecostal Movements: Migration, Mission, and Public Religion*, ed. Michael Wilkinson (Leiden: Brill, 2012), 38.

4 Edward Luttwak, "The Missing Dimension," in *Religion: The Missing Dimension of Statecraft*, eds. Douglas Johnston and Cynthia Sarnpson (New York: Oxford University Press, 1994), 8–19; Isaac Phiri, *Proclaiming Political Pluralism: Churches and Political Transitions in Africa* (Westport, CT: Praeger, 2001); Harvey J. Sindima, *The Gospel According to the Marginalized* (New York: Peter Lang, 2008); Harvey J. Sindima, *Introduction to Religious Studies* (Lanham: University Press of America, 2009).

5 Ruth Marshall, *Political Spiritualities: The Pentecostal Revolution in Nigeria* (Chicago: University of Chicago Press, 2009); Ruth Marshall, "The Sovereignty of Miracles: Pentecostal Political Theology in Nigeria," *Constellations* 17, no. 2 (2010): 197–223.

6 See also, Stephen Ellis and Gerrie ter Haar, *Worlds of Power: Religious Thought and Political Practice in Africa* (London: C. Hurst, 2004).

7 Ruth Marshall, "Destroying Arguments and Captivating Thoughts: Spiritual

contrast, scholars such as Paul Gifford do not see how prayers of spiritual warfare could have any meaningful impact on Africa's development in modern society. He argues that Pentecostalism functions within an enchanted worldview that perpetuates spiritualization of national politics. For him, this worldview hinders the development of scientific rationality that is essential for effective governance in modern societies.[8]

However, scholars approaching prayer from the context of ritual demonstrate the indirect impact of prayer in transforming the political landscape. They argue that prayer can easily be applied to new purposes and hidden sociopolitical agenda. Marcin Pomarański, for instance, stresses that prayer presents a paradox in political science. It is utilized as both a strategic tool in political struggle, and as means to legitimize political powers. Politicians tap into prayer as a social ritual to position themselves as generating their political authority from a divine source.[9] Anthropologists argue that ritual power is a factor in the politics of legitimization.[10] They demonstrate how political leaders use rituals to insert and justify their own political authority and agenda.[11] These scholars argue that many politicians seek to incorporate socially acceptable principles of legitimation. They generate and legitimize their power by appealing to the strongest rituals within society that integrate familiar beliefs and practices to popularize their hidden agenda.[12] Lisa Lucero notes that political association with religio-socially acceptable rituals could result in sacralization and uncritical acceptance of political powers, as subjects increasingly believe that their politicians have been appointed by the Supernatural Being.[13]

Warfare Prayer as Global Praxis," *Journal of Religious and Political Practice* 2, no. 1 (2016): 108.

8 Paul Gifford, *Ghana's New Christianity: Pentecostalism in a Globalizing African Economy* (Bloomington, IN: Indiana University Press, 2004); Paul Gifford, *Christianity, Development and Modernity in Africa* (London: Hurst, 2015).

9 Marcin Pomarański, "'God Bless America': Prayer as a Political Ritual in the USA", *Annales UMCS, Sectio K (Politologia)* 20, no. 1 (2013):139–150.

10 David I. Kertzer, *Ritual, Politics, and Power* (New Haven: Yale University Press, 1988); Eric R. Wolf, *Envisioning Power: Ideologies of Dominance and Crisis* (Berkeley: University of California Press, 1999); Roy A. Rappaport, *Ritual and Religion in the Making of Humanity* (Cambridge: Cambridge University Press, 1999); Lisa J. Lucero, "The Politics of Ritual," *Current Anthropology* 44, no. 4 (2003): 523–558.

11 Kertzer, *Ritual, Politics, and Power*, 42.

12 Max Weber, *The Protestant Ethic and the Spirit of Capitalism*, trans. Talcott Parsons (London and New York: Routledge Classics, 1930 [2001]); Kent V. Flannery, "The Cultural Evolution of Civilizations," *Annual Review of Ecology and Systematics* 3 (1972): 399–426; Pierre Bourdieu, *The Logic of Practice*, trans. Richard Nice (Stanford: Stanford University Press, 1990); Lucero, "Politics of Ritual," 523–558.

13 Lucero, "Politics of Ritual," 525.

The foregoing discussion could potentially lead someone to conclude that the ritual does not enshrine any subversive power of resistance against political manipulation. It is important to underline that the ritual is not in itself susceptible to political manipulation; rather, it becomes vulnerable when self-interest of the custodians overpower the will to watch over the interests of masses. Beyond the views of political scientists, sociologists, and anthropologists, theologians argue that prayer, like all other religious rituals, is embedded in subversive spirituality against evil forces.[14] They stress that if approached from a social analytical perspective, prayer situated in the public spaces has the potential to challenge the *status quo* and promote the rearrangement of social norms, love-driven politics, and the religious, economic, and cultural values of a particular community. In other words, prayer has the potential to be utilized as "the power of the weak."[15] This means there are some public prayers that have the potential to create a spirituality of resistance that could bring about a new social consciousness and lead to authentic political transformation.

On a Missio-political Prayer Approach

The chapter is based on a wider project that sought to capture Zambian pentecostal culture and identity that embodies its understanding of God's mission in the context of national politics.[16] The data was gathered from over 350 pentecostal ministers, leaders, and laity through a multidirectional approach that included face-to-face interviews, group discussions, surveys, and blogs in Lusaka and Ndola from March 2016 to October 2017.[17] This chapter specifically focuses on the link between Pentecostalism and political praxis in relation to the Day of Prayer. The findings show that there is a division within pentecostal communities. On the one hand, there are some Pentecostals, especially the elites, who have accepted the Day of Prayer to the extent of legitimizing and justifying

14 Harvey J. Sindima, *Religious and Political Ethics in Africa: A Moral Inquiry* (Westport, CT: Greenwood Press, 1998).

15 Victor Turner, *The Ritual Process: Structure and Anti-structure* (Ithaca, NY: Cornell University Press, 1969), 108; and for detailed discussion of the notion of "weapon of the weak," see James C. Scott, *Weapons of the Weak: Everyday Forms of Peasant Resistance* (New Haven: Yale University Press, 1987).

16 For more detail about research findings, see Chammah J. Kaunda, "'From Fools for Christ to Fools for Politicians': A Critique of Zambian Pentecostal Theopolitical Imagination," *International Bulletin of Mission Research* 41, no. 4 (2017): 296–311; Chammah J. Kaunda, "*The Nation That Fears God Prospers*": *A Zambian Pentecostal Theology of Nations* (Minneapolis, MN: Fortress Press, 2018).

17 The research grant was given by John Templeton Foundation, through the Nagel Institute for the Study of World Christianity under the theme, "Christianity and Social Change in Contemporary Africa," Grant ID: 2016-TH210.

political power and authority. On the other hand, there are also voices of dissent from the margins arguing for a critical approach to the Day of Prayer for the sake of advancing social justice and economic equality.

This chapter takes a missio-political approach to prayer. It argues that the phenomenon of prayer is empirical by nature because it is embedded within the faith communities' ongoing participation in God's missional activity in the world within a particular sociocultural context.[18] In this study, missio-political prayer refers to the public missional praxis of the church where the action of the state is put under God's eye.[19] Missio-political prayer does not separate the act of praying from political commitment to total liberation and social transformation.[20] Missio-political prayer does not depend on Christians having or exercising political authority by any means; rather, it seeks to create a critical safe space for the church to promote social healing and reconciliation indispensable for national building and social cohesion, justice and equality, human rights and good governance, resistance against corruption and sociopolitical and economic injustice, and unapologetic promotion of abundant life for all.

Since prayer is an aspect of practical theology, scholars suggest empirical theology as a methodological approach. Jan Jongeneel[21] and Tobias Faix[22] affirm that empirical research is a methodological foundation for missiology as well. In this approach, the study focuses on a particular religious phenomenon rather than the congregations.[23] Within an empirical missiological approach, the study is underpinned by Harvey Sindima's twofold model of missio political prayer analysis. The first is a type of prayer he calls "empty talk." This is a form of prayer with no sociopolitical impact. Sindima argues that,

> a prayer that does not initiate one into some kind of action, a transformation, a conversion, is an empty talk. At best, such prayer is therapy, an emotional catharsis that makes one feel good because deep inner

---

18 Tobias Faix, "The Empirical-Theological Praxis (ETP) Cycle as a Methodological Basis for Missiology," *Missionalia* 35, no. 1 (2007): 113–129.

19 See Allan A. Boesak and Charles Villa-Vicencio, eds., *When Prayer Makes News* (Philadelphia: Westminster, 1986); Christian Iosso and Elizabeth Hinson-Hasty, eds., *Prayers for the New Social Awakening: Inspired by the New Social Creed* (Louisville: Westminster John Knox Press, 2008).

20 Harvey J. Sindima, *The Gospel According to the Marginalized* (New York: Peter Lang, 2008), 47.

21 Jan A.B. Jongeneel, *Science and Theology of Mission in the 19th and 20th Centuries: A Missiological Encyclopaedia: The Philosophy and Science of Mission* (Zurich: Peter Lang, 1995), 182.

22 Faix, "Empirical-Theological Praxis (ETP)," 113–129.

23 Kaunda, "*Nation That Fears God Prospers,*" 69.

> feelings have been verbalized. That cannot be talking to and listening to God, but a need to hear oneself.[24]

The "empty talk" does not integrate prayer and political commitment with concrete social transformation through acts of resistance against political injustice and corruption. There are three characteristics of "empty talk" prayer. First, it is shaped by status-seeking motives which affect the church's ability to distinguish the mission of God in politics from politics itself, and as such, fails to challenge the *status quo*. Second, it tends to spiritualize politics and individualize social problems. Third, there is also very little theology of advocacy for the excluded and marginalized. Although empty-talk prayer is done in public, it has little concern for social transformation; rather, it unwittingly legitimizes political powers.

The second approach in Sindima's twofold model of missio-political prayer analysis is prayer as sociopolitical action. The approach seeks God's missional possibilities from countercultural and marginal spaces.[25] It perceives public prayer as a critical space for contesting the unquestioned neocolonial construction of dominant political imaginations, and for subverting the politics of corruption and repression inherent in the contemporary political order.[26] This is a form of prayer that seeks to shape political struggle for justice and human liberation. As Sindima describes it:

> Prayer is a silent revolution against evil in all its manifestations, individual and structural. To pray is to say the world is not as God intended it to be; it is no longer as good as it was at creation. To pray is to acknowledge that people have corrupted the world and that the whole creation groans as it awaits liberation. Prayer is ushering the rule of God into one's life and the world.[27]

Sindima perceives missio-political prayer as multidirectional in its orientation. It places emphasis on the constant interaction between words spoken to God, with concrete social actions aimed at transformation in relational, social, structural, economic, political, and cultural configurations of the national landscape. In other words, prayer as sociopolitical action is based on a vigorous and passionate search for the reign of God in the nation, as it is in heaven. Sindima believes that the authenticity of prayer as sociopolitical action is based on enactment of God's mission

---

24 Sindima, *Religious and Political Ethics in Africa*, 180.

25 Amos Yong, *The Missiological Spirit: Christian Mission Theology in the Third Millennium Global Context* (Eugene, OR: Cascade Books, 2014).

26 Chammah J. Kaunda, "Enabling Liminality Prophetic Witness to Xenophobia: Proposing a Missiological Spirit Response for the Church in South Africa," *KOERS—Bulletin for Christian Scholarship* 81, no. 1 (2016): 1–9, http://dx.doi.org/10.19108/ KOERS.81.1.2217.

27 Sindima, *Religious and Political Ethics in Africa*, 180.

through political struggle and includes resistance, public witness, speech, acts, and redemptive social actions. Through this model, it became clear that there are contestations among Zambian Pentecostals in their ways of engaging in the Day of Prayer.

Zambia's Lungu and Politicization of Prayer

The current president of Zambia, Edgar Chagwa Lungu, began as a Defense and Justice Minister in the late Michael Sata's Patriotic Front (PF) political party. Sata became the president of Zambia in 2011 and died in office in 2014. Lungu took up the office on October 28, 2014, until the presidential elections in January 2015. Sata did not groom a successor, and after his death, political factions and rivalry broke out over who should be the presidential candidate of the PF. Lungu was finally adopted as the candidate and won the election in January 2015 to finish Sata's term. While Lungu won the election, "tribalism" in voting patterns was more pronounced than in all the previous presidential elections.

In addition to these, Lungu's few months in office were also riddled with overwhelming economic challenges. The copper price on which the nation's 70 percent of export income is derived, declined and the currency plunged down to over 45 percent against the USD. The nation was experiencing falling water levels at hydropower plants, which triggered the highest load shedding ever. Alarmed, Lungu resolved to seek divine intervention. He declared October 18, 2015, a public holiday for a National Day of Prayer and Fasting, which included prayers for national repentance, forgiveness, and reconciliation. He instructed all bars, nightclubs, entertainment places, and all eateries, to be closed on the day, and the Football Association of Zambia to cancel all domestic games. The church leaders were encouraged to organize their members for prayer and fasting. On this day, the people of Zambia came together to seek help from the Lord.

On that day, Lungu first re-affirmed Chiluba's 1991 declaration of Zambia as a Christian nation, and added his own declaration: "Zambia set free from the dark forces of evil."[28] Second, he declared October 18 as an Annual National Day of Prayer and Fasting, which was also gazetted as a National Public Holiday. Third, on October 25, 2015, Lungu conducted a ceremony for the construction of the National House of Prayer (NHoP) to help actualize Zambia as a Christian nation.[29] The mission statement of the NHoP is to "establish prayer as a foundation for righteousness and

[28] Kamufisa Manchishi, "President Edgar Lungu Speaks at the Day of Prayer & Fasting," accessed October 18, 2016, https://www.youtube.com/watch?v=UDEw7zTM2rU.

[29] National House of Prayer, *National House of Prayer* (Lusaka: NHoP, 2016), 4.

justice, peace, and prosperity and co-existence in love."[30] The construction is still underway in a government reserved area in Lusaka. It is a ten thousand seat auditorium that is estimated to cost $10 million (USD). Lungu has also appointed twelve members of the advisory board, fundraising and technical committee, chaired by a pentecostal Bishop, Dr. Joshua Banda of the Northmead Assembly of God, to spearhead the construction of NHoP. Most members in the advisory board represent pentecostal forms of Christianity. Lungu's subtle association with Pentecostalism appears to have contributed to his victory in the 2016 presidential election.

In an almost appreciative manner for support that Lungu received from some Pentecostals during the presidential campaign, he introduced the Ministry of Religious Affairs and National Guidance (hereafter, the ministry). He also appointed a pentecostal lady pastor, Godfridah Sumaili,[31] as its head. The introduction of this Ministry came while the opposition party's petition over perceived electoral fraud during the presidential election on August 11, 2016, was still pending in the Constitutional Court.[32] Before Lungu was even inaugurated, he promised to introduce the ministry, arguing that it was imperative in the process of reaffirmation and actualization of the Declaration. The elections were regarded as manipulated, and the main opposition—The United Party for National Development (UPND)—demanded a recount of the votes. Lungu won the election with 50.3 percent to defeat Hichilema who got 47.6 percent. These political issues make it significant to analyze how Zambian Pentecostalism has responded to the Day of Prayer.

Prayerization of the Nation: Variety of Pentecostal Responses

This section interrogates the responses of Zambian Pentecostalism to the Declaration of the Day of Prayer. The responses are developed into three sections, as Evangelical Fellowship of Zambia (EFZ), pentecostal elites, and Pentecostals on the margins.

---

30 National House of Prayer, *National House of Prayer*, 3.

31 Rev. Sumaili is a pastor at Bread of Life Church International (BLCI), under Bishop Joe Imakando. This is the largest single congregation in Zambia, with over 12,000 members.

32 See *Zambia Reports*, "Pres. Lungu Wins Tight Presidential Election; ECL 1, 860, 877 Hichilema 1, 760, 347," accessed August 28, 2016, https://zambiareports.com/2016/08/15/pres-lungu-wins-tight-presidential-election-ecl-1-860-877-hichilema-1-760-347/.

The Response of EFZ

The response of EFZ can only be fully appreciated in comparison to the responses of its two counterpart churches' mother bodies in Zambia—the Council of Churches in Zambia (CCZ) and The Zambia Conference of Catholic Bishops (ZCCB). The CCZ, ZCCB, and EFZ, classified as three church mother bodies, have played a critical role in issues related to national politics and religio-social cohesion. They have often worked closely on many issues affecting the nation. In the late 1980s through to the early 1990s, the expression of ecumenism by these church mother bodies was increasingly described as "genuine ecumenism."[33] Nonetheless, the change in leadership has meant that the focus on the activities that seek to promote the common good have been overlooked. The fundamental quest appears to be nationalization of pentecostal-oriented morality in the nation. The demographic explosion of Pentecostalism and its increasing participation in EFZ has brought a paradigm shift in the organization's theological emphasis and missional orientation. The EFZ is now principally pentecostal in character with 90 percent of its Executive Board members identified as Pentecostals.[34]

Thus, the three church mother bodies no longer see eye-to-eye on many national issues. Even on the question of nationalization of prayer, they have responded in different ways. The two church mother bodies that house mainline churches—CCZ and ZCCB—have rejected the politicization of prayer. These two mother bodies foresee the possibility of the process resulting in religionization of politics. They also rejected the introduction of the Ministry of Religious Affairs and National Guidance. They argued that the introduction was both "unwise and unnecessary . . . in view of the various financial and economic challenges our country is currently facing."[35] They further argued that "Zambians want their country to be a democracy rather than a theocracy."[36] The two mother bodies had also rejected Chiluba's Declaration of Zambia as a Christian nation, as it was done without any formal consultation with the wider church but only one sector of the church, Pentecostalism. The

33 Paul Gifford, *African Christianity: Its Public Role* (Bloomington, IN: Indiana University Press, 1998), 188.

34 See EFZ, "Our Executive Board Members," accessed October 17, 2016, http://www.efzsecretariat.org). Other scholars have made this observation, too. See Gifford, *African Christianity*; Burgess, "Pentecostals and Political Culture."

35 Vatican News, "Catholics and Protestant Churches in Zambia against New Ministry of Religion," accessed October 28, 2016, http://en.radiovaticana.va/news/2016/09/21/catholics_and_protestants_in_zambia_against_new_ministry/125974.

36 Vatican News, "Catholics and Protestant Churches."

two mother bodies have always sought for more constructive engagement with social issues rather than using prayer as an excuse.

However, the introduction received indiscriminate support and was uncritically defended by EFZ. Even though it was the political context that gave rise to the Day of Prayer, some EFZ maintained that it has no political implications. In response to the Day of Prayer, some Pentecostals who describe themselves as prayer warriors have created a WhatsApp blog under the group name "One nation under Christ." This blog was created to coordinate the activities of the Day of Prayer and promote ongoing prayer for the nation. The group consists of over 92 participants across the nation and some from the diaspora, including some prominent pentecostal clergy, pentecostal politicians such as Honorable Rev. Godfridah Sumaili and Honorable Dr. Liya Mutale, and the General Secretary of EFZ, Rev. Pukuta Mwanza.

There are at least two diverging political theological ideas operating within the three church mother bodies. The first is the ecumenical political theology from the CCZ and ZCCB. These two mother bodies have well-developed theological ideals of social order and justice, and a long history and tradition of practical engagement with the state. The second is an evangelical/pentecostal political theology that informs EFZ's ideo-theological orientation. The EFZ political theology is shaped by theocratic politics rather than liberatory politics.[37] This theocratic imagination has little or no focus on authentic Christian faith shaped by missional activism. It seeks to impose a pentecostal nationalism with a morality dictated by pentecostal beliefs and practices. It is grounded on the triumph of Pentecostalism over other church denominations and religions and political parties not approved by a sect of pentecostal leadership.[38] It is not informed by the search for sociopolitical justice from the margins and by the marginalized, but rather a spiritual struggle to be addressed only through prayer and fasting. They believe that the root of political corruption, injustice, and human right violations are spiritual problems that are to be identified and dealt with in the spiritual realm.[39] Once this is done, the positive effects will be evident in the natural through divine intervention or miracle. For instance, Rev. Pukuta Mwanza of EFZ argues that "if

---

37 Ruth Marshall, *Political Spiritualities: The Pentecostal Revolution in Nigeria* (Chicago: University of Chicago Press, 2009); Nimi Wariboko, *Nigerian Pentecostalism* (Rochester: University of Rochester Press, 2014).

38 Susan M. Shaw, "The Political Theology of Trumpian Evangelicalism: God Sides with the Powerful," *Huffpost*, July 28, 2017, accessed February 26, 2018, https://www.huffingtonpost.com/entry/the-political-theology-of-trumpian-evangelicalism_us_597b6b35e4b06b305561d01e.

39 Clifton R. Clarke, ed., *Pentecostal Theology in Africa* (Eugene, OR: Pickwick, 2014).

we prioritize God, the material needs of our country will be taken care of by God's supernatural provision and blessings. First things first."[40] He believes that prayer cannot be politicked as it is in continuation with biblical tradition and the history of Zambia.[41]

Since Chiluba's Declaration of Zambia as a Christian nation in 1991, there has been ongoing theological conflict and confusion as to the role of the church in politics and society. The demarcation between religion and politics has become increasingly fluid and confused, especially by EFZ. In some cases, the church has allowed the state to set the agenda for its mission in the nation. The identity of the church is often muddled; its missional mandate is confused with promoting the interests of the reigning government. The church appears to have religionized the concept of political power, which is often placed in mystical dimensions. This approach to political power makes the president withdraw his political accountability from the voters and relocate it in the mystical realm as its authentic source. This also robs the church of the political mandate to call the state to account. In this context, the church is always seen as the servant of the state rather than a community with a mandate to call the state to divine accountability. This is an ancient problem in the history of the church and EFZ continues to demonstrate ignorance of history.

The Response of Pentecostal Elites

The second response emerges from some pentecostal elites who have uncritically affirmed the call for prayer in a way that appears to legitimize the status quo. Some pentecostal elites are persuaded that only prayer can liberate the nation from neocolonial challenges. In the speech on the first official commemoration of the Day of Prayer on October 18, 2016, The National House of Prayer Advisory chairperson, Bishop Joshua Banda, stressed that Lungu's Declaration "is an announcement of a new spiritual dispensation in Zambia." He underlined that "we are determined to raise a praying Christian nation . . . for without prayer, the life of the nation will be taken away."[42] Many Zambian Pentecostals would agree with his assertion as they perceive prayer as critical for political transformation, and transformation is impossible without prayer, especially spiritual warfare. But as Sindima argues, it is not every form of prayer that can bring about social transformation. Banda also does not explain what life of the nation he is talking about. Thus, while Banda's optimism about prayer

40 Pukuta N. Mwanza, "Justification for the Construction of the National House of Prayer—An Evangelical Reaction," unpublished paper, January 6, 2016, 2.

41 Mwanza, "Justification for the Construction," 4.

42 "Bishop Joshua Banda's Speech during National Day of Prayer and Fasting October 18, 2016," accessed October 28, 2016, https://www.youtube.com/watch?v=xLs2234nopQ.

has political implications in relation to social challenges, it is inadequate in that it does not promote prophetic criticism that can help in creating new political structures. This form of prayer is what Sindima classifies as empty discourse that legitimizes the political status quo and has no clear agenda for concrete political transformation.

The Declaration of the Day of Prayer made some Pentecostals believe that Lungu is the right president for Zambia. A pentecostal clergy and politician, Rev. Danny Pule, argues:

> I am supporting President Lungu because I believe he is the right man at the time that God has put in the national leadership. Of all the candidates, I can't see anyone who can help us advance Christian leadership. Lungu has shown it by declaring the Day of Prayer and reconciliation and annual holiday on which we'll remember to thank God and dedicate ourselves and our nation to the Lord. As a result, we are building a National House of Prayer which Chiluba did not do.[43]

Declaring the Day of Prayer was kind of Lungu's presidential debut among some Pentecostals. It made him a national religious celebrity, such that some Pentecostals even formed a Christian campaign wing called Christians for Lungu (vote for Edgar Lungu).[44] In an interview, the chairperson for the movement, who is also Pentecostal, Dr Liya Mutale,[45] argued that Lungu is a "*God ordained leader*" for Zambia. She emphatically argued that the August 11, 2016 presidential election was

> a spiritual election, a battle for the soul of Zambia. So, we have to ensure that Zambian Christian heritage is sustained, it's secured. And to keep it secure, we keep the man that God has called for the season. And we believe that Edgar Chagwa Lungu is that man, so as far as we are concerned, he is winning the election anyway.[46]

The spiritualization of elections emerging from Mutale affirms Sindima's argument that empty prayer tends to spiritualize the political realm. In fact, the two main presidential candidates Lungu and the opposition UPND led by Hakainde Hichilema—were categorized in terms of the struggle between good and evil. On the one hand,

---

43 Dr. Danny Pule, interview with the author, Pule residential house in Lusaka, June 11, 2016.

44 Christians for Lungu, "Christians for Lungu—Vote for Edgar C. Lungu," accessed October 28, 2016, http://www.christiansforlungu.org/.

45 At the time of the interview, Dr. Mutale was unemployed but immediately after Lungu won the August 2016 elections, she was appointed Permanent Secretary in the Ministry of Tourism and Arts.

46 Liya Mutale, interview with the author, Twin Palm Street, Lusaka, May 30, 2016.

Hakainde Hichilema was categorized as a Satanist.[47] This already made him an agent of darkness that some Pentecostals had to fight against in order to secure Lungu's winning. On the other hand, Lungu's declaration made him an angel of light—"*God ordained leader*"—as Dr. Mutale underlines. On the inauguration of Day of Prayer, Lungu argued, "I have done my part to reconcile the church and the state."[48] It appears that Lungu enacted the Day of Prayer as a political ritual through which he has won the favor of many Pentecostals. There is little prophetic criticism in the Day of Prayer. There has not been any engagement in authentic prophetic resistance against political corruption and nepotism; rather, it has helped reconstruct the image of Lungu as a Christian president. The Day of Prayer is not open to criticism and anyone who dares challenge the action is deemed an enemy of God and therefore an enemy of the nation and equated to being a Satanist. The fact that the Day of Prayer precludes intellectual discussions reinforces Lungu's sacralization. It functions as a vehicle for political legitimacy.

There are some Pentecostals who are against those who question the legitimacy of the Day of Prayer. They have argued that the Day of Prayer and politics are not related. For instance, a participant on the "One Nation under Christ" WhatsApp blog stressed: "Let's keep this page [Blog] for our specific purpose of 'One nation under Christ.' There is a myriad of things in the Kingdom. We must understand our portion. Please know the difference to keep our focus on our calling even for such a time as this. We cannot be in everything."[49] Another affirms: "I agree entirely. When I look at the ministry of our Saviour, he was focused on what the Father sent him to do. It is important for us to develop this discipline. We have limited time, strength, resources, etc. We cannot focus on everything. Our efforts will be spread and we will not achieve our mandate."[50] Another participant insists:

> Corruption is all over the world, never mind the indexes. There are very few countries that are pure. Dwelling on politics is wasted energy. In Jesus's days, Rome and the Herod were very unjust and corrupt. But Jesus stayed focussed on His mission and didn't remove the

47 General Kanene Feat Chester, "Ulemu Kwa Alungu (Reply to Pilato)" https://www.youtube.com/watch?v=8GHxr1OAHZw; Lusakatimes.com, "HH's Name Appears on the Register of the Freemasons, Bishop Chomba Tells Court," accessed October 30, 2016, https://www.lusakatimes.com/2015/01/09/hhs-name-appears-register-freemasons-bishop-chomba-tells-court/.

48 Edgar Lungu, "President Edgar Lungu—National Day of Prayer and Fasting," accessed October 28, 2016, https://www.youtube.com/watch?v=RPc-IzC_Tgc.

49 Blogger, "One Nation under Christ," WhatsApp Blog, October 14, 2017. The rest of references are from this page unless indicated.

50 Blogger, October 19, 2017.

> Herod etc. Let's stay focussed and let politics be handled (or mishandled) by politicians. There is one who is the god of this world. B[u]t we belong to the world whose ruler is the King of Kings and Lord of all.[51]

These Pentecostals advocate for prayer that promotes a radical flight from reality. While prayer is the soul and breath of authentic Christianity, prayer that does not translate into concrete political action cannot bring about social change. They promote empty-talk prayer based on personal repentance, forgiveness, and reconciliation as sufficient for the realization of peace and a transformed society.[52] But prayer without political activism is "faith without works," which James 2:14 classifies as "dead." However, there is a brand of Pentecostalism that is dissatisfied with prayer that does not translate into concrete actions. For instance, Rev. Elias Munshya categorizes prayer without action as good rhetoric that does not transcend emotional therapy.[53]

The Response of the Margins

The third response emerges within Pentecostals who are mostly from the margins. These have responded in ways that have the potential to promote a transformative political agenda. Perhaps, one of the values of the call for the Day of Prayer lies in the fact that it has engendered critical discussions among Pentecostals themselves. The discussants are seeking to understand how a movement grounded in such unparalleled theological diversity, inconsistency, and competition for public recognition can engage constructively in national politics. The scope of this chapter does not allow for engagement with such a broader question. Rather, this section is limited to analysis of the debates seeking to strike a balance between prayer and concrete political action. However, as already demonstrated above, some pentecostal elites argue that the Day of Prayer should not be interpreted in political terms, rather as a spiritual activity. However, this has not deterred participants on the "One Nation under Christ" WhatsApp blog from analyzing the Day of Prayer from a political perspective. For instance, one participant posted a lamentation:

> My heart is heavy, my spirit is low because of levels of corruption in my country, the country I love so dearly, the country of my fathers, the country that I will leave for my children. But what sort of country

51 Blogger, October 24, 2017.

52 Gregory Deacon makes a similar observation among Kenyan Pentecostals. See Gregory Deacon, "Driving the Devil Out: Kenya's Born-Again Election," *Journal of Religion in Africa* 45 (2015), 200–220.

53 Elias Munshya, "After We have Said 'Amen': Towards a Pentecostal Theology of Politics in Zambia," October 15, 2015, accessed October 25, 2017, https://eliasmunshya.org.

> are we going to leave for our children? With these levels of corruption, our country's future outlook does not look bright. Something must be done, and must be done now.[54]

This blogger is calling for prayer that can contribute concretely to human struggle in Zambia. Another participant questions: "You people of this group surprise me how do you want to pray for Zambia and yet you want to avoid discussing politics. The Bible [is] 80 percent politics and wars. I can't pray for the nation without talking about its politics and economics."[55] The blog creator, Rev. Derek Mutungu, posted prayer points under the heading "Prayer for the president is an urgent RED ALERT." He argued,

> I've heard an outcry at the throne of heaven concerning his Excellency and his cabinet. The main issue is for him to come into line with Psalm 72. This is the prime Scripture in the Bible concerning the calling, mandate, influence, and legacy of a godly king. He is a royal son, meaning one who is positioned as a vice regent on earth to the eternal king in heaven. S/he operates in the Office of Jesus as king of kings and Yahweh regent in the entire universe. [56]

The use of the word *outcry* is of interest, for, rarely would a Pentecostal use such a term on a social space accessible to politicians. Rev. Mutungu appears to position himself as a prophet revealing the mind and the feelings of God concerning the president of Zambia. This outcry is itself both confirmation that the president has not carried out the mandate of God in the nation and the seriousness of such disobedience. Rev. Mutungu clarifies: "We don't use the word king to mean that Zambia is a monarchy, but in the simple sense of a HEAD OF STATE."[57] This is a radical departure from the common Zambian pentecostal theology that tends to regard the president in monarchical terms. He quoted Psalm 72:1–4[58] where he underlined what he terms a "six specific prayer point" focus for praying for the president, as follows:

1. *ECL [Edgar Chagwa Lungu] to understand his relation to Yahweh as a ROYAL SON (v.1b). With that conviction, for him to pursue righteousness in his own life and demand it of his entire cabinet (v.2).*

---

54 Blogger, October 14, 2017.

55 Blogger, October 24, 2017.

56 Blogger, October 24, 2017.

57 Blogger, October 24, 2017.

58 "Endow the king with your justice, O God, the royal son with your righteousness. May he judge your people in righteousness, your afflicted ones with justice. May the mountains bring prosperity to the people, the hills the fruit of righteousness. May he defend the afflicted among the people and save the children of the needy; may he crush the oppressor" (Psalm 72:1–4 NIV).

2. *ECL to appreciate his calling as chief vice regent to Christ in Zambia for this brief moment. (Note the children "your people... your afflicted ones" in v. 2). Since the nation is covenanted to the Lamb, ECL is there to establish the purposes of Christ.*
3. *In that role HE [His Excellence] is to demand justice (v.2) in his personal dealings and establish a godly standard of distributive justice in the entire government and of retributive justice in the judicial system.*
4. *True prosperity to burst upon Zambia (v.3), and his own legacy before God and men hangs on the twin virtues of righteousness and justice from top to bottom and up again.*
5. *A preferential bias to the poor (v.4). That HE will truly "defend the afflicted... save the children of the needy and crush Zambians or foreigners who oppress the needy."*
6. *Saints, please understand that heaven is in a hurry to carve a righteous nation out of Zambia so she can be an outstanding sign and a beacon to other nations.*[59]

While Rev. Mutungu still uses terminologies such as "chief vice regent of Christ in Zambia," that could easily be misinterpreted as the president in a democratic society who draws the mandate and power to rule from the voters. He is rather calling for a presidency shaped by the struggles of the marginalized and excluded. He is calling for the presidency of the marginalized. In this form of presidency, the margins should become key actors in shaping how the president governs the nation and shapes public policies. This type of presidency could be classified as an incarnational presidency. The president of Zambia must fulfill its mandate by opting to be with the marginalized people of Zambia, "not out of paternalistic charity but because their situations testify to [structural wickedness of the nation] and their yearnings for life pointed to God's purposes."[60] Rev. Mutungu argues that the presidency must be reshaped in the encounter with the margins. This will help all politicians resist the forces of corruption, nepotism, and globalization, and reposition politics anew in response to human struggles.

In other words, the margins should inform the process of presiding over the nation, for "transformation never genuinely happens at the center but at the margins where the reality of people seeking 'fullness of life' ... becomes a 'new creative core.'" [61] They are challenging Pentecostalism to

[59] Blogger, September 7, 2017.

[60] Jooseup Keum, ed., *Together toward Life: Mission and Evangelism in Changing Landscapes* (Geneva: World Council of Churches Publications, 2013), 15.

[61] Chammah J. Kaunda and Roderick R. Hewitt, "Together towards Life: Reconceptualising Missio-Formation in Changing Landscape of World Christianity," *Pharos Journal of Theology* 96 (2015): 11.

resist assimilation by the state and the loss of its missional identity and prophetic responsibility to the marginalized.[62] They see sociopolitical prayer as a liberation, a movement from prayer as engaging God to prayer as engaging social actions in concrete terms. Prayer is God's design for engaging the world through speech acts, which materializes in the application of the redemptive and emancipatory mind of God in human struggles. Sindima classifies this form of prayer as multidirectional as it constantly interacts with God's redemptive and justice mind, with concrete social and political actions aimed at transformation in the political realm. This form of prayer finds its place in political and social practice. It exalts people to develop an oppositional lifestyle that subverts the dominant political culture of corruption and injustice, in daily activities of thinking, feeling, and acting. An oppositional lifestyle is a means to engage in powerful resistance to an oppression. It fosters questioning of the legitimacy of nationalization of prayer and has the potential to lead to understanding on how poor governance is reflected within the wider society and among the margins through violence, institutionalization of corruption, injustice, human rights abuse, and so on. It is still too early to demonstrate how the emerging prayer as sociopolitical action will contribute to the Day of Prayer and transformation of the political agenda. As Roderick Hewitt observes in the Jamaican context, missio-political prayer "suggests that the complex global and local factors that are negatively impacting on the contemporary nation's well-being, necessitates that other missional tools that can embody the spirituality of prayer but are more practically engaged in offering alternative models of national development must be explored by the churches and shared with the political and civil leaders for national implementation."[63]

Conclusion

This chapter demonstrates the centrality of faith assumptions in pentecostal notions of the Zambian national state. These assumptions are critical in understanding their responses to the Declaration of the Prayer Day in Zambia that was called by President Lungu. For most Pentecostals, prayer embodies the spiritual phenomena of power and political influence because its fundamental objective is to converse with God. The challenge is that their reverence and whole-heartedness in their faith assumptions

62 Allan Boesak, *The Tenderness of Conscience: African Renaissance and the Spirituality of Politics* (Stellenbosch: Sun Press, 2005).

63 Roderick Hewitt, "A Missio-political Critique of National Prayer Breakfasts in Jamaica since 1981," unpublished paper presented at the 14th Assembly of the International Association for Mission Studies, "Conversions and Transformations: Missiological Approaches to Religious Change," August 11–17, 2016, Seoul, South Korea, 11.

has meant they give little attention to seeking rational understanding of their missional identity in relation to political praxis. However, as the chapter argues, the Day of Prayer has provided an opportunity for some members of pentecostal communities to start raising uncomfortable contextual questions and to reflect on what it means to engage in public prayer in the context of economic crisis and political corruption, nepotism, human rights abuses, and veritable poverty. What is God's vision for Zambia? What is the missional role of Pentecostalism in bringing about God's kingdom in Zambia? In what ways can prayer help to bring about transformation of power structures? How can public leaders—both religious and political—be made fully accountable to the margins? There are some Pentecostals who are increasingly recognizing that God has a preferential option to work with, within, from, and through the people on the margins. They believe that missio-political prayer should move Pentecostalism to see, analyze, and denounce the systems of evil compromising the humanity and dignity of the majority of the Zambian people in concrete ways.

4

PRAYER, POLITICS, AND POWER

Jonathan Kangwa

Introduction

Anthropologists have underlined that rituals serve to negotiate, mediate, and enact power within religious and political relationships.[1] They demonstrate how politicians utilize religious rituals to foster unity in the country or to convince people that their presidency is God-given.[2] On the National Day of Prayer at the White House in 2017, President Donald Trump stated that "prayer changes hearts and transforms lives."[3] He further noted that prayer "inspires action and unites" people "all as one nation under God."[4] What Trump brings to the fore is that a strong belief in prayer is part of the history of the Americans and their political ideology. In this case, prayer is not perceived as a mere form of communication with God. Rather, it is a ritualized political action that embodies an ideology that unites the nation. Similarly, a review of how prayer and corporate worship are used in Zambian politics throws new light on the role of prayer as a ritual in the micro-politics of everyday life. It reveals the way in which Zambian politicians attempt to use prayer and religious

1 Rodney A. Werline, "Prayer, Politics and Power in the Hebrew Bible: Interpretation," *A Journal of Bible and Theology* 68, no 1 (2014): 5.

2 Anthropology explores human biological and cultural diversity. It seeks to examine the origins of, and changes in, human biology and culture. See Conrad P. Kottak, *Anthropology: The Exploration of Human Diversity.* 9th ed. (Boston: McGraw Hill, 2002), 27.

3 Speech by President Donald Trump on National Day of Prayer at White House in 2017, accessed January 1, 2019, https://www.youtube.com/watch?v=lzlpO2lj-JE.

4 Speech by President Donald Trump on National Day of Prayer at White House in 2017.

ritual to win the support of the electorate.[5] First, President Chiluba's declaration of Zambia as a Christian nation is analyzed to show how prayer can be used to foster a particular political ideology.

Zambia's Christian Declaration as a Political Action

On December 29, 1991, President Frederick Chiluba dedicated and declared Zambia a Christian nation. In the ritualized prayer, he declared,

> On behalf of the nation I have now entered a covenant with the living God. And therefore, I want to make the following declaration: I declare today that I submit myself as president to the lordship of Jesus Christ. I likewise submit the government and the entire nation of Zambia to the lordship of Jesus Christ. I further declare that Zambia is a Christian nation. That we will seek to be governed by the righteous principles of the word of God. Righteousness and justice must prevail in all levels of authority. And then we shall see the righteousness of God exalt Zambia. My fellow Zambians, let this message reach all civil servants in all government departments. The time of corruption and bribery is over. For too long, these wicked practices have been destroying and tearing down the nation. Now the hour has come for our building up. The hour has come for stability.[6]

In a ritual performed at the State House (the official residence of the president in Zambia), President Chiluba stated that the nation of Zambia had now come to God for repentance. For Chiluba, the people of Zambia have been wicked due to idolatry, witchcraft, occultism, immorality, injustice, and corruption—wicked ways that had violated God's laws. Chiluba went on to invoke the name of God in heaven (the Christian Creator God) and the blood of Jesus to cleanse the country of Zambia from all wicked ways and the consequences of wickedness—calling for healing, restoration, blessing, and prosperity.[7]

Consistent with the African worldview, the Declaration embodies a brief that Zambia's economic meltdown and social problems are due to

5 Chammah J. Kaunda and Mutale M. Kaunda have interrogated how the National Day of Prayer and Fasting declared by President Edgar Lungu on October 18, 2015, embodies "a religio-nationalistic character that blurs the distinction between religion and politics." Kaunda and Kaunda rightly observe that public prayer has been used by President Lungu to sacralize "the reigning political system and elevates it beyond human critique." See Chammah J. Kaunda and Mutale M. Kaunda, "'An Announcement of a New Spiritual Dispensation': Pentecostalism and Nationalization of Prayer in Zambia," *Journal of Theology for Southern Africa* 161 (2018): 72.

6 Declaration of Zambia as a Christian Nation by President Frederick Chiluba, accessed December 13, 2018, https://www.youtube.com/watch?v=RhFX5kywvCs.

7 Declaration of Zambia as a Christian Nation.

the people's failure to please the spiritual (invisible) forces. As Kaunda notes, it contemplates the link between the social and the spiritual realms.[8] David Gordon also makes this observation.

> By insisting on an autonomous relationship with God, Pentecostals offered an alternative morality to humanism. In part, Kaunda's regime succumbed to a revolution based on these pentecostal ideas. Instead of leading to a neoliberal multiparty democracy that entrenched individual rights, however, a politics of spiritual patrimonialism emerged. Blessing in this world devolved from prophets who had access to the spirit world. Those who sought power in this world, in the form of wealth or political influence, had to cultivate relationships with the spirit world through a new class of pentecostal "big men" and "big women." [9]

Gordon further notes that "Zambian Pentecostals wanted to rid the world of evil spirits, to defeat those who used spirits to bewitch others, and to harness the Holy Spirit to achieve prosperity. These ideas spread beyond the diverse collection of evangelical churches to Protestants and even to Roman Catholics."[10] In the same line, Kaunda notes that pentecostal Christians in Zambia have mined the belief in African culture that holds "that the authority and power of the ancestors is embodied in the king, who acts as the unionization of religion and political power in his body and personality."[11] This Christian-African worldview is illustrated below.

Figure 1: Showing a Zambian-African Worldview

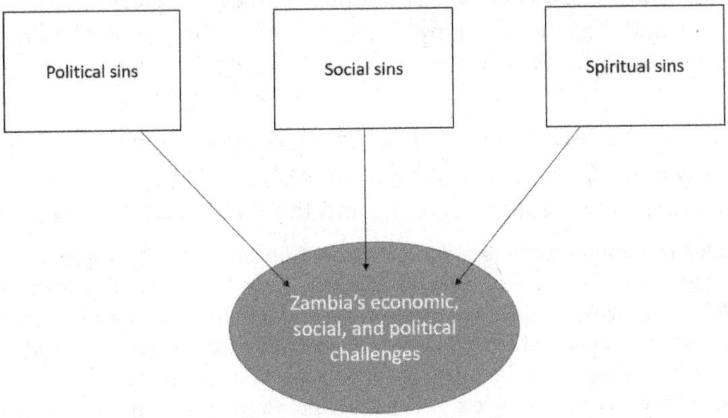

8 Chammah J. Kaunda, "'The Altars are Holding the Nation in Captivity': Zambian Pentecostalism, Nationality, and African Religio-Political Heritage," *Religions* 9, no 145 (2018): 4.

9 David M. Gordon, *Invisible Agents: Spirits in a Central African History* (Ohio: Ohio University Press, 2012), 182.

10 Gordon, *Invisible Agents*, 181.

11 Kaunda, "'Altars are Holding the Nation,'" 4.

The declaration that Zambia is a Christian nation attracted many pentecostal missionaries from America. It also opened the door for many Christians in Zambia to be actively involved in politics. Christians no longer made a distinction between Christian faith and the public role in politics.[12] Drawing on Proverbs 29:4, President Chiluba affirmed the biblical mandate for those in authority to reject bribery and uphold justice. He emphasized that bribery ruins the nation but justice brings stability.

Riding on an eschatological[13] political ideology of the Movement for Multiparty Democracy (MMD)—"The hour has come"—President Chiluba declared that the time for salvation had come for the Zambians. He challenged Zambians to wake up from the slumber because the new dawn had come (Romans 13:11). Chiluba invited Zambians to "live according to [God's] righteous laws."[14] This call for moral uprightness is consistent with the African belief that success can only be achieved within the religiopolitical moral system. Kaunda notes that in African culture, "the king's exercise of power is constrained with ancestral checks and balances within the religious moral system."[15] In this religiopolitical worldview, "morality originates and flows from Lesa (God, the ground of all beings and moral order) through the ancestors into the community and ecological order."[16] The leaders and members of the community are obliged to desist from any actions that could compromise the common good.[17]

Chiluba's declaration is consistent with the pentecostal-charismatic belief that anticipates God's blessings in the present life. Obedience to God's commandments brings abundant material blessings on earth. Prophecy and healing are emphasized to effect material blessings for Christians. Philip Jenkins rightly observes that Christianity in the Global South emphasizes prophecy and healing: "As in the early church, much of Global South Christianity today is a healing religion par excellence, with a strong belief in the objective existence of evil, and (commonly) a willingness to accept the reality of demons and the diabolical."[18] This belief can

[12] Jonathan Kangwa, *Pentecostalism, Mainline Churches, and Theological Education in Africa: The Case of the United Church of Zambia* (Dallas: St. Paul Press, 2017), 178; Isabel Apawo Phiri, "President Frederick Chiluba and Zambia: Evangelicals and Democracy in a "Christian Nation," in *Evangelical Christianity in Africa*, ed. Terence O. Ranger (Oxford: Oxford University Press, 2008): 96.

[13] Eschatology is a theological belief that the world will come to an end and judgment administered by God is the final destiny of human beings.

[14] Declaration of Zambia as a Christian Nation.

[15] Kaunda, "'Altars are Holding the Nation,'" 5.

[16] Kaunda, "'Altars are Holding the Nation,'" 5.

[17] Kaunda, "'Altars are Holding the Nation,'" 5.

[18] Philip Jenkins, "Christianity Moves South," in *Global Christianity: Contested Claims*, ed. Frans Wijsen and Robert Schreiter (Amsterdam, New York: Rodopi, 2007), 21.

be seen in many pentecostal churches that supported Chiluba's declaration of Zambia to be a Christian nation.[19]

The other thing we can note is that Chiluba used the church as a platform to promote his political ambitions. As the Zambian economy deteriorated, many Zambians found themselves living in abject poverty. After he left office in 2001, Chiluba was arrested for corruption and abuse of office.[20] However, the influence of Chiluba's declaration that Zambia is a Christian nation has endured in Zambian politics. Politicians have learnt that to associate themselves with the link between church and nation helps them to gain support from the electorate.[21]

In 2001, when Levy Patrick Mwanawasa became president, he had himself re-baptized to prove that he was a genuine Christian. Through the ritual of baptism, President Mwanawasa was admitted to the Zambian Christian community and thereby became a God-given leader. After being elected into office as president of Zambia in 2011, Michael Sata, a Catholic, attended a church service and after being prayed for by the parish priest, he declared that his rule of the country was based on the Ten Commandments.[22] The Roman Catholic Church supported Sata in the run-up to the 2011 presidential, parliamentary, and local government elections. At a campaign rally in Luanshya, Fr. Frank Bwalya, a Catholic priest and die hard supporter of the Patriotic Front, beheaded a chicken with a machete and sprinkled its blood on the ground in a ritual that symbolized the end of the Movement for Multiparty Democracy (MMD).[23] Such ritual acts had a strong impact on the minds of the Zambian people who were made to believe that the MMD had died. It is therefore not surprising that the MMD lost the elections.

President Michael Sata died in office on October 28, 2014, in King Edward VII's Hospital in London, United Kingdom, after an illness.[24]

19 See Chammah J. Kaunda, " 'Baptising Zambia's Edgah Chagwa Lungu': Critiquing the Utilization of the Declaration of Zambia during the Presidential Campaign of 2016," *International Journal of Public Theology* 13 (2019): 72–93; Chammah J. Kaunda, "The Day of Prayer and its Potential for Engendering Public Ecclesiology Ecumenism in Zambia," *Religions* 9, no 393 (2018): 1–13.

20 Kangwa, "Pentecostalism," 178.

21 Kangwa, "Pentecostalism," 178.

22 *Zambian Watchdog*, "Sata: I Will Govern According to Biblical 10 Commandments," (September 25, 2011), accessed February 1, 2019, https://www.zambiawatchdog.com/sata-i-will-govern-according-to-biblical-10-commandments/.

23 *Lusaka Times*, "Father Frank Bwalya Condemned for Beheading a Live Chicken at PF Rally,"1 September 1, 2011, accessed May 29, 2019, https://www.lusakatimes.com/2011/09/01/father-frank-bwalya-condemned-beheading-live-chicken-pf-rally/.

24 BBC news, "Zambian President Michael Sata Dies in London," October 29, 2014, accessed May 28, 2019, https://www.bbc.com/news/world-africa-29813612.

Mwenda and Sata report that "Mr. Michael Chilufya Sata died of a heart failure in London on October 28, 2014, at the age of 75, having endured poor health for almost seven years. He had been receiving treatment for over a week before he died."[25] Sata was succeeded by Edgar Lungu who was elected president on January 24, 2015. Lungu—who held two portfolios as Minister of Defense and Minister of Justice—was acting president at the time Sata died in London.[26]

Lungu used the platform of Christianity to come to power both in 2015 and 2016.[27] He has mastered the art of identifying himself with churches and the declaration of Zambia to be a Christian nation as a strategy to win the support of the electorate. In 2015, Lungu had his closest rival in the presidential election, Hakainde Hichilema of the United Party for National Development (UPND), de-campaigned on the basis that he was a member of the Free Masons, considered by many to be a cult.[28] Lungu's supporters, led by Bishop Eddie Chomba, accused Hichilema of being a member of the Free Masons and therefore a Satanist.[29] Bishop Chomba insisted that Hichilema joined the Free Masons "in April, 1999 and was initiated from Eagle Lodge number 7232EC which is the grand lodge in Zambia and has been a congregant of the Masons Temple located in Cha Cha Cha road, Lusaka."[30] Hichilema denied the allegations and sued Bishop Chomba in the courts of law. However, the accusation that Hichilema was a Satanist made many Zambians associate him with evil powers and the socioeconomic problems that the country was experiencing. In his analysis of the views of some Pentecostals in Zambia on the role of prayer in politics, Kaunda rightly notes,

> Lungu and the opposition UPND led by Hakainde Hichilema (HH)—were categorised in terms of the struggle between good and evil. On the one hand, HH was categorized as Satanist. This already made him an agent of darkness that some Pentecostals had to fight in order to secure Lungu's winning. On the other hand, Lungu's declaration made him an angel of light.[31]

---

25 Kasonde C. Mwenda and Mubanga B. Sata, *Michael Chilufya Sata: Passion Indelible* (Lusaka: Our Feet, 2017), 113.

26 Mwenda and Sata, "Michael Chilufya Sata," 113.

27 Kaunda, "An Announcement," 79.

28 In many places, the Freemasons are a social service organization of professional Christian men who support the community and are not considered a cult.

29 In Zambian Christianity, especially in pentecostal circles, members of groups such as the Free Masons are called Satanists.

30 *Tumfweko*, "HH is a Satanist, Insists Bishop Chomba," January 8, 2015, accessed January 5, 2019, https://tumfweko.com/2015/01/08/hh-is-a-satanist-insists-bishop-chomba/comment-page-2/.

31 Kaunda, "An Announcement," 83–84. See also Kaunda, "'Altars are Holding the Nation,'" 1–17; Kaunda, "Baptising Zambia's Edgar Chagwa Lung," 72–93;

The allegations that Hichilema was a Satanist pushed him to the margins of the society as no Zambian would want an evil person to be their leader. In their campaigns, member of the ruling Patriotic Front (PF) warned Zambians not to vote for Hichilema as he would sacrifice their sons and daughters to Satan. Many churches—especially those with pentecostal orientation—held prayer meetings to ask God to guide Zambians to vote for a Christian leader—and that suitable person was seen in Edgar Lungu. Many Zambians were persuaded to think that Hichilema was not suitable to be the president of a country that had been declared a Christian nation. Hence, Zambians voted for Edgar Lungu.

Politicians in the Patriotic Front have continued to refer to Hichilema as Satanist to prevent him from contesting in future elections. In 2017, Edwin Lifwekelo, a former spokesperson for the UPND, stated that Hichilema was a danger to society because he was a Satanist. Lifwekelo claimed that there was substantial evidence to show that Hichilema was a member of the Free Masons as Bishop Chomba had disclosed earlier.[32] These allegations are not mere religious claims; rather, they are politically engineered to tarnish the image of the opposition UPND.

Kenneth Kaunda's Dedication of Zambia

The other ritual act performed to promote a political ideology was the dedication of the nation by Kenneth Kaunda during the Africa Freedom Day celebrations on May 25, 2015. Barely four months after being elected into office as president, Lungu invited the first president of Zambia, Kenneth Kaunda, to bless the nation. President Lungu announced that Zambia was in a form of spiritual bondage that needed to be broken by Kaunda, the founding father of the nation. Kaunda pronounced a prayer to free Zambia from spiritual, economic, and spiritual bondage.

> I hereby pronounce today a blessing of peace, prosperity, and stability upon our nation of Zambia, the presidency, and the people of Zambia. I bless and therefore release the nation, its people, and the presidency from every negative force made against this nation. I submit the souls now living and in posterity and also its presidency to the salvation and Lordship of the Lord Jesus Christ and the Father. I further declare that Zambia shall forever enjoy tranquility and shall remain a united

Chammah J. Kaunda, "Christianising Edgar Chagwa Lungu: The Christian Nation, Social Media Presidential Photography and 2016 Election Campaign," *Stellenbosch Theological Journal* 4, no.1 (2018): 215–245; Chammah J. Kaunda, "'Baptising Zambia's Edgar Chagwa Lungu," 72–93.

32 *The Zambian Observer*, "I Ditched UPND because Hichilema is a Full Time Satanist says Edwin Lifwekelo," February 13, 2017, accessed January 5, 2019, https://www.zambianobserver.com/i-ditched-upnd-because-hichilema-is-a-full-time-satanist-says-edwin-lifwekelo/.

> and peaceful people under the motto; one Zambia one nation. The Lord bless Zambia and keep Zambia. God bless you all.[33]

The religiopolitical features of the prayer-ritual can be identified. Kaunda prays for peace, prosperity, stability, and tranquility in the country Zambia. He then submits "the souls now living and in posterity" to the Lordship of Jesus Christ. Further, Kaunda submits the presidency to Jesus Christ. These ritual pronouncements were believed to free Zambia and its citizens from blood covenants made by Zambians through cults in the past. Chammah J. Kaunda accentuates,

> This prayer is significant to Pentecostals as Kaunda was accused of opening national spiritual doors to the forces of darkness through his introduction of humanism and subsequent establishment of the David Universal Temple at the State House. The temple, named after Kaunda's father, David, taught Eastern mysticism (such as transcendental meditation, the heaven that is on earth, humanism, and reincarnation).Thus, Kaunda's so-called "spiritual release [of] the nation" is perceived to have had positively address evil forces, which he had allowed to enter the nation. Most Pentecostals saw the prayer as a public acknowledgement and renunciation of the cultic covenant, which Kaunda was [*sic*] allegedly entered. These Pentecostals believe that through this cultic covenant he made with forces of darkness, Kaunda opened spiritual gates of the nation, thereby exposing the national altar to these demonic forces that manipulated the nation politically and economically.[34]

As Kaunda shows above, his prayer is deeply rooted in the African worldview where it is believed that there is always someone or some spiritual forces responsible for one's failures in life. In African culture, the king, a priest, a diviner, a senior member of the family, or the parent can perform a blessing ritual to ask the ancestors for blessings, especially in difficult times.[35] Therefore, Kaunda's prayer is consistent with the observation that new forms of Christianity in Africa are retrieving elements of African indigenous culture, thereby creating a unique generic spirituality.[36] Philip Jenkins notes,

> Pentecostal expansion across the southern hemisphere has been so astonishing as to justify claims of a new Reformation. In addition, rapid growth is occurring in non-traditional denominations that

33 Charles Kachikoti, "Meaning of KK's Spiritual 'Release,'" *Times of Zambia*, May 28, 2015, accessed April 16, 2019, http://www.times.co.zm/?p=60354.

34 Kaunda, "'Altars are Holding the Nation,'" 8.

35 Kaunda, "'Altars are Holding the Nation,'" 4.

36 See Ogbu Kalu, *African Pentecostalism: An Introduction* (New York: Oxford University Press, 2008).

adapt Christian belief to local tradition, groups that are categorized by titles such as African instituted churches.[37]

Kaunda's prayer served the same purpose as President Chiluba's declaration of Zambia as a Christian nation. In fact, it reinforced the belief that Zambia is a Christian nation. But at the same time, it served as an affirmation of Lungu's presidency and his political party—the Patriotic Front. The prayer ordained President Lungu as a God-given leader—one who has the blessings and the approval of the ancestors and the Almighty God.[38]

New forms of Christianity in Africa believe in breaking generational curses. It is believed that if parents or ancestors consulted a traditional diviner or used any form of charms, the offspring would experience failures and all forms of social problems in life. Chammah J. Kaunda has shown how the belief in "politics and a sacred realm of contestations between forces of good and evil" is entrenched in Zambian Christianity, especially from pentecostal circles.[39] He reasons that this pentecostal worldview "is a continuation of traditional African religio-cultural ethnonational heritage."[40] In keeping with this worldview, Chiluba had to invite pastors to pray for the State House because Kaunda was associated with Eastern religion that was regarded as idolatry in Zambian Christianity. The ritual that Kaunda performed when he blessed President Lungu served almost the same purpose—to remove evil from Zambia and pronounce prosperity.

Prayer Rituals for Peaceful Elections and Economic Success

As already stated, President Lungu has continued to use the church as a campaigning platform for re-election.[41] Prayers are used by politicians to show that the economic challenges the country is facing are not due to poor leadership. Rather, they are due to the spiritual forces that hinder development and economic success. In 2015, the *Sunday Morning Herald* reported,

> God save the kwacha is what Zambian President Edgar Lungu is hoping as he urges his people to pray for a reverse in the decline of the world's worst currency to fix a litany of problems from plunging copper prices to electricity shortages. All bars, nightclubs, and entertainment venues have been instructed by the government to shut on

37 Jenkins, "Christianity Moves South," 18.

38 See Kaunda, "'Altars are Holding the Nation,'" 1.

39 Kaunda, "'Altars are Holding the Nation,'" 1–13; Kaunda and Kaunda, "An Announcement," 71–88.

40 Kaunda, "'Altars are Holding the Nation,'" 1.

41 Kangwa, *Pentecostalism*, 179.

> Sunday for a national day of devotion and fasting, while the Football Association of Zambia has cancelled domestic games.[42]

During the day of prayer and fasting on October 18, 2015, held at the Agriculture Showground in Lusaka, rituals to improve the economy and the Zambian currency were performed. First, President Lungu released a white dove from his hands during the prayers as a symbol of peace, love, reconciliation, and blessings on the nation.[43] He then declared Zambia free from evil, emphasizing that the desire by the nation to come before God in prayer was a sign of reverence to God. Lungu then declared October 18 as a public holiday on which Christians are expected to pray and fast for reconciliation, peace, and economic success.

The ritual of releasing a dove or pigeon is used in many cultures across the world. The dove is a symbol of love, peace, and prosperity. The ritual participants read the direction of the bird to get the message from God and the ancestors. If the bird flies up into the sky, it means that God has accepted the supplications for peace and prosperity. If the bird refuses to fly, it means that God is not happy and the supplications are rejected. The ritual, therefore, served to prove to the Zambians that God was happy with President Lungu's leadership and would bestow prosperity on Zambia.

Second, Kenneth Kaunda—the first president of Zambia—was invited to pronounce blessings upon President Lungu. Apostle Peter Ndhlovu, the overseer of the Bible Gospel Church in Africa (BIGOCA) was the presider over the blessings. Former President Rupiah Banda was also present. Again, the ritual of blessing done by Kaunda served to affirm President Lungu as a God-given leader.[44]

Third, Chief Chipepo of the Tonga-speaking people in Gweembe district performed a ritual to bless President Lungu and to ask God and the ancestors to bless Zambia. In his ritual prayer, Chief Chipepo invoked God's power to be upon the nation to fully benefit from minerals and other natural resources. Representing traditional leaders in the country, Chief Chipepo took some soil from the ground, blessed it, and pronounced peace and blessings upon the country, Zambia, and President

---

42 *The Sunday Morning Herald*, "Zambia's President Seeks Divine Intervention in a Declining Economy," October 20, 2015, accessed June 4, 2019, https://www.smh.com.au/business/markets/zambias-president-seeks-divine-intervention-in-a-declining-economy-20151020-gkd5es.html.

43 *Lusaka Times*, "The Day of Prayer and Fasting in Pictures," October 21, 2015, accessed May 1, 2019, https://www.lusakatimes.com/2015/10/21/the-day-of-prayer-and-fasting-in-pictures/.

44 Kaunda and Kaunda, "'An Announcement,'" 84; Kaunda, "'Altars are Holding the Nation,'" 6–8.

Lungu. The traditional leader charged that those who were against the prayers organized by the president were cursed by the ancestors as they did not want peace. Through this ritual, President Lungu was affirmed as a leader who is accepted by all traditional leaders.

During the same prayer meeting, the clergy and church leaders offered prayers for the country. Pastor Jeffrey Ngosa invoked the power of God to enable politicians to stop quarreling. Rev. Joyce Mwanza prayed for the media organizations to stop causing violence through reporting falsehood. Bishop Frank Mwiinga asked God to stop tribalism in the nation. Rev. Steven Mubanga prayed for peace during the forthcoming elections in 2016. He further prayed against gender-based violence (GBV) and the youth being used by politicians to cause violence. Pastor Joseph Honto prayed for the nation to have loving families and Bishop Harrison Sakala prayed for the nation's spiritual revival. The members of the clergy and traditional leaders called upon Zambians, including leaders of opposition political parties, to support President Lungu and declared that those who opposed him were inviting punishment from God.[45]

In 2015, the Zambian currency had a 45 percent slump against the USD. Zambia is the second largest producer of copper in Africa and its economy depends entirely on copper. However, the price of copper dropped in the international market. The slump in the mining industry hindered economic growth in the country. There was also a shortage of electricity. The water levels at the hydropower plants fell, triggering the most severe electricity shortage in the country. Amidst all this, President Lungu organized prayers and rituals to seek divine intervention.[46] President Lungu was supported by pastors especially from pentecostal churches. For example, Bishop Joe Imakando of the Bread of Life International Church in Lusaka "urged Zambians to pray for an improvement, referring to a call by King George VI of Britain in 1940 for a national day of prayer during World War II."[47] The implication of these prayer rituals is that the blame for economic and political decline was shifted to the spiritual forces that hinder development.[48] The president and the ruling party could not be blamed. Citizens ought to pray enough for development and economic success. There is therefore a need to analyze prayer as a political action.

45 *Zambia Daily Mail*, "Prayer Critics Risk Curse, Says Chief Chipepo," October 15, 2015, accessed May 1, 2019, http://www.daily-mail.co.zm/prayer-critics-risk-curse-says-chief-chipepo/.

46 *The Sunday Morning Herald*, "Zambia's President." Seeks Divine Intervention.

47 *The Sunday Morning Herald*, "Zambia's President."

48 Kaunda, "Altars are Holding the Nation," 9.

Prayer as a Ritualized Political Action

Prayer as a ritual has both political and ideological powers. A ritual is a "formal-stylized, repetitive, and stereotyped" religious action.[49] It is "a collection of culturally determined behaviors through which humans bodily participate in what is 'really real' to them and enact relationships with one another."[50] A ritual includes a sequence "of words and actions invented prior to the current performances of the ritual in which" it occurs.[51]

Anthropologists help us understand that religion is a cultural universal which consists of beliefs and behaviors concerned with supernatural beings and powers, and forces.[52] Religion embodies emotional, social, political, and ecological functions. Christians use prayer seemingly to influence the outcome on things over which they do not have technical and rational control. Prayer provides comfort and psychological security in times of crisis such as the economic meltdown or elections. As a ritual, prayers serve as "formal, invariant, earnest acts that require people to join actively in social collectivity."[53]

First, prayer and corporate worship are powerful political actions in which the participants experience an encounter with God or the supernatural force. However, these ritual actions are involved in politics and power dealings. Prayer and corporate worship are used by politicians to influence the electorates. And as Rodney Werline rightly observes, "power does not simply exist as an ideal, but in the ability of humans to influence the actions of other humans."[54] Zambian politicians go around to the churches making donations toward church projects. As Kaunda stresses, "politicians tap into prayer as a social ritual to position themselves as generating their political authority from a divine source."[55] They position themselves as God-fearing people and therefore good people for political leadership.

Second, anthropologists have established that rituals serve the social function of creating temporary or permanent solidarity among people forming a social community.[56] In Christianity, prayer plays an important role in this regard. Christian identity serves in the same way as a totem to indigenous tribes. Totems are sacred emblems symbolizing common

---

49 Kottak, "Anthropology," 491.
50 Werline, "Prayer, Politics and Power," 6.
51 Kottak, "Anthropology," 491.
52 Kottak, "Anthropology," 488.
53 Kottak, "Anthropology," 488.
54 Werline, "Prayer, Politics, and Power," 5.
55 Kaunda and Kaunda, "An Announcement," 74.
56 Kottak, "Anthropology," 495.

identity.[57] People relate to each other through their totemic association. The unity of the human social order is enhanced by symbolic association with and imitation of the natural order through a totem. In the same way, Christian identity shapes the way people relate to each other. Those who are not admitted into the Christian family through rituals such as prayer and corporate worship become social outcasts. Kaunda postulates,

> The process of making politicians spiritual brothers and sisters, has resulted in politicians perceiving themselves as spiritual leaders who are beyond criticism and who could demand an authoritarian or a monarchical form of respect afforded to traditional leaders. One of the challenges of pentecostal ontocracies is that they tend to demonize dissenting voices, especially those of opposition political parties.[58]

It was on this basis that Zambians did not vote for Hichilema of the UPND because of allegations of being a member of the Free Masons.

Third, there is a manner in which Christian prayer and corporate worship serve as a rite of passage. The concepts of liminality and *communitas* espoused by anthropologists such as Arnold Van Gennep (1960), Victor Turner (1967, 1969), Pierre Bourdieu (2003), and J. Willet and J.M. Deegan (2001), provide useful insights for understanding how prayer works as a ritualized political action. Life is characterized by transition from one social group or situation to another. Individuals pass through different ages, social relationships, and occupations.[59] Willet and Deegan underscore,

> Rites of passage are subdivided into three stages: separation (preliminal), transition (liminal), and incorporation (postliminal). Rites of separation symbolically detach the individual from an existing point in the social structure. After this separation, the former social status no longer applies to the individual. In the transition or liminal stage, the individual is a symbolic outsider with no clearly derived status or role. The liminal personae (or "liminar") reside at the margins of society while they prepare to adopt a new role. The final stage of incorporation allows the individual to adopt a new social status and re-enter society. If this re-entry does not occur, liminality does not end.[60]

---

57 Kottak, "Anthropology," 495.

58 Kaunda, "'Altars are Holding the Nation,'" 14.

59 Jeffrey Willet and Mary Jo Deegan, "Liminality and Disability: Rites of Passage and Community in Hypermodern Society," *Disability Studies Quarterly* 21, no 3 (2001): 137–152.

60 Willet and Deegan, "Liminality and Disability," 137–152.

We can see that society is a "structure of positions" and the liminal stage marks the transition between two socially viable positions.[61] The initiates are in a movement between fixed points. As Turner notes, the initiates "are betwixt and between the positions assigned and arrayed by law, custom, convention, and ceremony."[62] In this regard, ritualized prayers represent a liminal moment, a threshold moment. Through prayer, the person being prayed for crosses over from one status to the other.[63]

Pierre Bourdieu reasons that rites of passage mark a distinction between those who stand inside the group and those left outside.[64] Applied to the Zambian political situation, the ritual action of prayer brings the politician being prayed for into the group of the acceptable members of the Zambian Christian community while also assigning the politician a place within the power structure. The politician, ritual officiant, and participants invoke the creator God and the ancestors for blessings. Within the breakdown of social structures in ritualized prayer, the politician and the members of society unite with one another in resistance to social, economic, and political problems they are facing. Those who are not part of the community or are considered to have defied social categories or have social restrictions are in a sense, non-persons.[65] It is on this basis that people refuse to vote for a politician who is accused of being a member of a cult.

Prayer for blessings, cleansing, or sanctification marks a change in someone's social status. Prayers pronounced on President Lungu by Kaunda, chiefs, and the clergy marked a change in his status from one who is on the periphery of the Zambian-Christian community to one who is an insider and an acceptable member of the Zambian community. Given that prayers and other collective rituals often are cemented by *communitas*—a feeling of intense fellowship and solidarity—those politicians who go through this ritual process win the support of the electorate.[66] This is the reason why Chiluba invited pastors to cleanse the State House when he became the president and went on to declare Zambia a Christian nation. Mwanawasa was re-baptized and Sata was prayed for by priests

61 Willet and Deegan, "Liminality and Disability," 137–152; Victor Turner, *The Forest of Symbols: Aspects of Ndembu Ritual* (Ithaca NY: Cornell University Press, 1967), 93.

62 Victor Turner, *The Ritual Process: Structure and Anti-structure* (Chicago: Aldine, 1969), 95.

63 Werline, "Prayer, Politics and Power," 10; see also Turner, "Ritual Process," 94–130.

64 Werline, "Prayer, Politics and Power," 10; see also Pierre Bourdieu, *Language and Symbolic Power* (Cambridge: Harvard University Press, 2003), 117–119.

65 Willet and Deegan, "Liminality and Disability," 137–152.

66 Kottak, "Anthropology," 488.

before and after being elected president. The politicians, as initiates, are received in the life of Christian brotherhood and sisterhood (fellowship).

Lastly, rituals achieve social control.[67] Both Christianity and African culture have rituals that establish and maintain social control. They do this through a series of moral and ethical beliefs, along with real and imagined rewards and punishments internalized in individuals.[68] Christianity, therefore, achieves social control by mobilizing members of the community for collective action. Depending on how power is used, it can be abusive and destructive or it can result in something beautiful and life giving.[69] Prayer and corporate worship do not simply constitute symbolic actions about people's beliefs regarding life in heaven. Rather, prayer is power.[70] Therefore, prayer becomes a way to negotiate and to navigate power relations between citizens and politicians at the micro-political level. In the Zambian context, as Kaunda observes, "prayer should take the question of politics and religious abuse at the center of concerns."[71] In its missiological endeavor, the church should not leave any room for politicians to abuse people using religious rituals such as prayer.

Missiological Implications of Prayer as a Political Action

Christian prayer is a ritual. As a ritual, it is performed by the Christian community within a web of systemic interrelationships of rites and power that can transform the political and economic landscape.[72] These interrelationships of rites and power should be checked to ensure that they do not deny people the fullness of life. Regarding the role of the church in the present world, Jooseop Keum posits,

> Now people at the margins are claiming their key role as agents of mission and affirming mission as transformation. This reversal of roles in the envisioning of mission has strong biblical foundations because God chose the poor, the foolish, and the powerless (1 Cor 1:18–31) to further God's mission of justice and peace so that life may flourish.[73]

---

67 Werline, "Prayer, Politics and Power," 6.

68 Kottak, "Anthropology," 488.

69 Werline, "Prayer, Politics and Power," 6.

70 Werline, "Prayer, Politics and Power," 7.

71 Kaunda, "The Day of Prayer," 10.

72 Kimberly Hope Belcher, "Ritual Systems, Ritualised Bodies, and the Laws of Liturgical Development," *Studia Liturgica* 49, no 1 (2019): 89; Kaunda, "An Announcement," 73.

73 Jooseop Keum, ed., *Together Towards Life: Mission and Evangelism in Changing Landscapes* (Geneva: WCC Publications, 2013), 5.

As we have seen, poor and ordinary Zambians are the victims of poor governance due to corruption, poor allocation of resources by the government, and failing public infrastructure. Schools and hospitals are among the public institutions that struggle to keep up with the high demand resulting in a reduction of public and social services. These challenges are not necessarily spiritual, but rather reflect inadequate financing of public infrastructure and poor social planning. Poverty is a result of political injustice and economic exploitation.[74] The inequality and exploitation are perpetuated by the government machinery that rides on the declaration of Zambia as a Christian nation.

It is becoming increasingly clear that ritual communities forge new forms of expression in their ritual performance.[75] As Belcher notes, "a ritual system makes particular meanings seem natural, permitting some new liturgical developments."[76] In this regard, poverty-stricken Christian communities such as that of Zambia tend to forge new forms of worship and spirituality that give them comfort in their present circumstances. It is therefore not surprising that many Christians, including bishops, support prayer meetings organized by politicians to resuscitate the economy.

One of the major tasks for the church in Zambia is to construct a good theology that empowers the church to do its prophetic ministry. How we see God (theology) determines how we see humans (anthropology). How we see humans (anthropology) determines how we order our society (sociology). Our theological lens shapes our sociological lens. To say Zambia is a Christian nation is not enough. The Zambian society must be ordered in a way that respects the dignity of human life.

Jose Miguez Bonino reminds us that life-giving theology should be done in response to reality.[77] This involves "the recognition of social analysis as a constitutive moment in theological reflection on politics."[78] In other words, theology and Christian mission ought to engage with social and political structures that deny the majority of Zambians the fullness of life. There is no point in Christians and their bishops praying for the improvement of the economy while politicians are busy stealing public funds. Prayer should not be used to prevent people from questioning the

---

74 Chammah Kaunda, *"The King Said "Kwere-Kwere Must Go": Xenophobia as South Africa's Political Mirror,"* *CIHA* (2015), accessed on April 20, 2015, http://www.cihablog.com/in-the-news-the-king-said-kwere-kwere-must-go-xenophobia-as-south-africas-politic-mirror/.

75 Belcher, "Ritual Systems," 89.

76 Belcher, "Ritual Systems," 89.

77 Jose Miguez Bonino, *Toward a Christian Political Ethic* (Philadelphia: Fortress Press, 1983), 45.

78 Bonino, "Toward a Christian Political Ethic," 45.

government to deliver public services. Rather, prayer must be used to organize Christians to fight for their God-given right to a better life.

Prayer and Christian ritual can play an important role in the emancipation of people. Johan Cilliers reminds us that "worship services have been a platform from which many African communities have struggled against oppression, whether it is political, social, or economic."[79] Kaunda adds that prayer and corporate worship can be used as a means "to create a critical safe space for the church to promote social healing and reconciliation . . . social cohesion, justice and equality, human rights, and good governance." During the apartheid in South Africa, Christians organized themselves for worship and used prayer and music to confront the colonial authorities that denied black South Africans their freedom.[80]

The problem in Zambia is that prayer is used as an opium of the people to stop people from holding the government responsible for the suffering of the poor Zambians. Political and economic failures are blamed on the spiritual forces out there. Poor Zambians have to pray enough to break the spiritual forces that prevent economic development. It is a theological and spiritual paradigm that the church needs to change. Prayer and worship services should begin to empower Christians in Zambia to confront the political, social, economic, and political structures that perpetuate exploitation and manipulation of Christians. Such a commitment of the church could prove life-giving to people on the margins.

Conclusion

As Bell underscores, "rituals do not refer to politics . . . they are politics. Ritual is a thing itself. It is power; it acts and actuates."[81] Prayer is a Christian ritual and it embodies power. Ritualized prayer may function as the way in which the community formalizes disapproval or approval of people's actions. It may also function as the way in which political leadership ties place and people to a political ideology or as the way to resist social, economic, and political challenges. In the case of Zambian politics, politicians adapt ritualized prayer to new settings to meet their political needs. The language used in prayer conveys a Christian-African worldview of the participants.

Prayer and any form of ritualized supplication include embodied, non-discursive elements. They contain speech or discourse. Prayer organized by and for politicians is not essentially good or evil. Instead, the focus should be on whether such prayers promote power to give life or to

79 Johan Cilliers, *Transformation of Worship and Liturgy in Urban African Contexts* (South Africa: University of Stellenbosch, 2012), 5.

80 Cilliers, "Transformation of Worship," 8.

81 Cited in Werline, "Prayer, Politics and Power," 7.

destroy. As politicians emphasize the declaration of Zambia as a Christian nation, there is a need for the citizens to pay attention to how ritualized prayer embodies power and whether that power supports human dignity. The church should guard against potential abuse of power by politicians and failure to manage people's suffering.

5

WORSHIP SPACES OR POLITICAL ELECTION POLLING STATIONS?

Devison Telen Banda

Introduction

The 8th African Association for the Study of Religion (AASR) conference took place on August 1–4, 2018, under the theme: "Revisiting Religion, Politics and the State of Africa and the African Diaspora." Hosted by the University of Zambia, Department of Religious Studies, in collaboration with Justo Mwale University in Lusaka, the conference gave opportunities to revisit several aspects of the theme including the vexing question of "religion and politics." The relationship between religion and politics has always been ambiguous in the sense that in some settings, the distinguishing line is clearly marked, while in other settings, it is not so. When it comes to the use of spaces or premises, some spaces are exclusively marked out for religion and some are exclusively for politics. In other settings, however, there is a faint or an unmarked line that separates religion from politics. In political premises, religious slogans, language, texts, and prayers are used while, and on some religious premises, political language, symbols, and slogans are used too. In other settings, however, as aforementioned, religion and politics are mutually exclusive.

This study interrogates this ambiguous relationship between religion and politics in perception and space usage. The key concern is driven from the following questions: Do churches that offer worship spaces or premises for usage as elections polling stations compromise the holiness doctrine? Is using worship spaces for political polling stations, part of giving Caesar what belongs to Caesar and giving to God what belongs to God? Or does the practice compromise the sacredness of worship spaces? If elections of political leaders take place in the worship spaces, does politics remain a "dirty game"? The study hypothesis is that the trend is growing because of the emerging opinion of some leaders that usage of worship spaces as political election voting stations is part of giving to "Caesar what belongs to Caesar and to God what belongs to God." Such tendencies, however, lead to some split of opinion among followers and fail to distinguish politics from religion. The methodology applied is a combination of literature review and evaluative observation with some ordinary actors in church and politics.

Zambia 2016 General Elections: Experiences

In 2016, Zambia held a general election under a new constitution that for the first time introduced a fifty plus one (50 percent+1) threshold for the presidential candidates while the mayor of Lusaka would be elected with executive powers for the first time since independence. One can say in many aspects that this was a unique election that drew several interests. For the purposes of our study, one of the interests to pursue is that which was exhibited by religious actors. Not only did some religious organizations express their interests to send polling and monitoring agents, but also made their worship spaces polling centers. In this study, worship spaces refer to premises and facilities such as classrooms, offices, halls, or indeed any land belonging to religious entities that are given to the Electoral Commission of Zambia (ECZ) to be used for polling. The database of the Parallel Vote Tabulation (PVT)[1] group that operates under among other organizations—the Council of Churches in Zambia (CCZ)—contains polling stations in Lusaka, Chongwe, and Chilanga districts. Among the polling stations are churches and para-church institutions. Although data on electoral activities are scanty, an analysis shows some increased usage of religious spaces in the 2016 elections, particularly among some Christian churches. Not mentioning the religious groups that give out their worship spaces or premises for polling stations satisfices,[2] this study focuses on the theories behind this openness. Why do some religious groups open so much and deploy members to monitor elections and allow worship spaces to be used for electoral causes? To respond to this question, one must first examine the perceptions of politics.

---

1 The Parallel Vote Tabulation (PVT) is a quasi non-governmental organization formed by a consortium of religious organizations for purposes of safeguarding electoral credibility in Zambia due to growing allegations about vote rigging during centralized totaling. PVT agents are very active at the voting and totaling centers alongside ECZ as an official manager of elections.

2 This refers to a compromise between total failure and acceptance on a below average level or minimal requirement.

Conflicting Perceptions of Politics

It must be clearly pointed out that not all religious groups are so open to political elections to an extent of allowing worship spaces to be used as voting stations. For instance, it is only the Christian religious groups out of the three Abrahamic faiths[3] in Zambia that is open. While there are churches named as wards or voting stations in the PVT group database, no Muslim institution is indicated as having been used as a ward in the 2016 Zambian elections. In fact, even among various Christian churches, not all denominations allow the usage of worship spaces as wards for voting candidates into political office. Why are some religious groups allowing using their worship spaces while others are not?

The Perceptions of Politics as a Dirty Game

The perception of politics as a "dirty game" still exists. The word *politics* to some invokes memories of propaganda, empty promises, falsehood, and covert schemes and strategies that politicians employ against the opponents in order to be elected and continue to be re-elected at all costs. Politics in this way is perceived as falsehood, denial of the realities, violation of morals, and criminality to secure political fortunes. For example, after the first president of Zambia Kenneth David Kaunda lost the 1991 election, President Frederick T.J. Chiluba declared Zambia a "Christian nation." In spite of propagating Christianity and becoming popular among some faith brand, particularly in major cities, to the extent of some attempting to ordain him as a pastor, Chiluba ordered the arrest of his predecessor President Kaunda during Christmas festivities in 1997. How was it possible for a Christian to arrest another Christian during the Christmas season? Further, the Chiluba's regime quickly amended the republican constitution in 1996 where a controversial citizenship clause was introduced for political reasons. In part, article 34 of the Constitution of Zambia (as amended by Act No. 18 of 1996)[4] in clause (3) states that,

> A person shall be qualified to be a candidate for election as President if:
> (a) He is a citizen of Zambia;
> (b) Both his parents are Zambians by birth or descent.

---

3 This refers to faith communities that claim Abraham as their forefather. Common among these are Judaism, Christianity, and Islam. See "Abrahamic Religions," *Wikipedia*, accessed November 16, 2018, https://en.wikipedia.org/wiki/Abrahamic_religions.

4 See "An Act to amend the Constitution of Zambia," accessed November 16, 2018, http://www.parliament.gov.zm/sites/default/files/documents/amendment_act/Constitution%20of%20Zambia%20%20%28Amendment%29%2C%202016-Act%20No.%202_0.pdf.

Facts of the situation are that Kaunda decided to come out of retirement and challenge Chiluba on the ballot. When what had seemed to be empty threats began to form reality as Kaunda first toppled his own anointed successor Kebby Musokotwane in the ranks of the United National Independence Party (UNIP), became UNIP president again, and the old man was regaining ground, the Chiluba regime didn't want to take chances. They had to politically fix Kaunda by introducing a citizenship clause that demanded that for a person to qualify as a presidential candidate, both of his parents must be Zambians by birth or descent. This disqualified Kaunda's candidature because his parents came into Zambia as missionaries from Malawi. Kaunda's UNIP boycotted the whole election but the move did not help at all, as it sent the Independence Party into political oblivion where it hasn't managed to come out.

Much later in 2011, Michael Chilufya Sata won the presidential election and became the fifth Zambian president after resoundingly beating Rupia Bwezani Banda despite Banda's incumbency advantages. Soon after assuming office, Sata announced that he would rule Zambia by the Ten Commandments, yet his ruling party harassed the opposition parties and prevented them from mobilization, a political tactic that seems to have been adopted forever. Still in Zambia, during the 2016 general elections, allegations of a foreign national having been found in the strong room of the Electoral Commission of Zambia (ECZ) at the totaling Center have not been successfully put to rest but merely suppressed. All what happened to address the concern was the elimination of the Director of elections that seemed to have been a politically orchestrated move. The preamble of the Zambian constitution states in clear terms that the people of Zambia commit themselves "*to upholding the principles of democracy and good governance.*"

The Edgar Changwa Lungu presidency assented to the amended constitution in a fully-packed stadium on January 5, 2016. It is this constitution that carries the above-quoted commitment, yet, law enforcement wings like the Zambia Police have been tamed to an extent that they apply the law selectively, particularly the public order act. Cadres and sympathizers of the ruling party can carry out public demonstrations in favor or against anything while those in opposition are denied. Opponent parties can be denied a permit to organize a public rally over a reason that insufficient police officers would be unable to provide security, yet if the party insists, that party would find the venue sealed by heavily armed police officers.

Finally, we can look at the case of the Democratic Republic of Congo as we explore the nature of politics in Africa. Katongole laments about the Congo by arguing that institutions of governance and democracy have systemic weakness and paralysis to the advantage of the ruling elite who manipulate systems to favor them while the poor continue to suffer. The situation of the Congo is that,

> Modern Congo was a victim of one of the brutal episodes of colonial rule, when it was turned into the private business empire of King Leopard; under his reign and the subsequent rule by the republican Belgian government, the Congo's remaining customary chiefs were fought, co-opted, or sent into exile. Religious leaders who defied the orthodoxy of the European-run churches faced the same fate: the prophet Simon Kimbangu died after thirty years in prison for his anticolonial rhetoric. Mobutu just continued the same manipulative "taming" of state institutions and turned them into personal fiefdoms. He did so not only for private gain but also in order to prevent any challengers to his power from emerging, a policy that effectively ended up eroding that very power in the process.[5]

These samples signify that politics remains a dirty game as political actors do all they can to retain power even if it means "taming" governance to the detriment of the country. Politics remains a game that is so dirty that actors fail to see the things that threaten the country's future in the long term, as the politician sees vote bank that is the short term. In this perception, allowing worship spaces to be used as wards or polling stations becomes a compromise on the sacredness of the church. To sum up, these communities that view politics as a dirty game nevertheless, vote and allow some of their members to participate as monitors but resist availing facilities like church schools to be used as polling stations. In other words, political actors who share discomfort with the relationship that is too close between religion and politics, endeavor to create a distinctive line whereas religion and politics become mutually exclusive. This can be discerned in the position adopted by the forefathers of the United States of America, particularly those who were responsible for creating the constitution. According to the first Amendment to the Constitution of the United States of America,

> Congress shall make no law respecting an establishment of religion, or prohibiting the free exercise thereof; or abridging the freedom of speech, or of press; or the right of the people peaceably to assemble, and to petition the government for a redress of grievances.[6]

An analysis of this amendment brings out several observations. First, the "right to exercise religion" is placed on the same level with freedoms

5 Emmanuel Katongole, *Born from Lament: The Theology of Politics of Hope in Africa* (Grand Rapids, MI: Eerdmanns, 2017), 4.

6 The first ten amendments (Bill of Rights) were ratified effective December 15, 1791.

of speech, of the press, assembly, and petitioning government over any grievance. Second, politics and religion are separated in that political actors do not make laws that place religion either at an advantage or disadvantage. Putting it differently, as far as the relationship between politics and religion is concerned, each one is by default self-regulating. In a country whose religious inclinations are discerned even in the language of the currency,[7] one would have expected a constitution to reflect religious details, yet it does not. Why? Perhaps the religionization of politics or politicization of politics were avoided because of the nature of politics to retain itself as a dirty game no matter who is a player. In this regard, the vexing question is; why should there be voting in a dirty game? Before tackling this question, it is necessary to explore the other perception.

The Perceptions of Politics as a Noble vocation

While some view politics as a dirty game, others however, view politics as a noble calling. Under this view, politics translates the adjective *politiké*; a concept understood with an unexpressed noun. It is action in pursuit of the happiness of the *polis*, which is a city.[8] As Irwin argues; politics "deliberates and *decides* about happiness, it is the same *state* as *prudence*."[9]

In Nicomachean ethics, politics is concerned with "the application of prudence to political questions about the *good of the city*."[10] Thus, Aristotle contends that "the proper concern of the state and of political science is to achieve *happiness* for all citizens of the city,[11]" thereby rendering a human being as "political by nature (. . .) because only a political community develops his nature so as to achieve his complete happiness."[12] The view that politics is inseparable from community life as argued above, is well-summarized by Schumaker who in addressing great issues of politics persuasively contends that,

> We must first ask about the communities to which we belong or that we might join, as living within communities is a prerequisite for political life. People belong to many communities, and all communities are political. Families, religious organizations, workplaces, and other such associations pursue collective goals and distribute power and

7 The motto of the American dollar note is "In God We Trust."

8 Terence Irwin, *Aristotle* in *Nicomachean Ethics* (Indianapolis, IN: Hackett, 1999), 343.

9 Irwin, *Aristotle* in *Nicomachean Ethics,* 343.

10 Irwin, *Aristotle* in *Nicomachean Ethics,* 343.

11 Irwin, *Aristotle* in *Nicomachean Ethics,* 343.

12 Irwin, *Aristotle* in *Nicomachean Ethics*, 343; Kenneth W. Thompson, "Religion and Politics in the United States: An Overview," *Annals of the American Academy of Political Science* 483, 12–24; Jeffrey Haynes, *Religion and Politics in Europe: The Middle East and North Africa* (Abingdon, UK: Routledge, 2010), 2.

> privileges, leading us to speak of family politics, church politics, office politics, and the like. Because each of these families is political, their members could benefit by having conversations on the perennial political questions in order to develop a public philosophy to guide their politics.[13]

The key argument in Schumaker's quotation gives flesh to the Aristotelian view of humans as citizens of the city and man as a political animal by nature. This is because life in the city or community is about decision on the equitable distribution of "power and privileges," goods, and services. Therefore, political questions are questions about daily necessities of life in terms of goods and services like, good roads, water, electricity, farming inputs, food security, and healthcare to mention but a few. By design, it seems politics is a noble calling though by practice it can be dirty as argued.

It appears that religious groups, who view politics in this way, tend to develop a strong sense of civic responsibility. In this way, this perception leads to an involvement even in partisan politics in such a way that the distinguishing line between religion and politics is either faint or non-existent and using worship spaces as wards or center of voting candidates of political office flows without seeing anything odd. This is because giving spaces be it for worship or otherwise is viewed as a civic responsibility or patriotic dual citizenship: citizen of heaven and citizen of this world. Put differently, it is giving Caesar what belongs to Caesar, and giving to God what belongs to God.

In national contexts where religion and politics are not so distinctive as to be mutually exclusive, as political actors create constitutions, they infuse religion by stating the interplay between a particular religion and the state. Some of the clear examples of this claim are Zambia, which is a Christian nation, and Egypt, which is an Islamic Republic. As Zambia declares in the preamble of the constitution that Zambia is a Christian nation, so also Egypt declares that it is an Islamic country and its language is Arabic. In refrain from the details of these respective declarations, it satisfies the purposes of this study to observe that the line marking the religious radius from the political one is either faint or it does not exist at all. Both can intrude into each other and so, just as the state actors can take interest in religious affairs, equally, religious actors can take interest in political affairs including making available worship spaces for worship as wards or polling stations for political elections. What can be said further about this study? Even if material has been scarce and more investment

13 Paul Schumaker, *From Ideologies to Public Philosophies: An Introduction to Political Theories* (Malden, MA: Blackwell, 2008), 203.

into research could bring more insights, this "tip of the iceberg" leads to some meaningful concluding remarks as demonstrated below.

Conclusion

This study took off as an interrogation of the ambiguous relationship between religion and politics in so far as perception and spaces usage are concerned. Key research questions that spearhead the study included: *Do churches that offer worship spaces or premises for usage as elections polling stations compromise the holiness? Is offering worship spaces for use as political election polling ward or station part of giving Caesar what belongs to Caesar and giving to God what belongs to God or does the practice compromise the sacredness of worship spaces. If elections of political leaders take place in the worship spaces, does politics remain a "dirty game"?* The study reveals the growing trend, because of the opinions of some leaders, that usage of worship spaces as political election voting station is of giving to "Caesar what belongs to Caesar and to God what belongs to God."

This study has contributed on the subject matter of our pursuit by identifying the emerging issues as follows:

- Navigating the relationship between religion and politics and spaces thereof is a complex undertaking that cannot be resolved by simple "either/or" choices.
- Religion exists to address current and future needs of individuals within a given society holistically.
- Politics is about the common good and limit setting on destructive tendencies, yet it can be dirty if undertaken by corrupt people.
- Religion and politics are distinct and they possess distinct spaces while somewhat sharing a common claim of meeting human needs at the grassroots.
- Failure to distinguish leads to premature crisscrossing that superficially addresses the needs of religion and politics. There is no strong evidence that using worship spaces as polling wards is a legitimate way of rendering to *Caesar what belongs to Caesar and giving to God what belongs to God,* as the New Testament attributes to Jesus. As such, using worship spaces as wards or center of voting for political leaders must be re-visited *a priori* as it has potential to compromise the sacredness of worship spaces.

To conclude, there is need for a more detailed research in this field as part of the re-visitation of dialogue between politics and religion. Such a research could include widening the scope to a regional level.

PART II: RELIGION-BASED POLITICS AND SOCIAL ISSUES

6

RELIGION, SEXUALITIES, AND POLITICS

Adriaan van Klinken

Introduction

Exploring sexuality and nationalist ideologies in postcolonial Africa, Basile Ndjio distinguishes four strategic units that mark the deployment of sexual politics through nationalist discourse, specifically in the context of Cameroon.

> The first unit is the sublimation of procreative and reproductive sexuality, accompanied by the fetishization and ritualization of heterosexual relationships . . .. The second unit is the essentialization and racialization of native Africans' sexuality . . .. The third unit is the segregation and symbolic "othering" of homosexuals . . .. The fourth unit is the criminalization and demonization of homoerotic practices and other unconventional forms of sexual longing and expression.[1]

In this chapter, I use these four units distinguished by Ndjio, adopting them as an analytical frame to examine the different strategies and patterns in the politics of sexuality in postcolonial Zambia. Discussing these, I draw on material I used in previous publications, but in a more concise and systematized way here.[2] Although Ndjio's frame proves to be useful

1 Basile Ndjio, "Sexuality and Nationalist Ideologies in Post-Colonial Cameroon," in *The Sexual History of the Global South: Sexual Politics in Africa, Asia, and Latin America*, eds. Saskia Wieringa and Horacio Sivori (London: Zed Books, 2013), 121–22.

2 In particular, these publications: Adriaan van Klinken, "Homosexuality, Politics and Pentecostal Nationalism in Zambia," *Studies in World Christianity* 20, no. 3 (2014): 259–81; Adriaan van Klinken, "Sexual Citizenship in Postcolonial Zambia: From Zambian Humanism to Christian Nationalism," in *Christian Citizens and the Moral Regeneration of the African State*, eds. Barbara Bompani and Caroline Valois (London and New York: Routledge, 2018), 133–48; Adriaan

to analyze the Zambian context, there is one crucial difference between Cameroonian and Zambian postcolonial sexual politics: more than in Cameroon, in contemporary Zambia the politics of sexuality appears to be shaped by an explicitly Christian, mostly pentecostal, form of nationalism. This is the result of President Chiluba's 1991 Declaration, which in 1996 was enshrined in a preamble to the country's constitution and has given rise to a sense of pentecostal nationalism.[3] This became the ideology of nation-building, replacing the earlier ideology of "Zambian humanism" promoted by the first republican president, Kenneth Kaunda. Despite considerable differences, both ideologies reflect certain continuities that will become clear below. Let me make one caveat: while I discuss Ndjio's units one by one, it should not be interpreted as that they can be easily separated or are successive stages. Although it will become clear that there are certain historical developments, at the same time, the various units are intertwined and overlap in complex ways. Due to the limited space of this chapter, I choose not to give a full and detailed account but only highlight certain patterns.

The Sublimation of Procreative and Reproductive Sexuality

Sublimation here refers to the process through which heterosexuality is transformed into the pure, ideal form of sexuality, and is reimagined as of a culturally and socially higher order. According to Ndjio, this process served to "maintain the long durée of male sexual supremacy as the foundation of postcolonial political power."[4] In the Zambian context, a clear early manifestation of this unit can be observed in the discourse of Zambian Humanism, which was introduced by President Kenneth Kaunda in the mid-1960s, and became the ideology of Kaunda's United National Independence Party (UNIP) in the 1970s. It served as a socialist-inspired philosophy for postcolonial nation building and was based on what Kaunda saw as "a distinctively African way of looking at things" while also having a "Christian basis."[5] The latter is not surprising, given Kaunda's upbringing at the Presbyterian Lubwa Mission in Chinsali, Northern Province, where his father was an evangelist and teacher.

van Klinken, "Sexual Orientation, (Anti-)Discrimination and Human Rights in a 'Christian Nation': The Politicization of Homosexuality in Zambia," *Critical African Studies* 9, no. 1 (2017): 9–31.

3 Isabel A. Phiri, "President Frederick J.T. Chiluba of Zambia: The Christian Nation and Democracy," *Journal of Religion in Africa* 33, no. 4 (2003): 401–28.

4 Ndjio, "Sexuality and Nationalist Ideologies," 121.

5 Kenneth Kaunda, *A Humanist in Africa* (London: Longmans, 1966), 29, 38.

In 1975, at a time when, according to David Gordon, the repressive and intrusive tendencies of humanism became pronounced[6]—the UNIP Research Bureau published a document called *The Zambian Moral Code*. Here, the party (which, in the system of single-party democracy at the time, equaled the government), presented a program of moral regeneration based on humanist principles. The Code addresses issues in areas such as politics, economics, and labor relations, but also in the more individual sphere, with sections about smoking habits, love and sex, marriage, cosmetics and dress, and nudes. Already in the introduction, the Code expresses concern about the "considerable immorality" in Zambia, referring to mini-skirts, tight trousers, jeans, and unaccompanied girls in Zambian streets at night.[7]

Interestingly, in the section about love and sex, the Code repeatedly refers to the phenomenon of a "decent free love affair," which is considered acceptable on one condition: that it is man, not woman, who takes the initiative. Referring to Zambian customary law, the code literally states,

> The Zambian traditional customs and indeed the African custom in general, dictate that a woman shall at all times wait until she is loved or approached by a man to engage her in a decent love affair. On the contrary, it shall not be in her power to solicit for love or to engage herself in "Soho-Hyde Park" type of love affairs.[8]

Drawing on ethnographic accounts of gender and sexuality in southern Africa, Signe Arnfred points out that the "rules for a decent love affair" in traditional societies often reflect the sociocultural norm of discretion.[9] Here, women are allowed to engage in sexual relationships with men other than their husbands, as long as they keep a public image of shyness and modesty. Traditionally, these norms of sexuality are complex and subtle, and they allow for considerable levels of feminine power and agency in the negotiation of sexuality, especially in the matrilineal societies of many peoples in Zambia.[10] However, the rather bold statement of the Code that "it is immoral for a woman to solicit a man for love" appears to invoke a Victorian or Christian notion of im/morality and can be argued to reflect a patriarchal bias that, in the words of Ndjio, seeks to

6 David M. Gordon, *Invisible Agents: Spirits in a Central African History* (Athens, OH: Ohio University Press, 2012), 165.

7 Research Bureau, *The Zambian Moral Code—A Programmatic Approach* (Lusaka: Freedom House, 1975), 2.

8 Research Bureau, *Zambian Moral Code*, 16.

9 Signe Arnfred, "'African Sexuality'/Sexuality in Africa: Tales and Silences," in *Re-Thinking Sexualities in Africa*, ed. Signe Arnfred (Uppsala: Nordiska Afrika Institutet, 2005), 74.

10 For eg., see Karla Poewe, *Matrilineal Ideology: Male and Female Dynamics in Luapula, Zambia* (London: International African Institute, 1981).

"maintain the long durée of male sexual supremacy."[11] The next section of the Code, about marriage, further foregrounds how sexual morality is concerned with reproduction. The section states that it is allowed for husbands to exchange their wives, for a payment in money form or in kind, with other men, the first reason for this practice being the situation where the wedlock of the couple concerned may have had entangled into problems of childlessness.[12]

In the contemporary Zambian context, where public morality has been transformed by the rise of pentecostal forms of Christianity, it is unimaginable that "free love affairs" or the exchange of wives would be publicly promoted by political parties and leaders, in the way that Kaunda and UNIP did in the 1970s. Yet, the process of the sublimation of procreative sexuality can be observed here, too, although it manifests itself in new forms. For instance, prominent pentecostal pastor, Bishop Joshua Banda of Northmead Assembly of God Church in Lusaka, who is one of the strongest defenders of the Declaration, addressed all the wrongs of popular masculinity in Zambia in a series of sermons, "Fatherhood in the 21st Century," and sought to overcome these by promoting an ideal of biblical manhood. The sermons are interesting as they clearly illustrate Ndjio's point of the politics of sexuality being concerned with maintaining male supremacy. Banda in his sermons develops a relatively nuanced or even "soft" version of masculinity, as he denounces men's obsession with power, control, and supremacy and defines "biblical manhood" in terms of responsibility and "servant leadership."[13] Yet in the end, he bases his notion of manhood on biblical ideas of male headship, although he does endorse the equality of men and women, he simultaneously emphasizes that men have received a "primary" responsibility to provide leadership in the family, the church, and society at large.[14] What is relevant here is that Banda explicitly emphasizes the procreative nature of his Christian ideal of masculinity, and contrasts it to "alternative," that is, homosexual, lifestyles.

> Biblical fatherhood has in mind that a man, as God aimed him, in a family takes his role as a father, and a woman, as God has fashioned her, takes the role as a mother in the home, and the two become the

---

11 Research Bureau, *Zambian Moral Code*, 16; Ndjio, "Sexuality and Nationalist Ideologies," 121.

12 Research Bureau, *Zambian Moral Code*, 17.

13 For the notion of "soft masculinity" in relation to African Pentecostalism, see Ezra Chitando, "A New Man for a New Era? Zimbabwean Pentecostalism, Masculinities and the HIV Epidemic," *Missionalia* 35, no. 3 (2007): 112–27.

14 Adriaan van Klinken, "Pentecostalism, Political Masculinity and Citizenship: The Born-Again Male Subject as Key to Zambia's National Redemption," *Journal of Religion in Africa* 46, no. 2–3 (2016): 129–57.

> package that bring into this life, by procreation, a family through the offspring. And nothing else exists besides that. And why should those who take up a so-called alternative life style still take on the role of a mother and a father if they are [of the] same sex, and then go into adoption of children? We can adopt children in families and that's fine, but not in this fashion ... There is no substitute for fatherhood. It is rooted in biblical manhood, and biblical manhood is rooted in creation. And in creation God made them male and female. It is Adam and Eve and not Adam and Steve.[15]

Indeed, in his sermons Banda construes homosexual men as the counter-image of "biblical manhood," as they mix up the divinely ordained gender order and as such represent what he calls "the impairment of true manhood." The sermons provide an interesting twist to Ndjio's argument that postcolonial African politics of sexuality seeks to address the crisis of the *Muntu*—that is, the libidinous African heterosexual male. The sermons, like African pentecostal discourse more generally, seem to address this crisis of masculinity by domesticating masculinity, while simultaneously rendering the sphere of spiritual power as a key for the performance of masculinity in public.[16]

The Essentialization and Racialization of Native Africans' Sexuality

As part of the earlier mentioned discourse of Zambian humanism and its concern with moral regeneration, Kaunda in his 1975 Watershed Speech stated,

> There has been a successful invasion of our cultural values by those of the West. Any erosion, countrymen, of our cultural values is a threat to Zambian personality. While we are free to borrow positive aspects of foreign culture to enrich our own, we must defend ourselves against undermining our nationhood through cultural conquest . . .. This is Zambia with its own way of life and not Europe. This is Zambia and not the United States of America. We take our cultural values very seriously.[17]

---

15 Joshua Banda, "Fatherhood in the 21st Century—part 4," quoted in Adriaan van Klinken, "The Homosexual as the Antithesis of "'Biblical Manhood?'" Hetero-Normativity and Masculinity Politics in Zambian Pentecostal Sermons," *Journal of Gender and Religion in Africa* 17, no. 2 (2011): 129–42.

16 See Martin Lindhardt, "Men of God: Neo-Pentecostalism and Masculinities in Urban Tanzania," *Religion* 45, no. 2 (2015): 252–72.

17 Kenneth D. Kaunda, *The Watershed Speech* (Lusaka: Zambia Information Services, 1975), 28, 31.

The anti-Western rhetoric reflected here is linked to the anti-capitalist undertones of Zambian humanism, the idea being that humanism, different from capitalism, can provide a true moral basis to society. As part of the attempt to resist "immoral" Western cultural influences, Kaunda and UNIP banned "love-making films" to be screened on TV and "nude pictures" to be published in the media, because such things are considered to promote "prostitution in the nation."[18] The picture that emerges is one of "Western immorality" versus "Zambian moral purity." Although this was not only applied to matters of sexuality, the discourse of Zambian humanism does construe a notion of a pure, authentic, and "decent" Zambian sexuality, to be defended against immoral Western cultural influences.[19] No explicit reference is made to homosexuality—this apparently was not yet an issue of public and political concern at the time—yet it is obvious that this Zambian sexuality is thought of as strictly heterosexual.

Several decades later, when homosexuality had emerged as a key issue in the Zambian public sphere, the same binary scheme of Western immorality versus Zambian moral purity is evoked to explicitly denounce same-sex relationships and gay rights.[20] Thus, in the late 1990s, Kaunda's successor, President Frederick Chiluba, in response to the first Zambian person publicly coming out as gay, stated that "homosexuality is the deepest level of depravity," and is "unbiblical and abnormal," while reportedly insinuating that those advocating it "do so for financial favors from donors" and are "behaving like slaves ready to go against local morals because of poverty."[21] Two decades later, in 2013, then-Home Affairs Minister (and current Zambian President) Edgar Lungu, in response to the launch of a European Union funding program in support of the human rights of sexual minorities in Zambia, stated that homosexuality is un-Zambian; it is not part of our culture, while adding that he would closely watch which "money-hungry civil society organizations will fall for the money . . . and

---

18 Kaunda, *Watershed Speech*, 31.

19 Yet Kaunda did legalize abortion in 1972, which brought him into conflict with the Catholic Church. See Marja Hinfelaar, "Legitimizing Powers: The Political Role of the Roman Catholic Church, 1972–1991," in *One Zambia, Many Histories: Towards a History of Post-colonial Zambia*, eds. Jan-Bart Gewald, Marja Hinfelaar, and Giacomo Macola (Leiden: Brill 2008), 135–136.

20 Derrick M. Muwina, "Christianity, Homosexuality and Public Politics in Zambia," in *Christianity and Controversies over Homosexuality in Contemporary Africa*, eds. Ezra Chitando and Adriaan van Klinken (Abingdon,UK: Routledge, 2016), 85–97; Chammah J. Kaunda, "The Public Religious Speech That Does Justice: Reclaiming the Narrative of Resistance in the Context of Heterosexism," *Journal of Theology for Southern Africa* 155 (2016): 196–215.

21 Scott Long, Widney Brown, and Gail Cooper, "More than a Name: The Spread of Homophobic Rhetoric in Southern Africa," *Human Right Watch* (New York, 2003), 40; *Times of Zambia*, "Chiluba Blasts Gays," October 19, 1998.

start championing same sex marriages."[22] The notion of homosexuality as un-Zambian obviously implies that "Zambian sexuality" is essentially and normatively heterosexual. Lungu received support from the executive director of the Evangelical Fellowship of Zambia, Rev. Pukuta Mwanza, who referred to gay rights as "contrary to our fundamental Christian values and to our rich African and traditional beliefs and practices."[23] Further elaborating on his rejection of gay rights, Mwanza argued,

> There is a growing demand for human rights that are at variance against God. It is for this reason that we see a worldwide promotion of devious behavior and acts of pervasion such as homosexuality. Gay rights are ungodly because homosexuality is contrary to God's creative order of human beings. Human beings are not supposed to exercise a right in an area that God has forbidden.[24]

The above quotations from these political and religious leaders reflect a discursive process in which an authentic and pure Zambian sexuality is constructed, initially implicitly and later much more explicitly, and is defined as heterosexual, with homosexuality being represented as extraneous and autochthonous. This resembles a wider pattern across the continent with an emerging nativist construction of African sexuality, according to Ndjio.

> Sexuality has become a political and social landscape of privileged intervention by the postcolonial state, seeking to purify the body of the nation. It has also become a key site where the myth about African cultural unity is enacted by those who see a complex continent and its diverse populations through the lens of homogeneity and uniformity. In addition, sexuality has been made a cultural tool through which Africanity is expressed, and nativist ideologies are dramatized.[25]

What is different in the Zambian context, compared to the Cameroonian context as described by Ndjio, is that in recent years this logic of an "authentic" African sexuality is increasingly framed in and combined with Christian rhetoric about a divinely ordained sexuality, that is, sexuality as God intended it in the order of creation. This is reflected in Chiluba's reference to homosexuality as not only un-Zambian but also un-biblical, and in much greater detail in Rev. Mwanza's exposition

---

22 *Zambian Watchdog*, "Edgar Lungu Tells Off EU over Gay Rights Advert in Zambia," March 25, 2013.

23 Pukuta N. Mwanza, "Re: Call for Proposals in Support of Homosexuality" (Lusaka: Evangelical Fellowship of Zambia, April 2, 2013).

24 Pukuta N. Mwanza, "Biblical Reflections on the National Symposium on the Church and Human Rights" (Lusaka: Evangelical Fellowship of Zambia, June 2, 2015).

25 Ndjio, "Sexuality and Nationalist Ideologies," 126.

about gay rights as ungodly. Thus, both cultural and biblical arguments feed into the construction of an essentialized Zambian or African sexuality. In the contemporary Zambian context, both culture and the Bible serve as canons to define sexuality as purely heterosexual.

Although much of the concern with sexual purity in recent years appears to center around homosexuality in particular, it is worth keeping in mind—as Chammah J. Kaunda and Mutale Mulenga Kaunda prompt us—that "national sexual purity is not only about resisting homosexuality; it is defined based on the Christian traditional notion of family, which allows for expression of only heteronormative romantic love as God's ideal and excludes all other sexual expressions as forms of rebellion against God."[26] As examples, they refer to the recently established Ministry of National Guidance and Religious Affairs, which in 2018 warned Zambians against the use of sex dolls, as these would be inappropriate in a Christian nation, as well as to the National Zambian Arts Council banning the South African musician Zodwa Wabantu from entering the country as her performance would undermine Zambian values. These examples indeed illustrate that the concern with "decency" has much wider ramifications, as it is about controlling expressions of sexuality in the nation.

The Segregation and Symbolic Othering of Homosexuals

With Zambian sexuality being discursively constructed as strictly heterosexual, there is an increasing tendency to exclude Zambians who do not meet the standard of normative heterosexuality from the body of the nation. For instance, in 2013, Minister of Justice Wynter Kabimba reportedly stated that there is "no room for gays in Zambia," giving the following rationale: "As Zambians, we declared that we are a Christian nation and there is no way we can allow this un-Zambian culture. I want to urge all Zambians to rise and denounce this vice."[27] The implicit suggestion here is that good or proper Zambians are heterosexual, and that it is their patriotic duty to fight against all things gay. Indeed, in an analysis of discussions of homosexuality on Zambian online forums, I found several participants using explicitly patriotic language, with the defense of Zambia's sexual purity being represented as a critical nationalist as well as religious obligation. Zambian citizens who actively resist the acceptance of homosexuality are referred to as "warriors in prayer" and as the "new

---

26 Chammah J. Kaunda and Mutale Mulenga Kaunda, "Mobilising Religious Assets for Social Transformation: A Theology of Decolonial Reconstruction Perspective on the Ministry of National Guidance and Religious Affairs (MNGRA) in Zambia," *Religions* 9, no. 6 (2018): 7. https://doi.org/10.3390/rel9060176.

27 Chila Namaiko, "No Room for Gays in Zambia–Kabimba," *Times of Zambia*, April 22, 2013.

freedom fighters," and it is on the basis of the stance on homosexuality that "the true Christians will be separated from the false Christians and the patriot Zambians who cherish and protect the Zambian culture and traditions will be separated from the ones that do not love our land, traditions, and cultures and do not cherish what our freedom fighters fought for and what our fore fathers stood for."[28] This discourse illustrates Ndjio's observation of a "moral economy of alterity, which cultivates homogeneity and dramatizes authenticity, [in which] homosexuality and other transgressive desires have been denounced as influenced by neocolonialist forces attempting to re-alienate or re-acculturate the minds that African nationalists set free."[29] In this economy, Ndjio argues, there is a "growing tendency among the local population to equate heterosexuality with patriotism, localism, and Africanness, while homosexuality is generally associated with globalism and strangeness."[30] Critically, in the Zambian version of economy, not only gays themselves, but also the people who support their case are excluded from the body of the nation. For instance, when a Zambian NGO, Dette Resource Foundation, came out in 2012 in support of LGBT rights, the organization received enormous backlash, with the Home Affairs Minister Edgar Lungu even calling for a criminal investigation.[31]

One of the direct consequences of this discursive and symbolic othering and exclusion of sexual minorities can be observed in the area of public health, in particular, HIV prevention and treatment programs. In 2010, former president Kaunda while speaking at an event of the organization Champions for an HIV-free generation, reportedly called for a legal ban on the "promotion of homosexuality," with reference to Zambia's character as a Christian nation. The irony of making such a statement at an HIV prevention event is painful, especially when realizing that sexual minorities are among the key targets. It reflects the deeply rooted idea of HIV in Zambia, and in Africa more generally, being a heterosexual pandemic—an idea that itself is based on the notion that African sexuality is heterosexual.[32] Indeed, reviewing Zambian sexual health policy documents, Julius Kapembwa observes that they "contain no discussion of homosexuality despite the purported strong link between men who have

28 Quoted in van Klinken, "Homosexuality, Politics," 268.

29 Ndjio, "Sexuality and Nationalist Ideologies," 128.

30 Ndjio, "Sexuality and Nationalist Ideologies," 128.

31 Adriaan van Klinken, "Christianity, Human Rights and LGBTI Advocacy: The Case of Dette Resource Foundation in Zambia," in *Public Religion and the Politics of Homosexuality in Africa*, eds. Adriaan van Klinken and Ezra Chitando (London: Routledge, 2016), 231.

32 See Marc Epprecht, *Heterosexual Africa? The History of an Idea from the Age of Exploration to the Age of AIDS* (Athens: Ohio University Press, 2008).

sex with men (MSM) and HIV and AIDS."[33] In 2013, First Lady Christine Kaseba, the wife of then President Michael Sata, a medical doctor herself, caused national and international headlines by openly denouncing the silence on the phenomenon of men who have sex with men, and underlining the need to allow open discourse on the matter and mainstreaming this key population in HIV service provision.[34] Although Kaseba does claim that, notwithstanding the criminalization of homosexuality in Zambia, "access to HIV services including anti-retroviral treatment is open to all" regardless of sexual orientation, her speech draws attention to the critical fact that the culture of stigma, taboo, and criminalization of same-sex practices has serious health consequences and hampers effective HIV prevention and treatment. The uproar her comments provoked illustrate the long way that Zambia still has a long way to go in adopting a "truly holistic and cross-sectoral approach to HIV and AIDS and other sexual health and human rights discussions."[35]

The Criminalization and Demonization of Homoerotic Practices

As far as the criminalization of same-sex practices is concerned, Zambia's Penal Code (Chapter 87, section 155), which dates to the colonial period, criminalizes "carnal knowledge against the order of nature," with a penalty of fourteen years imprisonment. Although several Zambian politicians have suggested that the government would, or should, introduce stiffer laws against homosexuality and the "promotion" of it—inspired by the example of countries such as Uganda and Nigeria—so far, this has not yet translated into substantial legislative steps. However, the existing colonial law in recent years has been frequently used to prosecute people—mostly men, but in some cases also women—suspected to have violated this law. Moreover, Zambia has witnessed intensified prosecution of people advocating for the rights of sexual minorities, the highest profile case being against the activist Paul Kasonkomona who was arrested in 2013 at the MUVI TV studios after speaking in a live program, where he called for the inclusion of men who have sex with men in HIV prevention and treatment strategies. He was charged for "promoting homosexuality," which made one commentator—the Zambian, US-based Episcopal priest, Rev. Kapya Kaoma—ask whether speaking about gay rights is already seen as

33 Julius Kapembwa, "A Critical Appraisal of Heterosexism in Zambia," *South African Journal of Philosophy* 37, no. 3 (2018): 245–260, 253.

34 Dr. Christine Kaseba, "Speech by Dr. Christine Kaseba, First Lady of the Republic of Zambia," Lusaka, November 5, 2013.

35 Epprecht, *Heterosexual Africa?*, 29.

a crime in present-day Zambia.[36] The *Zambia 2017 Human Rights Report* by the United States Department of State concludes that the police contribute to the climate of systematic harassment and intimidation of sexual minorities.

> Rather than submit cases for trial, police on several occasions arrested suspected LGBTI persons on bogus charges, forcing them to spend at least one night in jail. In most cases, police demanded bribes before releasing the individuals. Police increasingly charged transgender persons with "impersonation" and subjected them to verbal abuse and harassment while in detention. The charges generally could not be prosecuted successfully and detainees were released. For example, on August 30, police in Kapiri Mposhi town arrested and charged two men for same-sex sexual conduct. The case was being tried at year's end.[37]

According to the same report, this culture of abuse and intimidation perpetuated by the police also legitimized societal violence against people belonging to LGBTI communities, resulting for instance in their discrimination in employment, housing, and access to education and health care. All of this illustrates Ndjio's argument that as a result of widely publicized anti-homosexual discourses, "lesbians and most notably gays are viewed as aliens to the nation . . . By this process of uprooting, alienation, and estrangement, gays and lesbians become lesser persons, deprived of their most basic rights as citizens."[38] At the root of this process, he argues, is the logic of demonization.

Ndjio suggests that in the context of Cameroon, the process of demonizing gays and lesbians is reflected in discourses centering on the "pervasive figure of the gay/lesbian witch," which reflects wider concerns with witchcraft in the country. In the Zambian context, discourses of witchcraft appear to be less prominent in relation to homosexuality. Yet, in true pentecostal style, demonization occurs even more literally here, through a discourse about the devil and demonic forces. Indeed, the public debate about homosexuality and gay rights in Zambia has become "eschatologically enchanted through millennialist thought."[39] The pentecostal imagination of politics as a site of competition between God and the devil, and the millennialist's expectation of the return of Jesus Christ

36 Kapya Kaoma, "Is Speaking on Gay Rights a Crime in Sata's Zambia?," *Tumfweko*, April 10, 2013.

37 *Zambia 2017 Human Rights Report*, United States Department of State, Bureau of Democracy, Human Rights and Labor, 22.

38 Ndjio, "Sexuality and Nationalist Ideologies," 134.

39 Adriaan van Klinken, "Gay Rights, the Devil and the End Times: Public Religion and the Enchantment of the Homosexuality Debate in Zambia," *Religion* 43, no. 4 (2013): 519, https://doi.org/10.1080/0048721X.2013.765631.

being preceded by intensified demonic attacks through personified "antichrists" and "false prophets" means that international bodies such as the European Union, and international leaders such as the former United Nations Secretary General Ban Ki Moon are seen as agents of the devil seeking to impose gay rights on Zambia as a Christian nation. It is not a coincidence that Edgar Lungu, at that time acting president, warned against homosexuality, same-sex marriage, and gay rights and called upon the Christian church to strongly oppose these vices together with the government, while delivering the opening address of the "21 days Jesus is Coming Again Crusade," of the Seventh Day Adventist Church (SDA).[40] Although the SDA that historically has a strong presence in Zambia is not a pentecostal denomination, it has a profound millennialist outlook, similar to many pentecostal churches, and it has played a critical role in framing the politics of sexuality in Zambia in an apocalyptic discourse of the end of the world being near.[41] Not only international organizations and leaders, but also local Zambians who advocate for the recognition of the human rights of sexual minorities are being demonized. Lungu, this time in his role as Home Affairs Minister, in 2013 stated: "Those advocating gay rights should go to hell, that is not an issue we will tolerate."[42] In the same year, another government minister (of youth and sports), Chishimba Kambwili, reportedly called in during a live panel discussion on Radio Phoenix to refer to defenders of LGBT rights as "agents of the devil."[43] Obviously, this demonizing discourse of political and religious leaders fuels homophobic hate speech and incites physical violence at a grassroots level as well; it reinforces the de-humanization of gays and lesbians, the denial of their human rights, and their exclusion from the body of the nation.[44]

Conclusion

The above analysis has demonstrated that sexual politics in postcolonial Zambia to a considerable extent is shaped by Christian beliefs and convictions. This is true implicitly for the discourse of Zambian humanism and its agenda of moral regeneration under Kaunda's UNIP administration,

40 "Anybody Engaging in Vices Like Gay Marriage Would be Arrested and Prosecuted–Lungu," *Lusaka Times*, April 8, 2013.

41 "SDA Says Call by Ban Ki-moon to Respect Gays a Sign That End is Near," *Zambian Watchdog*, February 26, 2012.

42 Paul Mwitwa, "Go to Hell, Edgar Lungu tells Gay Rights Activists," *Zambia Reports*, May 21, 2013, https://zambiareports.com/2013/05/21/go-to-hell-edgar-lungu-tells-gay-rights-activists/.

43 Human Rights Watch, "Zambia: Stop Prosecuting People for Homosexuality," May 20, 2013.

44 Van Klinken, "Gay Rights, the Devil," 530.

in the first decades after independence. This discourse continued the earlier "civilizing mission" of the Christian missionaries during the colonial period. It is much more explicit in the discourse of Christian nationalism, inaugurated by Kaunda's predecessor, Chiluba, which has shaped Zambia's sense of national identity since then, as a result of the growing influence of pentecostal churches. Here, let me make two caveats. First, as much as sexual politics in postcolonial Zambia generally has been heteronormative, and, especially for the past ten years, also overtly homophobic, it is important to acknowledge that these politics are not monolithic and static, but reflect changing political dynamics. In this regard, the premature death of President Michael Sata in 2014 is particularly sad, as there is ground to believe that Sata was committed to a different, more inclusive form of body politic. Second, as much as the above account underlines the role of pentecostal Christianity, which undoubtedly has contributed to the policing of the sexual purity of the nation and to the demonization of sexual "others," Zambian Christianity is highly diverse. The Catholic Church has consistently opposed the constitutional declaration of Zambia as a Christian nation, and has also expressed a more nuanced stance on matters of homosexuality.[45] How the politics of sexuality will develop in Zambia in the foreseeable future is difficult to predict. The current Lungu administration, which actively propagates pentecostal political rhetoric and has reinstalled the Ministry of National Guidance and Religious Affairs (currently led by a pentecostal ordained minister), gives little ground for optimism for the adoption of a more inclusive definition of sexual citizenship in the country. Yet politics, including sexual politics, is always subject to dynamics of change—for the worse, or for the better.

45 Van Klinken, "Homosexuality, Politics," 266–267.

7

RELIGION, GENDER, AND POLITICS

Chammah J. Kaunda
Nelly Mwale
Mutale Mulenga Kaunda
Joseph Chita

Introduction

This chapter explores a life trajectory of a female pentecostal clergy, Rev. Godfridah Sumaili, and her contributions to the religious and political discourse in the public sphere in order to understand the intersection of religion, gender, and politics and in turn make a critical contribution toward the evolving Zambian scholarship in the same field. The inquiry was sparked by the concern regarding scarcity in literature on gender and religion (that largely focuses on the religion's role in gender inequality) and gender, development, and politics (that often portrayed women subordination and disadvantaged position in development), thereby neglecting the active contribution of women to development in different contexts within Zambia. For example, it was observed that women's experienced considerable disadvantage and discrimination in societies perpetuating gender-differentiated structures.[1] At the same time, the growing popularity of female Pentecostals in Zambian politics in the public sphere could not be ignored. Therefore, it acknowledges the two notable pentecostal women politicians in Zambia today—namely, Rev. Godfridah Sumaili, the first Minister of National Guidance and Religious Affairs and a pastor at the neo-Pentecostal Bread of Life Church International (BLCI), and Dr. Liya Nawa Mutale, the Permanent Secretary Ministry of Home Affairs-Republic of Zambia, a medical doctor by profession and pastor in

1 Hurriyet Babacan, "'Women Hold Up Half the Sky': Gender Mainstreaming and Women's Inequality in Australia," *Gender Development Journal* 64 (2004): 49–52.

a pentecostal church, who was instrumental during the 2016 presidential campaign. Dr. Mutale formed a campaign wing called "Christians for Lungu" and after Lungu's election win, this campaign wing became defunct.[2] This chapter focuses on Rev. Sumaili's narrative in the public sphere for purposes of documenting women's life narratives in Zambia's public sphere through the intersection of religion, gender, and politics.

In doing so, the chapter reflects on the increasing debates regarding the relationship between religion and gender,[3] and extends this interaction to politics. A significant part of such research is based on the assumption that gender roles are primarily constructed through religion, culture, lifestyle, and upbringing[4] and women are reportedly more inclined to participate in religious life[5]. This chapter extends women's participation in the religious and political spheres and argues what the life trajectory of Rev. Sumaili demonstrated. First, contrary to the popular portrayal of women in religion as being oppressed, unemployed, and alienated, a pentecostal woman has contributed to the religious, gender, and political nexus by being an example of a symbol of this intersection. Second, this nexus is a mirror of a gendered religious and political discourse in contemporary Zambia.

In this chapter, religion is acknowledged as playing a vital role in different spaces, deeply rooted in peoples' experiences, and has influenced the socioeconomic and political direction of societies.[6] Scholars have also admitted that religious beliefs are central in everyday life, for religion provides the moral codes by which people live.[7] Most importantly, given that religion both shapes, and is shaped by society,[8] Rev. Sumaili's narrative in

---

2 Mutale M. Kaunda and Chammah J. Kaunda, "Pentecostalism, Female Spirit-Filled Politicians, and Populism in Zambia," *International Review of Mission* 107, no. 1 (2018): 28.

3 Peter Hopkins, "Women, Men, Positionalities and Emotion: Doing Feminist Geographies of Religion." *ACME: An International E-Journal for Critical Geographies* 8, no. 1 (2009): 1–17; Stephanie Seguino, "Help or Hindrance? Religion's Impact on Gender Inequality in Attitudes and Outcomes." *World Development* 39, no. 8 (2011): 1308–1321; Sanjukta Chaudhuri, "A Life Courses Model of Human Rights Realization, Female Empowerment, and Gender Inequality in India," *World Development* 52 (2013): 55–70.

4 Ursula King, "Introduction: Gender and the Study of Religion," in *Religion and Gender*, ed.Ursula King (Oxford: Blackwell, 1995): 1–38.

5 Claire M. Renzetti and Daniel J. Curran, *Women, Men, and Society* (Boston: Allyn and Bacon, 1999).

6 Roger W. Stump, *The Geography of Religion: Faith, Place and Space* (Lanham: Rowman and Littlefield Publishers, 2008).

7 Cliford Geertz, "Religion as a Cultural System," in *The Interpretation of Cultures: Selected Essays* (New York: Basic Books, 1993), 87–125.

8 Dodd, Sarah Drakopoulou, and Paul Timothy Seaman, "Religion and Enterprise:

the public sphere is used to mirror how religion has contributed to the gender and politics discourse and how society has shaped religion (motivated religion) in the gender and politics discourse. It is clear that most studies on religion and gender have focused on the status of women in religions,[9] and this chapter gives a shift of the discourse to the ways in which religion has permeated the political sphere through the active participation of the women clergy in the public sphere.

Methodology

Grounded in the interpretivist paradigm, this chapter is informed by insights from a narrative research design that seeks to give an account of Rev. Godfridah Sumaili's contributions to the religion and politics discourse in the public sphere in Zambia. Narrative research is understood as research concentrated on studying one or two individuals, gathering data through their stories, individual experiences, and chronologically ordering (or using life course stages) the meaning of those experiences.[10] In this study, we have adopted a biographical approach in which the researcher wrote and recorded the experiences of another person's life.[11] Because the interest of the study is to understand a woman's life trajectory in the public sphere, the main method of data collection was content analysis. The documents in the form of memos, official correspondence about the individual, and photographs among others were conveniently selected.[12] The central question addressed in the study is understanding the discourse surrounding the portrayal of Rev. Sumaili through the prism of the gender, religion, and politics in the public sphere in Zambia.

The data was analyzed through the narrative research restorying approach in which the narratives about Rev. Sumaili were reorganized into some general type of framework. This framework consisted of gathering stories from documentaries, social media, newspapers, internet, and archives, and thematically analyzing them by coding them into key themes

An Introductory Exploration," *Entrepreneurship Theory and Practice* 23, no. 1 (1998): 71–86.

9 Katherine Young, "Introduction," in *Women in World Religions*, ed. A. Sharma (Albany: State University of New York Press, 1987), 1–36; Renzetti and Curran, *Women, Men, and Society*; Margaret Ojo Yemisi and Matthias Ojo Olufemi Dada, "Gender and Religion: The Changing Status of Women within Religious Context," *Journal of Social Sciences and Humanities* 1, no. 3 (2015): 245–248.

10 John W. Creswell, *Research Design: Qualitative, Quantitative and Mixed Methods Approaches* (London: Sage, 2003).

11 Kathleen Casey, "The New Narrative Research in Education," *Review of Research in Education* 21, no. 1 (1995): 211–253.

12 John W. Creswell, *Qualitative Inquiry and Research Design: Choosing among Five Approaches* (Thousand Oaks: Sage, 2007); Louis Cohen, Lawrence Manion, and Keith Morrison, *Research Methods in Education* (London: Routledge, 2007).

organized according to the period, place, and activities and then rewriting the narratives chronologically.[13]

A Trajectory of Rev. Godfridah Nsenduluka Sumaili

Family, Pastor, and Banker

In the public sphere, first, Rev. Godfridah Nsenduluka Sumaili is described as having different roles in the family, church, and society. To start with, she is a family woman. She was born on May 26, 1957, is married to Fanuel Sumaili and has five children and four grandchildren,[14] and thus not only represents the family but also represents the societal expectations of a woman to have a family in that sense. Further, Sumaili is described as a human rights commissioner, president for Jesus Cares Ministry, chairperson for the Children in Network (CHIN), board member for National Credit and Savings Bank (NATSAVE), qualified banker, civic leader, and an ordained pastor at Lusaka's Bread of Life Church International and, most of all, woman, wife, mother, and grandmother, and that Sumaili's story has washed down the ancient assumption that a woman's temperament makes her unfit for leadership, thereby disapproving the second-class theory about the women-folk that is continuously reinforced by custom and tradition.[15] This portrayal of Rev. Sumaili's family further signifies the notions of family emphasized by Sumaili as the foundation for national values.[16]

Sumaili was also a pentecostal pastor at Bread of Life Church. She is inspired by the life of Mother Teresa, who gave herself to serving humanity and giving dignity to vulnerable people; and appreciates Bishop Joseph Imakando, her spiritual father and mentor who ordained her as pastor.[17] While there is a debate on Pentecostalism and women empowerment through the pentecostal gender paradox,[18] this depiction has resonated with the view that pentecostal churches have been advancing women's empowerment in the public sphere.[19] The churches have shown how pen-

13 Anne J. Ollerenshaw and John W. Creswell, "Narrative Research: A Comparison of Two Restorying Data Analysis Approaches," *Qualitative Inquiry* 8, no. 3 (2002): 329–347.

14 Christine Chisha, "Rev. Sumaili Passionate about Poverty Eradication," *Daily Mail*, December 4, 2016.

15 Gethsemane Mwizabi, "Zambia: Prominent Rise of Zambian Women," *Times of Zambia*, June 9, 2007).

16 Ministerial report, November 16, 2017, National Assembly of Zambia.

17 Joseph Mwenda and Stella Goma, "Sumaili Explains Her Plan for Religious Ministry," *News Diggers Newspaper*, April 9, 2017.

18 Kaunda and Kaunda, "Pentecostalism."

19 Charlotte Spinks, "Panacea or Painkiller? The Impact of Pentecostal Christianity on Women in Africa," *Critical Half* 1, no. 1 (2003): 21–25; Mariah

tecostal movements are a resource for empowering women to reject the sociocultural *status quo* of marginalization in patriarchal societies, and legitimizing ambitious women's achievement of economic, social, and political independence.

In addition to representations of a family woman and female pastor, Sumaili has also been represented as a woman graduate with a professional life. "A graduate of Master of Business Administration, she did her internship at Citizen Trust Bank in Atlanta, United States of America, and had a flourishing career in the banking sector."[20] As a banker, Sumaili worked for City Bank as treasurer, before joining Standard Chartered Bank in 1993. Her outstanding contribution was setting up a treasury: "I set up the department of treasury. There was no treasury then but I set it up by the grace of God, then I moved on to a very senior position in the bank."[21]

While working at Standard Chartered Bank, she had a religious encounter and, as she often puts it, "met God at the bank."

> Somebody shared with me. . . somebody talked to me about Jesus . . . somebody here at the Bank. This person told me how wonderful Jesus was, and how he could transform your life. It was the truth. And so I gave my life to Jesus then and there-right in the Bank, I gave my life to Jesus . . .[22]

Her contributions to the banking sector were also through serving on the National Savings and Credit bank of Zambia board.

Community Worker, Founder of Jesus Cares Ministries and Board Member

Sumaili has further been portrayed as a woman of care and concern as demonstrated through the setting up of an orphanage for homeless children. "From the activities of her organization, it could be deduced that she was passionate about development in areas such as poverty eradication and reducing inequalities with a view to reaching out to the vulnerable, especially women and children."[23] Sumaili was fully involved in community work after she left the flourishing banking career in 2001 to devote her time to the orphanage and establishing an organization, Jesus Cares Ministries. The beginning of the orphanage was traced to the time

Farn-Arp, "Pentecostal Charismatic Christianity and the Making of Female Managers," *Focus* 62 (2011): 47–53.

20 Chisha, *Daily Mail*, December 4, 2016.

21 Mwenda and Goma, *News Diggers*, April 9, 2017.

22 Godfridah Sumaili, "I Met Jesus at the Bank," in *Creative: Standard Chartered Bank* (Lusaka: Standard Chartered Bank, 2003).

23 Chisha, *Daily Mail*, December 4, 2016.

at the bank, when she began to feed children on the streets every Friday after her office hours in 1995. She would set up some tables for food on a street corner two blocks from Standard Chartered Bank's headquarters in downtown Lusaka and feed the children on the street. Alongside feeding physically, Sumaili enriched the children spiritually, too, through songs. She recalled that, "On that first Friday evening, fewer than 20 children came and ate. The following Friday, over 50 children showed up for a meal. On the third Friday, it was more than 70. And then the number was too great to count."[24] Sumaili also started preaching to street kids on Friday nights before serving them food.[25] Soon, it became apparent that feeding the children once a week was not enough. Consequently, she began to contemplate on finding a home. She stresses, "So I found a home where we could bring them . . .. And then I found a bus so that on the weekends we could pick them up and take them to the house."[26]

An American Christian Group which documented and aired what Sumaili was doing on television directly contributed to the establishment of an orphanage. After watching the documentary, one woman who had a house (that was once a bar not far from the center of the city) approached Sumaili saying that her property could be used to shelter the children. Following discussions, the woman allowed Sumaili to have it for six months free of rent, thus the Jesus Cares Ministries was born anchored on Luke 4:18 and has grown into a big interdenominational organization, based in Lusaka. According to Sumaili, it aims to embody the ministry of Jesus Christ while He was on earth and the initiative's main emphasis is on evangelism.[27] Jesus Cares Ministries also has many other mercy ministries that support orphans and prisoners, and engages in issues of child labor, the sick, and the poor.

> I set up a ministry called Jesus Cares Ministries. It is an inter-denominational [organization] and has members from various churches. The thing that holds members together is that you need to have a passion for evangelism to preach the work for his gospel and you also have to have a heart of compassion for the vulnerable, for the orphans, the widows, and the poor. So, it's a developmental organization that has grown from zero to now serving the nation of Zambia . . . It is working with a number of donor agencies including US Aid, UNICEF, ILO.[28]

---

24 Sumaili, "I Met Jesus at the Bank."

25 Goodson Machona, "Jesus Care Ministries Preaches To Street Kids," *The Post Newspaper*, June 7, 1999.

26 Sumaili, "I Met Jesus at the Bank."

27 Naar M'fundisi, "Pentecostal and Charismatic Spiritualities and Civic Engagement in Zambia (1964–2012)," PhD diss., University of Birmingham, 2014.

28 Mwenda and Goma, *News Diggers*, April 9, 2017.

A stunning success story of the Jesus Cares Ministries was liberating 5,000 children from various types of labor including 3,000 from stone crushing and integrating them into the formal school system while others were put in the Jesus Cares Ministries community schools across the country.[29] Sumaili's concern for children has not only been through actions (of feeding, caring, housing, and visiting the children in the University Teaching Hospital (UTH)), but also through advocacy. For instance, she called for support for the children in the wake of increasing numbers of children on the streets. Rev. Sumaili noted that "Orphans and vulnerable children require special attention from stakeholders.. . . increasing number of street kids is worrying and requires combined efforts from Non-Government Organizations (NGOs) that should supplement government interventions."[30]

Jesus Cares Ministries also established a development center in Mtendere township of Lusaka where children salvaged from child labor and streets are reformed before they are taken into mainstream education systems.[31] Sumaili is not only concerned with the children but also for the women too. For example, Jesus Cares Ministries has trained 120 women in various skills such as tailoring, knitting, cookery and entrepreneurship. These women are drawn from Chipata, Mtendere, Chawama, Kanyama, and George townships of Lusaka. Sumaili believes that women and children comprise the majority of the poor people in Zambia just like in various nations, many of whom are also doubly disadvantaged as they are illiterate.[32] The program is intended to acquaint women with various micro-business skills as a sustainable solution to poverty and combating child labor is linked to the empowerment of the community and education of vulnerable children. Although Sumaili and the organization have not focused on the possibility of education of women, they are serving the Zambian community especially in Lusaka in ways that assist the government in poverty eradication. The hope is that these skills such as knitting, tailoring, and cooking are a stepping stone to women's empowerment.

In 2010, Sumaili was also recognized for her initiative of the Jesus Cares for Souls 2010 event held in Lusaka whose aim was to launch a mission to win 100,000 souls for Jesus Christ in 100 days in all provinces of Zambia. This was also combined with prayers for various socioeconomic and sociopolitical issues in the nation. The Jesus Cares for Souls event was not intended to challenge the state but, instead, against demonic structures as

29 Integrated Regional Information Network, "Crushing Stones Is Not Child's Play" (Lusaka, September 6, 2006).

30 *Times of Zambia*, December 27, 2011.

31 *Times of Zambia*, March 24, 2005.

32 Mwizabi, *Times of Zambia*, October 1, 2004.

they were deemed responsible for Zambia's socioeconomic challenges and injustices, and in turn proved the tendency to spiritualize social structures that were problematic.[33] This tendency continued to characterize such gatherings as opposed to placing the blame on poor governance. While there may be demonic activity in the spiritual realms, there are also physical demons that the government needs to deal with within its system, such as not giving women and children space to flourish. As a minister of religious affairs and national guidance, she is in a powerful position now to speak and act regarding the way the government is running the nation. Prayer has its place and physical action and praxis is just as important as prayer. One cannot simply focus on prayer and neglect the action aspect that is more crucial. Sumaili's calls for prayers in the face of the country's challenges such as cholera[34] could easily be linked to the days of her Jesus Cares Ministries. However, much more is desired than just prayers, as a minister, Sumaili has a position and voice to make government work better. Her position in the government is strategic and needs to be utilized to bring about change and development in the nation.

Sumaili is further portrayed as serving on the boards of many government arms such as the Anti-Corruption Commission, Human Rights Commission, and as chairperson of the children's rights committee to promote and protect children's rights. All these government arms are strategic and can bring about a turnaround in the country if Sumaili and the committees are able to establish ways of meeting the needs of the nation, especially people on the grassroots. Sumaili noted that,

> While I was still serving in the communities and reaching out to the orphans, the late President Levy Mwanawasa appointed me as Human Rights commissioner that's where I served for six years and after that, the late President Michael Sata appointed me to be commissioner of Anti- Corruption Commission.[35]

Political Engagement

Her prominent representation was perhaps in the political sphere. While Sumaili had left the corporate world to start the Jesus Cares Ministries, this call into ministry collided with her joining politics, though at that time, her initial stay in politics was short-lived. For example, she was the first chairperson of Heritage Party, a position she held for two years before she resigned to join full-time ministry. With regard to her current political

33 M'fundisi, Pentecostal *and Charismatic Spiritualities*

34 "Government Declares One week of National prayer and Fasting for Cholera and Rains," *Lusaka Times*, January 14, 2018; "Those Mocking Cholera Prayers are under Devil's Attack—Sumaili," *Zambian Observer*, January 17, 2018.

35 Mwenda and Goma, *News Diggers*, April 9, 2017.

affiliation, Sumaili openly disclosed her political affiliation by acknowledging that "yes, I am PF [Patriotic Front] but I can tell you that in my approach, I am very balanced because of the work, the assignment that I have. I have to deal with everybody, everybody needs to be guided."[36]

There are lacunae in her position regarding how she interprets "very balanced." As a minister of religious affairs, she has not been inclusive of other religious groups besides the Christians. Therefore, her "very balanced" stance in the above statement is questionable. While in her private life she has been working hard to alleviate poverty and foster development for women and children, the same vigor seems to be lacking in her political space and position. Sumaili is renowned for her current political position as the first minister for the newly created Ministry of National Guidance and Religious Affairs (MNGRA). Suffice to note that Sumaili did not run for a Member of Parliament seat in the 2016 general elections, but instead received a nominated seat from Edgar Lungu on September 15, 2016. Seen through the pentecostal gender discourse,[37] this confirms how Pentecostalism has been seeking to empower women to gain access into public spaces based on male merit. It is also probable that it was this pentecostal gender discourse that accounted for Sumaili's appointment being applauded by the male pentecostal clergy such as Pastor Choolwe, the founder of Gospel Envoys Ministries.[38]

Thus, while representing a female pentecostal's rise to political position, Sumaili's narrative also reveals emerging challenges on the gender, religion, and politics discourse in the public sphere. To start with, Sumaili's appointment brought to the fore the debates on how the ministry was being used to reward Pentecostalism's role in the 2016 general elections. For example, it was observed that some people believed that the introduction of MNGRA was to show appreciation for the pentecostal sector that supported President Lungu during the campaign.[39] This position also resonated with the fact that while other church mother bodies contested the formation of the ministry, it was supported and affirmed by many pentecostal ministers and thus the appointment of Rev. Sumaili and the resulting debate could perhaps be partly understood as a product of the context in which the ministry was formed.

In addition, Sumaili was associated with contentions surrounding the gendered religion and politics discourse in the public sphere. This was

36 Mwenda and Goma, *News Diggers*, April 9, 2017.

37 Kaunda and Kaunda, "Pentecostalism."

38 "Pastor Choolwe Welcomes the Appointment of Pastor Sumaili as Minister of Religious Affairs," *Kitwe Times*, September 16, 2016.

39 Kaunda and Kaunda, *Pentecostalism;* Elias Munshya, "When the State Becomes a False Prophet: How Rev. Sumaili's Views Threaten Zambia's Constitutionalism," in Elias Munshya Blog, May 22, 2017.

partly because she brought to the fore her notions of how gender informed her connection of religion and politics. The prominence of these notions was equating the nation to the home by advancing a paternalism that was not envisioned by the constitution of Zambia.[40] In particular, Sumaili used the analogy of the home and a nation by noting that just as a home has values, a nation needs to have values too, a position that was critiqued in the public sphere. For example, Munshya argued that,

> Zambia is not a home with a father and mother ruling over children in a household. The biblical model of a home cannot be extrapolated to the Zambian state. Zambia is a republic with a constitution that assigns roles to each branch of government. Zambian citizens are responsible adults with rights and privileges afforded to them, not by custom, or the Bible, but by the constitution of the republic. . . Values in the home are not the same as values that keep a democratic republic viable. You can't stand up to your father in the home, but our constitution allows citizens to stand up to political leaders. Mr Lungu is head of a democratic state and not a monocratic home.[41]

Munshya's critique was re-echoed in observations that the "housenization"[42] of the nation by granting Lungu the title "father of the nation" while appalling, was a cultural transposition of wifely submission to politics in that Sumaili used cultural notions to morality in politics by combining cultural and religious pentecostal aspects, which in turn constructed her as an empowered subservient woman.[43]

Apart from representing Sumaili as fundamentally out of line with the constitution and advancing a paternalism not supported by the constitution, Sumaili's narrative also points to a gendered woman's role of cleaning the homestead. This found expression in different ways in which Sumaili attempted to instill a moral order in the nation. For example, this was manifested through attempts to regulate the church as expressed in her "Ministerial statement on the Mushrooming of False Churches and Prophets, and Measures Being Put in Place" in which she underscored the abuse of the favorable environment of a Christian nation by new pentecostal movements and the consequent need to clean up the nation. Sumaili's attempts to shape the country's moral order ranged from among

40 Munshya, Zambia BlogTalk Radio, May 22, 2017.

41 Munshya, "When the State Becomes a False Prophet."

42 The concept of "housenization" has been coined by Chammah J. Kaunda and Mutale Mulenga Kaunda in their article, "Pentecostalism."

43 Kaunda and Kaunda, "Pentecostalism."

other actions, condemning homosexuality,[44] banning sex toys,[45] deporting artists such as Zodwa Wabantu and Koffi Olomide who were deemed to corrupt the morals of the Zambians,[46] and prophets such as Prophet Uebert Angel[47] to prohibiting reality TV shows such as the "Lusaka Hustle," which portrayed the daily lives of three Lusaka celebrities.[48]

Sumaili's narrative not only showed a public critique of her actions, but also a call for her resignation. These calls were due to dissatisfaction from some sections of society such as Munshya who argued that since Sumaili had not demonstrated a religious and theological understanding of the constitution and her job, she needed to step down. Munshya argued that,

> Rev. Sumaili does seem to suggest that Zambia must be led according to the Bible, but she fundamentally misunderstands the practical application of such a concept. . . Theologically, the Holy Bible is God's word. It is the rule of personal faith and conduct; it is not the rule of Zambia's constitutionalism. The Holy Bible is not the constitution of Zambia and is not a source of Zambian law. Zambia is not a church; it is a republic . . .. Rev. Sumaili makes no legal sense and she certainly makes no theological sense. A government minister who fundamentally misunderstands and undermines the constitutional structure of our republic is unworthy to serve the people of Zambia. I call upon her to resign.[49]

Other sentiments on resignation were from the Zambian singer Chama Fumba, popularly known as Pilato who argued that Sumaili was using the church to advance her political agenda contrary to the expectations that the ministry would guide the government.[50] Similarly, the National Revolution Party demanded that Sumaili resigns on moral grounds.

> Mumba claims Rev. Sumaili has failed to guide the nation spiritually .... Rev. Sumaili has failed to unite the nation especially political party leaders in the national dialogue process which stalled for a long time.

44 Melody Mupeta, "Perpetrators of Homosexuality to Face Prosecution—Minister," *Zambia Daily Mail*, November 23, 2017.

45 Aislinn Laing, "Zambia Announces Crackdown on Immoral Sex Dolls," *The Sunday Times*, March 12, 2017.

46 "Religious Minister Says South African Controversial Dance Artist Won't be Allowed into Zambia," *Lusaka Times*, March 2, 2018; "Koffi Olomide Not Allowed in Zambia—Godfridah Sumaili," *Lusaka Voice*, July 16, 2018.

47 Christine Chisha, "Zambia No Haven for False Prophets—Sumaili," *Daily Mail*, May 7, 2017.

48 Angela Muchinshi, "Minister Bans Gay Show," *Daily Mail*, February 3, 2019.

49 Munshya, "When the State Becomes a False Prophet."

50 "Resign Now, Pilato Tells Religious Minister," *The Zambian Observer*, December 15, 2018.

> Rev. Sumaili is the one that was supposed to bring President Lungu and his opposition counterpart Hakainde Hichilema in the stalemate they were in before the three church mother bodies came in.[51]

While these calls represented a male dominated voice for resignation, it was probable that they pointed to a cultural context in which men took a lead to offer critique in the public sphere.

Conclusion

While Sumaili's narrative was still unfolding, it was clear that at the start of 2019, her narrative was still associated with growing debates on gender, religion, and politics in the Zambian public sphere. The chapter attempted to portray Sumaili's narrative in the public sphere mirroring her different roles in society were a product of the interplay of culture and pentecostal religiosity that raised an ongoing debate on how religion and politics were related in the Zambian context. At the same time, the narrative pointed to a gendered religion's relevance to politics in contemporary Zambian society by reflecting how a woman minister's trajectory not only ignited debates but also cemented the relationship between religion and politics in Zambia.

51 "Cosmo Wants Sumaili Out," *Zambian Eye*, November 28, 2018.

8

RELIGION, HUMAN RIGHTS, AND POLITICS

Godfrey Msiska

Introduction: Religious Demography

The influence of religion on Zambian politics is blinded by the very diverse types of religious expression. The last census in Zambia was carried out in 2010. Under the Census and Statistics Act,[1] a census is valid for ten years. According to the 2010 census, the population is 13.1 million of which 87 percent are Christians; 1 percent is Muslim or Hindu, and 12 percent adhere to other belief systems, including indigenous religions. Many people combine Christianity and indigenous beliefs. Zambia is officially a "Christian nation" according to the 1996 constitution. However, it respects other religions, too. In terms of religious affiliation, 75.3 percent of population are Protestants and 20.2 percent are Catholics. Muslims make up 0.5 percent, other religions make up 2 percent, and non-religion 1.8 percent.[2] It is worth noting that in Zambia, religion is treated as a social feature of the population. This is because religion is classified as part of the social components of society.

Religion, Religious Identity, and Religious Plurality

The term *religion* can be unpacked in both cultural and structural ways. Culturally, we speak of the way religion functions in creating core values for particular religious communities within a society. One test of the formation and articulation of these values for Zambians asks how well religious norms serve to promote religious plurality and deconstruct power. Structurally, I speak of religion as an institution, organization, or

1 Constitution of Zambia, Chapter 127 of laws of Zambia.

2 "Social Characteristics, Zambia 2010 Census," Zambia 2010 Census of Population and Housing Lusaka: Central Statistical Office, 2014.

association. The British Court of Chancery, for example, makes no distinction between one religion and another, unless the tenets of a sect inculcate doctrines averse to the very foundations of all religions. The case of *Thornton v Howe*[3] is cited for the proposition that, as between different religions, the law stands neutral, but it seems that any religion is at least better than none.[4] This is to suggest that the Zambian people would see this to be the case. Religion is by self-definition public in character, both in the practice of religious rituals and in the way that religious adherents educate their children to assume their adult roles in life.[5]

Christian political philosopher James W. Skillen argues that it is hard to define religion because of the strict separationist view that defines religion as a private domain. This view is narrow and confines most religious expressions to a private sphere.[6] In Zambia, the strict separationist view is more characterized by self-designation of a religion as non-secular, meaning the government makes this distinction and defines religion in relationship to secularism. This suggests that religion has a majoritarian control over the government. In practice, religion has control over the government in the "Christian nation" provision. A strict separationist position maintains that religion and religious organization are strictly separated from the political realm. It is assumed that the separation of religion and state helps to preserve the well-being of both religion and society. The roots of this view are from Enlightenment liberalism, with its emphases on individual autonomy and choice. The Enlightenment designated religion as private and politics as secular.

Religious identity and religious plurality meet in the context of definite communities, especially our primary communities of family, church, mosque, and temple. How do we embody openness and plurality within our communities of different identities? How is the plurality embodied in the present understanding of nationhood in Zambia? A core question poses this respect: Does religious language assist in the movement toward positive plurality or hinders in general? The challenge for religious language is to move from the notion of possessing the truth, of speaking in absolutes, to naming and opening up possibilities. All religious language comes from experience, but experience, though real for each, remains

---

3 Thornton v Howe (1862) 31 Beav. 14, 19–20, in *The All England Law Reports* (London: Butterworth, 1947).

4 Paul H. Richards and Leslie Basil Curzon, eds., *Longman Dictionary of Law*. 8th ed. (Edinburgh: Longman Group, 2011), 401.

5 Richards and Curzon, *Longman Dictionary of Law*, 401.

6 James W. Skillen, "Theoretical Roots of Equal Treatment," in *Equal Treatment of Religion in a Pluralistic Society*, eds. J.C. Soper and S.V. Monsma (Grand Rapids, MI: Eerdmans Publishing, 1998), 55.

partial, concealing as much as it reveals.[7] It is easy to observe that religious identity in Zambia is profoundly Christian, but in reality, Zambia is a secular state without state religion. This is because state and religion are separate, even though the Zambian Constitution guarantees freedom of religion—meaning any one is free to practice religion of their choice.

In my view, religious language must strive to name and open possibilities that assist in the movement toward possible plurality. To do this, religious language needs to be redefined and reconstructed. This is a mammoth task, but it should be developed even further in order to create a positive religious pluralism. As far as religious education in Zambia is concerned, efforts have been to develop a pluralistic religious language in the public sphere. It is also worth noting that various religions in Zambia co-exist pleasantly and collaborate at the local and national levels by holding interfaith prayers on specific important national occasions and on issues of common interest or national significance.[8] For example, Zambia Inter-faith Networking Group on HIV/AIDS (ZINGO) is a composition of national religious bodies of Christians, Hindus, Muslims, and Baha'is. The vision of this organization is to build "an interfaith community contributing to national development." Whereas, its mission is "to coordinate, network, mobilize resources, and build competencies among ZINGO members for a holistic and compassionate approach to responding to the impact of HIV/AIDS and other related development issues." This is an organization that is beneficial to all.[9]

When Christians are in dialogue with Muslims or Hindus, it is easy to recognize similarities and overlap, and religions may even challenge each other to revitalize certain hidden treasures in their respective traditions. Theologically, they are likely to discover that they are complementary parts of a wider religious unity that actually exists already, but has not yet been formulated adequately. Such complementarity is the ultimate of interreligious dialogue. Regrettably, in Zambia, I hardly see a Christian theological rationale for such complementarity or a more general will for

---

7 Gillian Walters, Steve Martin, and Cochrane James R., *Constructing a Language of Public Religion in Public Life: Summary Analysis of the Proceedings of the Preparatory Multi-Event 1999 Academic Workshop Papers* (Cape Town: University of Cape Town, 1999), 5–6.

8 The Zambia Inter-Faith Networking Group on HIV/AIDS was formed in 1997 to assist religious communities to become more involved in HIV/AIDs. It included the Council of Churches in Zambia, the Evangelical Fellowship of Zambia and Zambia Episcopal Conference, the Independent Churches of Zambia, the Islamic Council of Zambia, and representatives of the Baha'i, and Hindu communities.

9 See "Zambia at 20: Celebrating Lifesaving Partnerships on World AIDS Day," accessed May 30, 2020, https://www.pciglobal.org/zambia-anniversary-20-years-wad2016/.

Christians to work with other religions, isolated interfaith efforts such as ZINGO notwithstanding.[10]

It is evident in Zambia that a good deal of the Christian thought has been transplanted into civil society of Zambia. In my view, contemporary experiments of legal transplantation in a Christian nation of Zambia need to be examined carefully so that they may not affect the exercise of religious rights. Article 18 of Universal Declaration of Human Rights defines religion as,

> Everyone has right to freedom of opinion and expression, the right includes freedom to hold opinions without interference and to seek, receive, and impart information and ideas through any media and regardless of frontiers.[11]

This institutional legal instrument provides very broad definitions of religion. The Universal Declaration of Human Rights makes a sweeping guarantee. The declaration's conflation of terms like religion, thought, conscience, and belief continue in subsequent institutional instruments—most notably the compulsory 1966 Convention on Civil and Political Rights and 1981 Declaration on the Elimination of All Forms of Discrimination based on religion or belief, the fullest institutional statement on religious rights.[12]

Keeping this in mind, the functional and institutional dimension of religion deserve the strongest emphasis in defining the field of human rights. This is because religion in the broadest terms embraces beliefs and actions that the ultimate origin, meaning, and purpose of life, of existence is from God.[13]

Conceptualizing Politics

Conceptually, it is possible to define politics, what politics is and what it is not. However, it should be mentioned from the onset that politics may mean different things in different contexts. Reflecting on the struggle of Zambian politics, it is easy to see that politics is a government's arena of managing and running public affairs. The public affairs are activities that are carried out by people with qualities to manage. While the term *politics* can be used to mean a singular or plural, I have tried to be consistently

10 Leo J. Koffeman, "Differences Do They Still Make a Difference? A Response to Martin Brinkman," *Exchange Journal* 32, no. 20 (2004): 112–119.

11 United Nations, "World Press Freedom Day, 3 May," https://www.un.org/en/events/pressfreedomday/background.shtml, accessed September 3, 2019.

12 Andrew Fagan, "Philosophical Foundation of Human Rights," in *Handbook of Human Rights*, ed. Thomas Cushman (Abingdon: Routledge, 2012), 9–22.

13 Michael Goodhart, "Democracy as Human Rights," in *Handbook of Human Rights*, ed. Thomas Cushman (Abingdon: Routledge, 2012), 68–76.

to use the term *politics* when referring to its generic properties. The word *politics* is derived from *polis* (Greek), meaning literally city-state. This means the largest and the most desirable form of social organization. Politics is often portrayed as the cradle of democratic government.[14] In many cases, people are said to be in politics when they hold public office. In other words, politics has to do with matters that concerns the state. Politics takes place within a polity, system of some organization. Politics is practiced by politicians, civil servants, and lobbyists. Scholars stress that politics is an activity concerned with creating a just society.[15] In a sense, politics is the study of government and its functions, associated organizations, and institutions. Along with that, politics is concerned with the behavior of groups and individuals in matters that attract the course of government.[16] It can be stated that politics is a distribution form of rule and yet not all forms of rule are expressions of politics.

Weale defines politics as a collective choice that is best understood as a kind of market-place in which people pursue their interests in such a way as to maximize their benefits and minimize their costs.[17] This definition of politics advances the argument that people choose between particular courses of action aimed at achieving desired ends under circumstances when their resources are scarce and their wants are many. Politics is the way in which free societies are governed.

Burden of the Past: Colonization, Democracy, and Human Rights

Competitive politics in Zambia led to democratic replacement of the first republic President Kenneth Kaunda through the ballot box in 1991. This was a transition from one party participatory democracy to multiparty democracy, however, this transition had better opportunities for success than transition from colonial rule in Zambia. In a way, the process of democratization in Africa helped African societies confront their colonial legacy that helps in understanding of the post-independence erosion of democratic institutions in Africa. From the onset, colonization was not a democratic system and the so-called colonial masters were not teachers of

14 Adrian Leftwich, *Redefining Politics, People, Resources and Power* (Abingdon: Routledge, 2010), 11.

15 Lloyd P. Gerson, ed., *Aristotle Critical Assessments* (London: Routledge, 1999), 186–202.

16 Adrian Leftwich, ed., *What is Politics: Activity and Its Study* (Oxford: Blackwell, 2004), 1–22.

17 Albert Weale, "Politics as Collective Choices," in *What is Politics: Activity and its Study*, ed. Adrian Leftwich (Oxford: Blackwell, 2004), 86–99.

democracy because they took self-governance away from Africans.[18] It is evident that colonial experience was one of a minority imposing its will on a majority—here was legislation for Europeans, but Africans were relegated to customary laws. This is the background of African politics that during the colonial era, African dignity was denied because the Africans were regarded too incompetent to understand their own rights.

It is clear that colonization had destroyed indigenous democratic values and institutions without building stable replacements in contrast with current concepts of democracy. In contemporary Africa, the state is the major violator of human rights in Africa. Inasmuch as the rights and freedoms are written into African constitutions, they were modeled after the United Nations Universal Declaration of Human Rights. Thus, there is need for Africans to be educated in these human rights as a means to encourage people to know and defend their rights.

Democracy: Direct and Representative

Democracy has a Greek etymology *demos* (people) and *kratein* (to rule), thus, rule by the people for the people.[19] From this definition, the people and rule are not explained. However, Freire and Faundez have argued that the ruling should not be done for the people but with the people. Saying that democracy is the rule for the people seems to exclude the people or makes them passive as their representatives tend to rule for them. Here, the second republic president of Zambia Frederick Chiluba suggests that democracy should be redefined for Zambians.[20] Chiluba defines democracy as rule by the people and representative government as the means of that rule.[21] Democracy, as Chiluba says, values individuals as rational beings and recognizes the rights and capacity to self-governance. Democracy, in Chiluba's view, is human supremacy and owes its existence to its people.[22] Hence, democracy is a principle of legitimacy. In addition, because democracy accepts the consent of the people, leaders become accountable to the electorate through the rule of law. From this description, Chiluba does not explain the term self-governance and how it works but only the meaning. However, Chiluba understands human supremacy to include community; democracy advocates individual liberty rather than society as a whole, thus it is liberal democracy. It is obvious that Chiluba

18 Sahr John Kpundeh, *Democratisation in Africa: African views, African voices* (Washington DC: National Academic Press, 1992), 7–8.

19 Paulo Freire and Faundez Antonio, *Learning to Question: A Pedagogy of Liberation* (Geneva: WCC, 1993), 63.

20 Frederick JK Chiluba, *Democracy: The Challenge of Change* (Lusaka: Multimedia, 1995), 4.

21 Chiluba, *Democracy*, 2.

22 Chiluba, *Democracy*, 4.

fails to address the fact that this consent can be mere presumption by those in leadership. It is therefore misleading to think that the electorate is enough to determine consent since it is the people who cast votes.

Direct democracy—this holds that the entire society must be involved in decision making and governance. The level of involvement may vary but requires popular participation and political quality. It argues that political equality is vital to proper governance. Political equality here refers to equality of power in determining the outcome of decisions.

Power is decentralized and decisions are reached through common consensus and leaders are elected frequently; however, leaders are not entitled to personal or party policies but act as messengers of the electorate. This type of democracy assumes that every decision has to wait for everybody's opinion before society can move.[23] Here, De Gruchy argues that democracy should have a necessary vision of a just social order, which challenges individualism and promotes the welfare and fulfilment of society as a whole. For the same reason, De Gruchy insists that the concept of the common good will provide an important challenge to the possessive individualism that lies at the heart of liberal democratic capitalism, and to the sacrifice of human rights by social collectivism. He adds that the relationship between power and powerlessness has always been a struggle for democratic theory and the church's role is important in keeping those who are in power accountable. He proposes that the democratic system should have constitutional principles and procedures, and the democratic vision, which is the hope for society of equality, freedom, and justice.[24]

In my opinion, democratic vision in Zambia should originate in the message of peace from the Bible. In order to establish a just world order, De Gruchy envisions the common good as binding its members together in mutual accountability and as a process rather than static set of principles and at the same time empowering those who are weak to exercise their rights for the good of the whole society.[25] Here, he challenges the notion that a democratic system will produce morally responsible citizens as a matter of course, and argues that it is those who are morally informed and empowered that are able to make democracy work.[26] Based on this, it is clear that direct democracy demands that citizens need to be informed in order to make it work.

On the other hand, representative democracy is the most advocated form of democracy. In this system, some people are elected to represent

---

23 John de Gruchy, *Christianity and Democracy: A Theology of Just World* (Cambridge: CUP, 1995), 18.

24 De Gruchy, *Christianity and Democracy*,18.

25 De Gruchy, *Christianity and Democracy*,16–17

26 De Gruchy, *Christianity and Democracy*, 16–17.

citizens through the parliament in which the ordinary people are qualified to make political decisions through representatives. It is therefore wrong to suggest that only the elite must vote since every person has the right to choose who should represent and rule in their interest. As such, representatives are accountable to their electorate. This democracy rests on trust. All adults must choose from several parties. Elections must be held under fair conditions and the party with a majority vote should win. We can therefore conclude that representative democracy is not possible in countries where the majority are ignorant and in poverty since those wealthy are likely to bribe voters. This type of democracy depends on material progress and education of the masses for it to work well.

From this account, majority rule is not the basis of modern African democracy. Majority rule is likely to serve the interests of many at the cost of the minority. In Africa, the poor are the majority, conversely, the poor majority have the right to vote that the wealth is shared equally, however, this is not the case. It is easy to see that the real ground for the poor rests with the rich. Chiluba argues that the majority of opponent parties are a result of economic hardship.[27] For the same reason, Freire and Faundez have argued that the poor have gone through the university of life, which most intellectuals are completely ignorant about.[28] I get an impression that those who hold political power are not aware of this, and however this awareness needs to be discovered, if not, the political structures remain the powerhouses of the oppressors. If the political structures can take seriously the human rights, this situation would be resolved.

Human Rights and Its Purpose

Conceptually, human rights foster freedom to all. Human rights are rights inherent to all human beings, irrespective of nationality, domicile, gender, national or ethnic origin, color, religion, language, or any other status. We are all equally entitled to our human rights without discrimination. These rights are all interrelated, interdependent, and indivisible. Universal human rights are often expressed and guaranteed by law, in the form of treaties. Donnelly says, "human rights are the rights one has because one is a human."[29] From this definition, human rights are a basis of moral authority. One bases their belief in the moral authority of a doctrine. Gewirth explains, "human rights are derived from the necessary conditions of human action. Human rights are of supreme importance and are central to other moral considerations, because they are the rights of every

---

27 Chiluba, *Democracy*,126–132.

28 Freire and Faundez, *Learning to Question*, 13.

29 Jack Donnelly, *Universal Rights in Theory and Practice* (New York: Cornell University), 10.

human action."[30] It means, human beings are entitled to human rights. Human rights were accepted in principle by all governments irrespective of their ideologies, political aspiration, economic, and social status in the world.[31] The principle of universality of human rights is the cornerstone of international human rights law. This principle, as first emphasized in the Universal Declaration of Human Rights in 1948, has been reiterated in numerous international human rights conventions, declarations, and resolutions.

Dworkin says that it is time for us to take religious rights seriously—to shake off our political indifference and narrow-minded self-interest and to address the plight and protection of people of all faiths.[32] This is supported by the Bible in Matthew 7:12, "Do unto others as you would have them do unto you." I opine that religion must thus be seen as an indispensable ally in the modern struggle for human rights. To ignore them from the struggle is impossible and indeed a problem. To embrace them —to enlist their unique resources and to protect their unique rights—is important to enhancing and advancing the regime of human rights.[33] I propose that human rights should adopt the methods and insights of religion, law, theology, and jurisprudence to communicate, protect, and promote these rights.

Human Rights—from International to African Regional Systems

When human rights were declared in 1948, it was barely after three years of serious war in Europe, mainly. The aftermath of war was the official birth of the United Nations in 1945. It can be said without doubt that the basis on which the United Nations Universal Declaration of Human Rights was formed, among other reasons, was first, to heal the wounds of the war victims in Europe. Second, it was to create an impression to the colonies that it wanted to free them. The original purpose of the human rights when they were created did not have the context of Africa in mind since at that time, no African continent leader was present during the declaration. At that time, Zambia was still a British colony, and it took 16 years after the 1948 human rights declaration for Zambia to gain its political independence. The colonial masters did not see that political

30 Alan Gewirth, *Human Rights: Essays on Justification and Applications* (Chicago: Chicago University Press, 1982), 3.

31 Thomas Cushman, ed., *Handbook of Human Rights* (Abingdon: Routledge, 2012), 1–4.

32 Ronald Dworkin, *Taking Rights Seriously* (Massachusetts: Harvard University Press, 1977), 184.

33 John Jr. Witte, and Johan D. Van der Vyver, *Religious Human Rights in Global Perspective, Religious Perspective* (Hague: Martinus Nijhoff Publishers, 1996), 17.

independence was a human right, and thereby did not enforce human rights at that time.

From the outset, when the human rights were formulated, Africa was not kept in mind. However, the idea to initiate human rights by Africans emerged in 1969, six years after the formation of the Organization of African Unity (OAU) in 1963, when the first African human rights were enforced. It was then transformed into the African Union (AU) in 2002. Despite the divergent and competing national interests among the member states, AU represents Africa's collective efforts in search of formal integration and development. The African Charter on Human and Peoples' Rights came into effect on October 21, 1986. Over a decade later, in 2001, African Experts on the Rights and Welfare on Human and People's Rights was formed by the African Union. In 2004, the African Court on Human and People's Rights was established. In 2005, the Rights of Women in Africa was founded.

The advent of AU has brought new institutions and prospects of better respect for human rights in the continent such as the New Partnership for Africa's Development (NEPAD), which has its primary focus on human rights and good governance; African Peer Review Mechanism (APRM), which is important for determining best practices of human rights and democracy in the continent of Africa. In 2013, Zambia came before the APRM forum. The APRM always considers in implementation reports the states that have undergone reviews and adopted a national program of action to address the issues identified through the process. Although Zambia has signed many UN and OAU documents that spell out these rights and duties, the government has not included them in the basic laws of the land, and implemented laws and statutory instruments.

Experimenting Constitutional Reforms and Human Rights

As we shall observe, religion's argument for democracy streams from human dignity and not from human sovereignty since sovereignty belongs to God.[34] The concept of democracy is enshrined in the Universal Declaration of Human Rights that states,

> The will of the people shall be the basis of the authority of the government, this will shall be expressed in periodic and genuine elections which shall be by universal and equal sufferings and shall be held by secret vote or by equivalent free voting procedures.[35]

34 William Temple, *Essays in Christian Politics and Kindred Subjects* (London: Paternoster Press, 1927), 73—74.

35 United Nations Universal Declaration of Human Rights (1948, Article 21).

It is clear that a democratic state must be aware that the electorate must be involved in the exercise of government. In my view, government exists for the people, by guaranteeing welfare, peace, and exercise of fundamental rights.

In every democracy, the constitution as the fundamental institution is for checks and balances. The greatest protection of human rights emanates from a democratic framework grounded in the rule of law. In a truly democratic society, there must be separation of powers of the legislative, executive, and judiciary. To gauge the grasp of the constitutional rights in Zambia, a survey of national constitution was conducted in all the four constitutions. In this chapter, I define constitution as one that refers to the frame or composition of a government. A written constitution is an act of deliberate creation, a code or charter of the government.

First, the independence constitution of 1965, which was tailored at Lancaster by the British with zero input from Zambians. Even the first president was installed by the British without taking Zambians into confidence.

Second, the one-party state constitution of 1973 by which the president announced the cabinet's decision that Zambia should become a one-party state. Consequently, the government appointed a Constitutional Review Commission under the chairperson of the Vice-President Mainza Chona. In 1973, the country became a one-party state with United National Independence Party's UNIP as the sole legal party, with an amended constitution. Again, Zambians had no opportunity to debate on the kind of constitution they wanted.

Third, for the 1991 constitution, a Constitution Review Commission was appointed under the Inquiries Act headed by Prof. M. Patrick Mvunga to examine and determine a system of political pluralism that would ensure a government, which would be strong enough to rule Zambia.[36] Subsequently, in June 1995, the Mwanakatwe Review Commission, named after its chair John Mwanakatwe, released its report in recommending a constituent assembly to adopt the constitution. The government rejected 70 percent of its recommendations. Next, the Mungomba Constitution Review Commission headed by William Mungomba was announced in April 17, 2003, by President Patrick Mwanawasa. The president indicated that the people of Zambia should accept the mode of adoption or alteration of the constitution, and the government will endeavor to implement the will of the people. It is worth noting that the efforts to come up with a Zambian constitution that can stand the test of time have proven futile as the past constitution reviews have lacked legitimacy and moral authority.

[36] *Constitution of Zambia*, The Inquiries Act, Chapter 41 of the Laws of Zambia.

In my opinion, people can exercise their power to adopt a constitution either directly at referendum or through constituent assembly. It must be emphasized that adoption through a constituent assembly or at a referendum should be preceded either at the drafting stage or after, through serious discussion of the constitutional proposals as wide as possible.

In this chapter, it is clear from the case study of Zambia that the practice of coming up with a constitution starts by appointing a Constitution Review Commission under Inquiries Act, a practice that has been criticized as being undemocratic because the president has overwhelming powers to select persons of his choice to draft the constitution. The president is at liberty to either accept or reject the recommendation tendered. In my view, the ideal way of enacting the constitution rests with the people and their role in government thereby imparting legitimacy to the constitution.

In 1995, the three church mother bodies in Zambia, namely, the Council of Churches in Zambia, Evangelical Fellowship of Zambia, and Zambia Episcopal Conference gave the press release with a view of campaigning the need for a new Zambian constitution.

Keeping this in mind, issues that can be said to violate God's law in the Zambian constitution are first, human dignity is undermined according to the Gospel of John 10:10 in which Jesus Christ said, "I have come that they may have life and have it to the full." From this passage of Scripture, the attempt to re-construct human dignity is emerging powerfully. People are valuable and they deserve respectful treatment because of the truth that they are created in God's image and likeness. Second, Economic, Social, and Cultural Rights (ESC) have not yet been encompassed in the constitution of Zambia. According to Exodus 3:7–10:

> The Lord said, I have indeed seen the misery of the people in Egypt. I have heard them crying out because of their slave drivers, and I am concerned about their suffering. So, I have come down to rescue them from the hand of the Egyptians and bring them up out of the land into good and spacious land, a land flowing with milk and honey—the home of the Canaanites, Hittites, Amorites, Perizzites, Hivites, and Jebusites. And now the cry of the Israelites has reached me, and I have seen the way the Egyptians are oppressing them. So now, I am sending you to Pharaoh to bring my people the Israelites out of Egypt.

God spoke this to Moses regarding the Israelites' passage from slavery in Egypt to enter Canaan. God told Moses to negotiate the settler position of God and his people to occupy the promised land. The constitution of Zambia does not adequately address the promotion and protection of economic, social, and cultural rights of vulnerable groups within the country of Zambia. The government of Zambia needs a mechanism to effect legislative changes and to provide specific and practical tools to supplement these changes. This way, Zambia can render a great contribution to the global community on protecting and promoting human rights.

In this regard, we can refer the discussion on economic, social, and cultural rights as meaning those rights that mandate that social conditions be adequate for meeting the physical, moral, and biological requirements for every class of people. They aim at ensuring everyone's access to resources, opportunities, and essentials for an adequate standard of living. The Bill of Rights embodied in Part III of the Zambian constitution provides for protection of fundamental rights and freedom. However, the rights pertaining to the improvement of the welfare of the citizens such as education, health, housing, employment, and social security are not placed in the Bill of Rights even though Economic, Social, and Cultural Rights (ESC) have been recognized to be important in the realization of political and civil rights. These rights are placed under part IX of the constitution, which deal with the Directive Principles of State Policy and Duties of Citizens, and may be attained in so far as state resources permit.[37]

It is clear in the Zambian constitution that ESC rights are under the Directive Principles of State Policy, which means a successful attainment of ESC rights is quite elusive because they are not enshrined in the constitution in an enforceable character. Hence, strong demands arise that stress a moral obligation for the government to consider enshrining ESC rights into the Bill of Rights. This means, of course, that the government must facilitate a Referendum process to allow for the amendment of Part III (Bill of Rights) of the constitution as demanded by article 79(3) (Constitution of Republic of Zambia, 1996, Chapter 1).

Third, consultation—the disciples were consulted to choose the seven people who would be responsible for distributing the resources (Acts 6:1–7). This necessitates that citizens must be sufficiently consulted. It can be said without doubt that the power to enact the constitution resides in the people. It institutionalizes the people and their role in government, thereby imparting the same in the constitution. In my view, in order to have a real human development, Zambia needs to have a republic constitution that has a clear and comprehensive Bill of Rights. Human rights are important because they help to condemn, and overcome forms of systematic human suffering. This is the matter of greatest moral urgency.

The justification for human rights is aimed at establishing the opportunities for all human beings to lead a good life. Here, Wina makes it clear that during the colonial days, the human dignity for people in Zambia

37 *Constitution of Republic of Zambia*, 1996, Chapter 1.

was undermined by colonial masters. He adds, "Liberation from economic slavery but [also] the liberation from all human indignities that we suffer across the continent in Black Africa. The liberation from structures that produce the teeming millions of refugees that we have on [the] continent."[38] He further underscores that "the church in Africa needs to define its role that keeps the initiative at this critical moment in the development of our peoples as they struggle for complete liberation."[39]

With respect to Wina's observations regarding human rights in Africa, the church in Zambia needs to be more proactive in addressing issues of human rights. Yet, it is necessary to make such a review of colonial legacy. Here, Maluleke finds,

> This may sound trite, but Africans are humans before they are Africans. The unique thing about African Christianity is, it is human Christianity. The African in African Christianity is the human. Therefore, there is nothing so essential about being African that justifies considering Africans outside of the human quest. The quest for African Christianity is the quest for a more humane and a more human Christianity. The struggle of African Christianity is for a more human and more humane world. It is therefore not helpful to study African Christianity outside of the quest for a better humanity in the service of God.[40]

African Christianity can advocate for a more humane world by manifesting Christianity in the democratic public sphere. Christian traditions represent a vital contribution to democratic pluralism and even to non-religious citizens. Even if Christianity does not have legal status, it includes an open, transparent, and regular dialogue between human rights and politics. Modern Africa falls short sharply in ensuring such opportunities to all. The hope for Zambia is still to be made in the serious analysis of human rights practices.

Keeping this in mind, the Bill of Rights in the Zambian constitution should seriously consider economic, social, and cultural rights because these rights mandate the social conditions to be adequate for meeting physical, moral, and biological requirement for every category of people. They aim at ensuring everyone's access to resources, opportunities, and essentials for an adequate standard of living. The methods of interpretation

---

38 Sikota Wina, "From Inertia to Energy," in *Christian Press in Africa: Voice of Human Concern*, ed. E. Charles Makunike, 1st ed. (Lusaka: Multimedia Publication, 1973), 26–37.

39 Wina, "From Inertia to Energy."

40 Tinyike S. Maluleke, "Of Africanised Bees and Africanised Christians: Ten Theses on African Christianity," *Missionalia: South African Journal of Mission Studies* 38, no. 3 (November 2010): 369–379.

of sacred texts and traditions can be designed to recover and transparent these religious teachings and activities conducive to human rights.

From this evaluation, it is clear that human rights are inherent in human dignity and the government's task is to protect and promote these rights. It is worth noting that human dignity is declared to be universal. Human rights and human development must walk hand in hand. However, the United Nations Development Programme indicates that Zambia's human development ranking in 2017 was 144 out of 189 countries.[41] The contributing factor for the poor human development in Zambia, first and foremost, is the quality of health, education, and living standards that are abysmally low. Second, the way Zambia is enforcing the fundamental human rights treaties does not have a bearing on the quality of human development. Such treaties include the International Convention of Elimination of All Forms of Racial Discrimination (ICERD) of 1965, enforced in Zambia in 1972; International Convention on Civil and Political Rights (ICCPR) of 1966, enforced in Zambia in 1984; International Convention on Economic, Social, and Cultural Rights (ICESCR) of 1966, enforced in Zambia in 1984; Convention of the Rights of Persons with Disabilities (CRPD) of 2006, enforced in Zambia in 2010. From these treaties, ICESCR and United Nations Universal Declaration of Human Rights form the International Bills of Human Rights. From these outlines of human rights treaties, it is clear that the way these treaties are enforced determine the quality of human development.

In 1987, a joint pastoral letter was issued by ecumenical mother bodies, namely, Council of Churches in Zambia, Evangelical Fellowship of Zambia, and Zambia Episcopal Conference under the theme—Christian Liberation, Justice, and Development: The Churches' Concern for Human Development. It emphasizes that rights should be promoted and respected by the state that is responsible for the common good and for each of those under its care.[42] The churches' efforts to unite were made with the view of suggesting socioeconomic betterment of Zambia as a country.[43] The ecumenical document used social analysis and theological reflection to come up with the document. The main concerns in this document were questions on relationship between the church and state, work and ownership, national solidarity, materialism and ideology, and democracy and participation.[44]

---

41 United Nations Development Programme, Indices and Indicators, 2018 Statistics (New York: UNDP, 2018).

42 Joe Komakoma, *The Social Teaching of the Catholic Bishops and other Christian Leaders in Zambia: Major Pastoral Letters and Statements 1953–2001* (Ndola: Mission Press, 2003).

43 Komakoma, *The Social Teaching.*

44 Komakoma, *The Social Teaching.*

Here, the World Bank defines governance "as the manner in which power is exercised in the management of a country's economic and social resources for development."[45] The World Bank's definition of governance is concerned with a country's efficiency and the capacity of the state institutions beyond the private sector for rules and institutions that creates a predictable and transparent framework for the conduct of public and private business, as well as accountability for economic and financial performance.

New State and Church Distanced Relationship

In the twenty-first century, the church-state relationship in Zambia, is at the crossroad, whether the church can comment on the state or not. If criticized, the state will be unhappy with the church. On the other hand, the state would easily criticize the church if the church gets involved in the politics or state affairs. It is found that the authority of the state cannot be questioned by the church. Whenever the leaders are elected into political office, it is accepted in Zambia that the authority of the political leaders was given by God. So, political leaders in the government refute genuine criticisms by the church. Therefore, the authority that the state possesses has no checks and balance as per the church's perspective. However, my view is that there is a need for a distanced relationship between the state and the church.

Durham and Scharffs find the view of John Rawls, as being based on the notion that,

> In a liberal constitutional democracy, when citizens or officials seek publicity to justify their policies, they should rely only on reasoning accessible to all rational citizens, and should refrain from invoking reasons, such as religious justifications, that are not cogent to all rational people.[46]

According to this argument, the state that imposes the doctrines of one religion either directly or indirectly on others is nothing but ruined of its religiousness and that state has no common depth upon which to build its democracy exercise.[47] One of the responsibilities of the church is to be prophetic to the government, because of its biblical position as salt and light to the nation. This works well when there is unity between the state and the church. When democracy is not fully implemented in a country,

---

45 *Managing Development: The Governance Dimension, A Discussion Paper* (World Bank, 1991).

46 John Lock quoted in W. Cole Ir Durban and Brett C. Scharffs, eds., *Law and Religion: National, International and Comparative Perspectives* (New York: Aspen Publishers, 2010), 551.

47 Lock, in Durban and Scharffs, *Law and Religion*, 551.

there is need for high political check and balance from the civil society. Democracy means people's participation in policy-making processes in a country. As Zambia has a weak civil society, it has not yet developed a strong system of check and balance of government power, and high standards of democracy.

The second responsibility of the church is to ensure that the public sphere has good representatives, accountability, and efficient government. Third, the church should recognize that the state is a keeper of public space—where the private and public are conflated. It is sensible to ask the keepers for permission to observe and share those observations. On top of that, the church should acknowledge that she is overshadowed by the declaration of Zambia as a Christian nation, however, this makes the church less serious in engaging the state. Because Christianity in Zambia is less visible, churches cannot identify with the ambiguity of declaration of a Christian nation and its interpretations. The church finds it difficult to claim, perform, and display its Christian identity in society. It is difficult in Zambia to reconcile the religious rights and state authority. Ironically, the Zambian situation illustrates that the state cannot abuse its authority. The Zambian condition is different as the church has not been keen in criticizing the state for decades.

Conclusion: Toward New Paradigm of the Role of Religion

Religion has played a crucial role in politics in Zambia. The struggle over power in Zambia is noted in the political and religious history of competing worldviews established by the respective leaders. My goal has been to advance the following argument: Under certain sociopolitical and cognitive conditions, the appearance of Christianity in the opinion-oriented public sphere can have an inherent value for democratic life. From the perspective of discursive relation between Christianity and democracy, the main role of Christianity is in the public culture, in those components of the public sphere that are the primary bearers of cultural and ethical meaning and value—universities, religious communities, the world of arts, and journalism. However, it is only after processes of selective interpretation and transformation through inclusive discursive practices that religious semantic contents may legitimately influence decisional interpretations of constitutional principles and rights.

To conclude, I suppose that one of the most essential problems of contemporary Africa is that the states have always monopolized the right to define and shape the principal components of public space. The state is restricting the right of individuals to shape the public space. I would like to reiterate that Africa needs a radical change in the state society paradigm, that is to say that state should maintain an equal distance with all faiths. The state should give up the discourse of tolerance, and generate an alternative discourse of respect and equality.

9

RELIGION, EDUCATION, AND POLITICS

Judith Lubasi Ilubala-Ziwa

Introduction

In Zambia, religion, politics, and education have closely affected each other to such an extent that it is difficult to isolate one from the others. The three institutions have been extensively defined and studied from diverse perspectives. In this chapter, the term *religion* is used to encompass the different churches in Zambia. A church is simply a large, bureaucratically organized religious institution that is closely integrated into the larger society.[1] In sociology, the word *church* is most often used in a technical sense to refer to the one dominant religious institution in a religious monopoly state such as the Roman Catholic Church in Italy, Spain, and Poland. Closely related to the term church is the term *denomination*, which is often used in religiously pluralistic states to refer to a church. For instance, in the United States, what one finds is not churches in a technical sense but denominations competing with no one group prevailing as dominant.

About politics, Kasomo defines the term as the art and science of directing and administering states and political units. So, he considers politics as the art of governance that deals with the affairs of the state.[2] According to Kastfelt, politics is based on the view that individuals, families, and various groups that compose the civic community are aware of

---

1 Eileen Berker, *New Religious Movements: A Practical Introduction* (London: HMSO, 1987).

2 Daniel Kasomo, "An Examination of Co-existence of Religion and Politics," *International Journal of Sociology and Anthropology* 1(2009): 124–131.

their own insufficiencies.[3] Many people living in one group make up the political community and these may be inclined to diverse ways of doing things. Hence, human authority is needed to regulate the people's behavior and to direct their efforts toward attaining the common good. Going by Kastfelt's explanation of politics, Hansen concludes that all people who make up a political community are called politicians. He adds that politicians may criticize their government, but politics entails much more than that. For Hansen, politics refers to all the activities of the government and the governed, including education.[4]

Emile Durkheim, the early sociologist of education, defines education as the influence exercised by adult generations on those that are not yet ready for social life. Durkheim further states that education is a social function because it is the "means by which a society prepares, in its young, the essential conditions for its own existence."[5] The objective is to develop in the child's physical, intellectual, and moral aspects that which are necessitated by both the political society as a whole and the environment for which the individual is a part of. Additionally, in its 1991 world education report, the United Nations Educational, Scientific, and Cultural Organization (UNESCO) describes education as an organized and sustained communication process designed to bring about learning.[6]

The three terms—church, politics, and education—are used in this chapter as they are understood in the public domain. The term *church* entails individual Christian denominations in Zambia and the three church mother bodies—the Council of Churches in Zambia (CCZ), Evangelical Fellowship of Zambia (EFZ), and the Zambia Episcopal Conference (ZEC). *Politics* is used to mean political governing and non-governing bodies that use their power in public life to influence the decisions that affect the country and the welfare of the people. *Education* is used to mean formal and organized learning that takes place in schools from primary through to secondary school.

Church Involvement in Politics

The presence of the church in Zambian politics is currently experienced by the formation of church-related programs in the political arena. For example, soon after President Edgar Chagwa Lungu became the republican

3 Niels Kastfelt, *Religion and Politics in Nigeria* (London: British Academic Press, 2004).

4 Michael Hansen, *Religion and Politics in East Africa* (London: James Currey, 2002).

5 Emile Durkheim, *Anomie and the Moral Structure of Industry, and the Social Bases of Education*, in *Emile Durkheim: Selected Writings*, ed. A. Giddens (New York: Cambridge University Press, 1972), 203.

6 UNESCO, *World Education Report* (Paris: UNESCO, 1991), 16–19.

president following the death of the fifth republican president Micheal Chilufya Sata on October 28, 2014, the church worked as the chief architect and guardian of the Declaration of October 18 as a public holiday for the National Day of Prayer and Fasting. The church also masterminded the introduction of the Ministry of National Guidance and Religious Affairs (MNGRA), which is headed by a female pentecostal pastor, Godfridah Sumaili.[7] In her paper, Sumaili stated that one of the key roles of MNGRA is to stimulate Faith Based Organizations (FBOs) and religious communities' interest, support, and participation in the pursuit of social reconstruction and transformation of the nation.[8] Regardless of this noble purpose, the birth of the ministry gave a leeway to the church to take center stage in the national politics. It is no wonder Chammah and Mutale Kaunda asserted that following the introduction of the MNGRA in Zambia, some sections of the church became partisan as they took part in promoting defamatory discourse against the main opposition political parties.[9]

Regardless of any unintended outcomes, the current developments in the Zambian churches have come as a pointer to their desire to occupy center stage in the administration of the state. The MNGRA therefore provides a platform for the church to add its voice in the administration of the state as well as allowing political will to have space in the organization of faith-based institutions. The church has also proved to be a key stakeholder in various educational reforms undertaken by the government. An example to mention here is the objection by the church when the Mwanakatwe Commission of 1976 excluded religious education from the school curriculum.

However, some prominent organizations have accused the church of performing its duties away from biblical functions. In a joint statement, the Zambia Conference of Catholic Bishops (ZCCB) and the Council of Churches in Zambia (CCZ) rejected the introduction of the MNGRA, describing it as both "unwise and unnecessary" in view of the various economic and political challenges faced by the Zambian citizens. They

---

7 *Zambia Reports*, "Pres. Lungu Wins Tight Presidential Election; ECL 1, 860, 877 Hichilema 1, 760, 347," August 15, 2016, accessed September 24, 2018, https://zambiareports.com/2016/08/15/pres-lungu-wins-tight-presidential-election-ecl-1-860-877-hichilema-1-760-347/.

8 Godfridah Sumaili, "Role of Ministry of National Guidance and Religious Affairs," Paper presented at National Symposium, "Equipping People of Faith to Face the Challenges of Today," Lusaka, Zambia, March 20, 2018.

9 Chammah J. Kaunda and Mutale M. Kaunda, "Mobilising Religious Assets for Social Transformation: A Theology of De-colonial Reconstruction Perspective on the Ministry of National Guidance and Religious Affairs in Zambia," *Religions* 9, no. 6 (2018): 176, https://doi.org/10.3390/rel9060176.

further argued that Zambians wanted their country to be a democracy rather than a theocracy.[10] The church's duty is to consolidate the moral and spiritual strength of the society, which has little or nothing to do with politics. The church is expected to follow the model set by Jesus Christ when he was on earth. The two organizations argued that though Jesus lived at a time when political tension was at its peak in Jerusalem and surrounding areas, he did not take part in politics.

Other scholars have argued that it is appropriate for the church to intervene in the political matters that affect its people. For example, Davies writes that Christians living in countries where there is exploitation of the poor are bound to be involved in politics.[11] His argument is that though the main task of the church is the preservation of her members' faith, she has the duty to fight the evil that prevailed in the society. Davies views Christianity to be within the social and political spheres of life. For this reason, he argues that Christians become involved in the mitigation of the social problems of the contemporary world. He cites the church in Brazil whose many priests underwent a change of direction, in their thinking and conduct, by abandoning the old moral standpoint of saving one's own soul. They were also against the view that the political function was an essential component of the social life. Davies further asserts that for every action, there was a force that made groups to abandon the status quo. He further notes that Jesus provided no ground for Christians to deny their political responsibility. Jesus himself was "apolitical," that is, he was not a member of a political party and did not give any solid teaching on the separation of politics from religion.

The church involvement in the political affairs of a society seems to be the most effective means by which the nation can ensure that justice prevails in the society. McGracken reports how the Free Church of Scotland in Malawi worked hard to prepare a small group of nationalists for their political independence. This small group reflected some missionaries' attitude toward colonial rule and African affairs. According to McGracken, in the 1920s, the political activities in Malawi were intimately linked to the impact of the Livingstonia Mission during the previous thirty years.[12] Thomas also mentions the Presbyterian Church that fought for fair treatment of Christians in Labadi and Akropong districts

---

10 *Vatican News*, "Catholics and Protestant Churches in Zambia against New Ministry of Religion," accessed September 24, 2018, http://en.radiovaticana.va/news/2016/09/21/.

11 John G. Davies, *Christian Politics and Violent Revolution* (New York: Orbis Book, 1976).

12 John McCracken, *Politics and Christianity in Malawi 1875–1940* (London: Cambridge University, 1977), 257.

in 1921.[13] The Presbyterian Synod reported to the District Officers that their Christians received unfair treatment among the local communities. Later clarifications were made concerning the right of self-government and racial equality in the government and church involvement in politics. Furthermore, Ozigi and Ocho note that though the Christian missionaries' major objective of establishing schools was the propagation of Christianity, their greatest legacy was their contribution to the educational and political development of the indigenous people. They summarized the contributions of religious education brought by Western missionaries as follows:

> Facilitation of political, social, and moral development of the Nigerian people. For example, the Hope Waddell Training Institution (HWTI), Calabara Presbyterian Institution, provided early incubation for budding nationalist politicians; many Nigerian statesmen can trace their beginnings to staff-supported school debates. Frontline Nigerian politicians and nationalists like Dr. Nnamdi Azikiwe, first Nigerian president; Sir Francis Akanu Ibiam, HWTI's principal at independence, and the eastern region's first Nigerian governor; Dr. Mbadiwe, federal minister of communications and aviation; and Dr. Eni Njoku, minister of mines and power, and the first indigenous vice-chancellor, University of Lagos, were among the people that influenced the shaping of Nigeria as a nation.[14]

Regardless of the above cited positive impact of the church in social reformation, the basis for the church's involvement in the political arena is still questioned and doubted. For example, Bigo also emphasizes the need for the church to be apolitical and justifies his argument by using the Marxist philosophy. He views church and politics through a philosophical perspective. He argues that church and politics cannot be treated as one since their roles are different. He further argues that Christ gave his church no proper mission in the political, economic, or social order, and that the purpose that Christ set before the church was a religious one.[15] It is this religious mission that unites humanity. If the mission of the church unites humanity, it is necessary that the church is involved in the political affairs of any nation so that the symbiotic relationship could help strengthen the society.

---

13 Thomas R. Kanza, The *Churches and Ghana Society 1918–1955* (Leiden: Bull, 1963), 181–184.

14 Albert Ozigi and Lawrence Ocho, *Education in Northern Nigeria* (London: Allen & Unwin, 1981), 142–144.

15 Pierre Bigo, *The Church and the Third World Revolution* (New York: Orbis Book, 1974), 137.

Involvement in Religious Education

The relationship the church has with politics in Zambia might leave either a positive or negative influence on religious education. The relationship might also affect the content in religious education and the nature of democratic values and skills the subject seeks to impart in the learners, whether they are political or religious in nature. The next section therefore discusses how religious education promotes critical consciousness among learners. To do this, we focus on religious education syllabus 2046 (which is taken by most of the learners) offered at the senior secondary school level. The section first draws the attention of the reader to the historical relationship of the church, education, and politics in Zambia before and after independence. In the main, this chapter seeks to answer the question: whose agenda does religious education promote—church or government/political agenda?

Missionary Era (1890–1924)

From the missionary era, the church has been collaborating with the state in provision of education and health care. Provision of education by the church in Zambia traces its beginning to the work of David Livingstone, who was the first missionary to come to Zambia. Hinfelaar reports that Livingstone, through his sermons, inspired other missionaries so much that they were moved to do more by providing education to the Africans.[16] One such missionary was Frederick Stanley Arnot who introduced the first school in Zambia in Barotseland. The account on Arnot's visit to Zambia has it that upon being granted permission by Lewanika, he opened his first school at Limulunga, Lewanika's summer capital, in March 1883. This first school in Northern Rhodesia (now Zambia) began with an enrolment of three boys as pupils. Though the school did not last for many years due to prolonged illness of the founder, it paved way for the next group of missionaries who introduced modern education to a larger population of the people in Barotseland and Zambia at large. These included the Paris Evangelical Missionary Society (PEMS), the Jesuits, and the Catholic Capuchin missionaries who came later in 1935.

In this era, the curriculum was based on literacy to enable the local people to read the Bible that was also the main textbook. Children who attended such schools were expected to become adherents to the church running the school. Though schools were considered as the most effective means for Christianization by the missions, the education laid a foundation for political, cultural, economic, and intellectual colonization of Africa. Commenting on the state of affairs in this era, a Nigerian Catholic

16 Hugo F. Hinfelaar, *History of the Catholic Church in Zambia* (Lusaka: Bookworld, 2004).

bishop observed that those who owned schools held the country, its religion, and the future together.[17] Similarly, the missionary education in Zambia laid the foundation for the local people to be enlightened on their political affairs. However, the religious education offered at the time was biblically oriented and could not help learners be critical to the prevailing political conditions.

Colonial Era (1925–1963)

When the colonial office took over the running of the government in 1924, the church became active in its spiritual and political roles. During June 9–15, 1924, a General Missionary Conference (GMC) was held in Kafue Town where the missionaries continued to press for the rights of Africans.[18] At this conference, the colonial government was urged to do more for the education of natives. This was because, except for the National School in Barotseland, the government had shown no practical interest in the native education anywhere else in the territory. The conference pointed out that all the 500 voluntary schools in the country were entirely sustained by the funds from various missions. It further reminded the colonial government that primary and secondary education was to be undertaken in mission schools with the help of the government. Later, in 1935, the missionaries voiced the interests of Africans and spoke out not only to the Northern Rhodesian government but also to the mother government, namely the British government. However, their outspokenness did not go without reprimand from political officials. This came after the Copperbelt miners' strike of 1935 in which six strikers were killed.

A Commission of Enquiry was appointed to investigate the cause of the disturbance by the governor. Bishop May and Rev. J.G. Saulby, the acting president of the General Missionary Conference, objected to the composition of the Commission of Enquiry. They argued that an impartial commission should be appointed for that type of investigation. The governor of Northern Rhodesia, Sir Hubert Winthrop Young, attended the conference and reprimanded the missionaries for associating themselves with government activities. In reaction to the reprimand, Reverend Saulby said,

> We claim the right to criticize when criticism is obviously deserved and our criticism is offered in kindness and with a desire to help both

17 Michael, J. Kelly, *The Origins and Development of Education in Zambia: From Precolonial Times to 1996.* A Book of Notes and Readings (Lusaka: Image Publishers Limited, 1999), 29–31.

18 Jesuits Archives, Xavier House/Proceedings of the General Missionary Conference of Northern Rhodesia held at Kafue, June 9–15, 1924 (Lovedale Institution Press, 1925).

> Europeans and natives and also the government. We think it does not quite deserve the castigation which it has received this morning.[19]

This brief history testifies how the church has been actively involved in the politics of Zambia from as far back as the missionary era (1890–1924) through to the colonial era (1925–1963). The church did become mute after this era. This was because the winds of change enhanced by the extreme inevitable spirit of nationalism enabled the newly formed independent state of Zambia to take over the control and administration of most schools formerly administered by missionaries.[20] As an example, the Free Church of Scotland missionaries aimed at offering good education to fulfill their objective of bringing about radical thinkers among Africans. Their main aim was to produce an educated elite group of nationalists that would dislodge the colonial rule. This is further witnessed in Kaunda's (Zambia's first president) words of gratitude to mission education.

> We were taught by great educationalists such as my father, Rev. and Doctor David Brown and Rev. Maxwell Robert. Dr. Brown went around for clerical and teaching work. Maxwell later opened up Chalimbana College in Lusaka. These were not simple people but capable men who made learning very enjoyable. Without education, we were not going to achieve political freedom. The education from Lubwa made us to do what we did towards independence. At the same time, Christ's message made us what we were and what we have been. No matter how little the education was, it helped us to organize ourselves politically.[21]

From the year 1945, the General Missionary Conference was called the Christian Council of Northern Rhodesia and upon independence in 1964, it was named the Christian Council of Zambia (CCZ). Thus, CCZ along with other church mother bodies (EFZ and ZEC) continued to take part in the political debates of postcolonial era with the basis of securing the civic and social rights of the Zambian people. Religious education continued to be controlled by the church and offered in schools as religious instruction.

---

19 Jesuits Archives, Xavier House/BQX 3736 Mis/, The General Missionary Conference of Northern Rhodesia: Report of Proceedings of Seventh Conference Held at Ndola June 7–13, 1935 (Lovedale Institution Press, 1925), 9–12.

20 Farrelli Hambulo, "Catholic Secondary Education and Identity Reformation in Zambia's Southern Province," Unpublished PhD diss., University of South Africa, 2016.

21 Kenneth D. Kaunda, interview by Margaret Musonda Chileshe Kabulonga, Lusaka, Zambia, November 17, 2006.

Postcolonial Era (1964–to date)

The period stretching from 1964 to 1991 is well marked in Zambian politics as a transition from one-party state to multi-party state. The church did not remain silent on this development as it took a leading role in uplifting Zambia's political status to a different level. For example, Komakoma cites an account of how the church acted as the voice for the poor from 1953 to 2001 through its famous pastoral letters.[22] Additionally, according to Mwale, the pastoral letters and statements by the CCZ, ZEC, and EFZ did not only alleviate poor people from various hardships in that space of time but also provided a model to be emulated by the present and future church.[23]

It is also important to mention that during this transition era, church and politics performed their functions simultaneously. While ensuring political and social transformation, the two institutions also ensured that there was transformation in the education system. Thus, Cheyeka asserts that during the one-party state era, the Zambian church worked hard to have the philosophy of humanism fused into the education system to foster a moral and material discipline of the Zambian people, especially those in leadership positions. This was also in line with the desire by the first republican president, Dr. Kenneth D. Kaunda to build a united Zambia in which he saw that the use of education was the best way to achieve his mission. Cheyeka concluded that it was the formation of the philosophy of humanism that led to the formation of the one-party humanist state with its tendency toward tyranny and absolutism in the second republic (1973-1991). [24]

The church did not end with welcoming the philosophy of humanism but also backed President Kaunda's agenda to have it fused into the religious education syllabi. During this period, Kaunda in his capacity as the republican president took keen interest in the religious education offered in schools. For example, in his advice to the curriculum developers at Curriculum Development Centre (CDC), Kaunda called for a curriculum that would enable teachers to address the task of stimulating the pupil's emotional, spiritual, and moral growth. He emphasized that the principle

22 Joe Komakoma, *The Social Teaching of the Catholic Bishops and Other Christian Leaders in Zambia: Major Pastoral Letters and Statements 1953—2001* (Ndola: Mission Press, 2003), 31.

23 Nelly Mwale, "Religion and Development in Zambia: The Role of the Roman Catholic Church in the Political Development of Zambia 1890—1964," *Alternation Journal* 11 (2013): 122–124.

24 Austin Cheyeka, "The Role of Zambian Humanism in the Development of Plural Religious Education in Zambia, 1972 to 1990," *The University of Zambia Institute for Social Research: African Social Research* no. 52 (Lusaka: University of Zambia Press, 2006), 22.

was important; hence, the need for it to be maintained and reinforced.[25] Though the church worked side by side with the government in the implementation of different policies on education, it did not support ideas that were intended to remove elements of religion from education. The church did not intend to witness the natural distinction of religious education in the school curriculum.

The antagonistic relationship of religion, politics, and education in Zambia did not end with the Kaunda regime. The coming of the Patriotic Front party into power in 2011 triggered the already existing need for education reforms to be more useful than they were at inception. In its content, the educational reform aligned itself with the new ruling party's manifesto and ideology as well as Vision 2030 whose objectives include "a common and shared destiny, equitable integrated and democratic in governance" among others. Cheyeka cites Michael Chilufya's speech when he attended midmorning mass on September 25, 2011, at St. Ignatius Church in Rhodes Park two days after his inauguration as the fifth republican president of Zambia.[26] He announced to the church and nation at large that his government would abide by the biblical teachings of the Ten Commandments and that it was easy for the society to learn from the commandments on how to behave and conduct itself. At CDC, religious instruction (RE) curriculum specialists took note of the "Rule by Biblical Principles" pronouncement and included it in the preface of the religious education syllabi 2044 and 2046.

> It is hoped that teachers will use this syllabus to inculcate in learners a deeper appreciation of other religions, deeper understanding of Christian values, and application of biblical principles to everyday living. The moral aspect has to do with values and morals while the spiritual is provided for in living in harmony with self, with others, and with the supernatural.[27]

So, the church in Zambia has been actively involved in politics and has not restricted its influence to the political domain only but it has also ensured that its ideas are fused in the education system. Similarly, the government, through the Ministry of Education (MoE), uses religious education to impart civic awareness among the learners to help them understand that one way they could fight for their rights is through political participation.

---

25 Kenneth Kaunda, *Letters to My Children* (London: Longman, 1973), 28.

26 Austin Cheyeka, "*Zambia*," in *Worldmark Encyclopedia of Religious Practices*, ed. T. Riggs (Detroit: Gale, 2014), 556–566.

27 Ministry of General Education, *The Zambia Education Curriculum—Framework* (Lusaka: CDC, 2012), 1–8.

Civic Competence in the Religious Education syllabus

According to Komalasari, civic competence refers to someone's wish to become an active member of a democracy or it is a social conscience.[28] Civic competence could also be described as a person's understanding and desire to be an active member of his country. A person who possesses civic competence is therefore involved in community activities and has patriotic feelings about his country. It helps individuals to become competent citizens who are aware of their obligations and responsibilities. Developing civic competence is synonymous with developing a social conscience. This means appreciating diversity and patriotism, having the ability to make informed decisions, and understanding the rights and responsibilities of citizenship.

Carpini and Keeter further explain the concept of civic competence by segmenting it into three facets—namely, civic knowledge, civic skills, and civic disposition. They describe civic knowledge as citizens having an understanding of the political system and of their own political civic rights and responsibilities; for example, the right to freedom of expression and to vote and the responsibilities to respect the rule of law and the rights and interests of others. Civic skills refer to the citizens' ability to use their knowledge to participate in civic and political processes; for example, to monitor the government's performance or mobilize other citizens to take part in communal or national activities. Civic dispositions are defined as the citizen traits necessary for a democracy such as tolerance, public spiritedness, civility, critical mindedness, and willingness to listen, negotiate, and compromise.[29]

Religious education as a subject is taught from primary, secondary, and tertiary level. Unlike other subjects, the existence of religious education in the Zambian education curriculum has more to do with the influence of the government than the church. As mentioned earlier, the first and earliest schools in Zambia were mission schools whose main textbook was the Bible translated in local languages. Children who attended such schools were expected to become adherents of the church running the school. Religious Instruction (currently called RE) was an important subject in the school curriculum. Carmody asserts that RE was taught in each school according to the doctrines, beliefs, and values of the particular mission church running the school or the dominant Christian

---

28 Kokom Kolamalasari, "The Effects of Contextual Learning in Civic Education on Students Civic Competence, Faculty of Social Science Education," *Journal of Social Sciences*, no.5 (2009): 261–270.

29 Michael X. Delli Carpini and Scott Keeter, *What Americans Know about Politics and Why it Matters*? (New Haven, CT: Yale University Press, 1996).

denomination in the area. As such, Carmody concludes that the mission school was an extension of the parish through the teaching of RE.[30]

Unlike its conversional objective as initially designed by the missionaries, RE is currently taught in line with the MoE ideology, the 1996 national policy on education, and vision 2030 as partly stated below:

> The aim of spiritual and moral education is to foster development of personally held civic, moral, and spiritual values. The learners are expected to attain a suitable level of competence in knowledge and understanding of spiritual, religious, and moral values and the traditions within which they have developed. The appreciation of other religions should be drawn from the four main religious traditions in Zambia, (namely Christianity, Hinduism, indigenous Zambian beliefs, and Islam).[31]

It is also important to mention that the quest to make RE educational and instrumental for attaining vision 2030 has not translated in the church losing control of the subject. The church has remained as an important stakeholder in that mission schools do not offer syllabus 2046, which is considered to be more Protestant than Catholic oriented. To some extent, this is the reason why RE in Zambia is commonly referred to as Christian Religious Education (CRE). However, the revision of the syllabuses is controlled by the government through the MoE. It is no wonder the 2013 revised curriculum has included governance as an important cross-cutting issue to be taught in all the subjects. The RE syllabuses read in part:

> Governance issues are an integral part of every society and therefore, should be included in the curriculum. The type of leadership in place has an influence on the social, economic, and political development. It is important that learning institutions expose learners to good governance by upholding democratic tendencies. It is, therefore, important that learning institutions include activities and practices in programmes that promote good governance.[32]

The Zambian government might be influential in terms of funding for syllabus formulation and revision; however, the content in the RE syllabuses is predominantly Christian. In view of this, the remaining part of this chapter presents topics from grade twelve 2046 syllabus (the syllabus that is most popular among the learners) to substantiate our standpoint.

---

30 Brendan Carmody, *Education in Zambia: Catholic Perspectives* (Lusaka: Bookworld Publishers, 1999).

31 Ministry of General Education, *The Zambia Education Curriculum Framework* (Lusaka: CDC, 2012), i–ii.

32 Ministry of General Education, *Zambia Education Curriculum Framework*, 21–23.

The grade twelve 2046 syllabus has the following topics: Early Church, Christian Witness, Life in the Early Church, Christian Attitudes to Work, Christian Attitudes to Leisure, Christian Attitudes to Money and Possessions, Christian Attitudes to Leadership, Christian Attitudes to Sex and Marriage, Husband and Wife Relationship, and Relationships between Parents and Children. From these topics, only one topic partially addresses issues to do with civic competence as shown below.

Topic	Sub-topic	Knowledge	Skills	Values
Christian attitudes to leadership	Bible teachings on leadership	**Israel's rejection of God:** • (1 Sam 8:4–9,19–20; 9:2) **Types of leadership:** • Bad leadership (Judg 9:1–15; Ezek 34:1–10) • Good leaders (Ezek 34:11–16; 34:20–31; Mark 10:35–45; Ps 72:1–14; John 13:3–15)	Application of teachings on leadership from the Bible.	Appreciating the virtues of patriotism and selflessness in leadership.
Christian attitudes to rulers	Attitudes to rulers in Christianity and other religions.	**Christian attitudes to rulers:** • obey good rulers • denounce bad rulers • pray for rulers **Attitudes to rulers:** • Christianity—a leader must be humble, willing to serve, listen, and learn. • Islam—cooperative, confident, and God-fearing; of God's great influence. • Hinduism—take advice, guide, sacrifice, devotion for the welfare of the people. • Zambian tradition—demands special treatment because of his position, gets into power through inheritance and consensus.		Appreciating positive attitudes of the rulers.

Generally, the topic "Christian Attitudes to Leadership" describes the qualities of good leaders and the need for learners to obey such leaders. However, the topic does not help learners with ways of participating in elections or contributing to the politics of Zambia other than through elections. So, though the Zambian government proposes the need for learners to acquire civic competences, the RE syllabuses do not fully help learners to be competent in civic matters. One might argue that senior school learners are helped to become good citizens by learning civic education as a school subject. However, the challenge is that under the "Vocational and Technical Career Pathway" of the 2013 revised curriculum, civic education and RE are offered as optional subjects.[33] This means that graduates of this pathway, who did not show interest in civic education and opted to study RE, may lack civic skills and dispositions. They may have no ability to analyze, evaluate, and defend their country's norms and values. They may also fail to use their knowledge to participate in civic and political processes, for example, to monitor government performance or mobilize other citizens to participate in community activities.

Thomas Dee, for example, asserts "it is widely believed that education is an essential component of a stable democratic society because it encourages citizens to participate in democratic processes and prepares them to do so in an informed and intelligent manner."[34] For him, education promotes civic engagement in future citizens as they acquire cognitive ability to process complex political information, to make decisions, and to circumvent the various bureaucratic and technological impediments to civic participation. Dee argues that educational attainment, especially one that is holistically designed, has large and statistically significant effects on subsequent voter participation and support for free speech. This assertion is in harmony with Kunkler and Lerner's findings on their comparison study on "Religious Education and Democracy in Indonesia and Israel." The study suggests that in Indonesia, the inclusion of a secular curriculum in religious education in the 1970s should be seen as one of the factors promoting the production and dissemination of "rationalist approaches to religion" and bringing religious actors on board with democratization. While in Israel, the exclusion of a secular curriculum from ultra-orthodox schooling has, over time, undermined civic commitments among ultra-orthodox Jewish citizens and weakened Israeli democracy.[35] In Zambia, instead of being purely religious and morally based, RE should

---

33 Ministry of General Education, *Zambia Education Curriculum*, 43–46.

34 Thomas S. Dee, "Are there Civic Returns to Education?" *Journal of Public Economics* 88, no. 9–10 (2004): 1698.

35 Mirjam Kunkler and Hanna Lerner, "A Private Matter? Religious Education and Democracy in Indonesia and Israel," *British Journal of Religious Education* (2016): 1–16.

strengthen the civic values and skills and provide a benchmark for the learners' involvement in politics.

Conclusion

The chapter has analyzed the relationship of church, politics, and education in Zambia from the missionary era through to the present time. The account shows that the three institutions have been working symbiotically where any of the three used the others to achieve its ideas. Based on this relationship, the chapter has extended its analysis of the three institutions by assessing grade twelve 2046 RE syllabus with a view to ascertain whether its content supports civic competence as demonstrated by the Zambian government through the MoE. The content of the syllabus suggests that grade twelve RE, as it is also the case with other grades, does not have much to do with political literacy. Most of its content addresses issues of moral and religious literacy. Thus, RE in Zambia currently promotes the MoE agenda as opposed to church agenda that was common during the missionary era. Its content is inclusive of other religions but highly Christian.

The chapter has also shown that, to a great extent, RE promotes democratic values and political literacy among learners. With regard to RE promoting the political debate about religion, this is not the concern of the subject. Instead, the chapter has shown that, to an extent, RE promotes critical consciousness among learners to help them participate in national politics. However, in order for learners to be fully involved in the politics of Zambia, the current relationship of church-politics-education should be strengthened by allowing for more dialogue among the groups so that the syllabus content could be inclusive of civic competences in all the topics. Additionally, all learners in secondary schools in Zambia should take RE as a compulsory subject so that the principles, values, and skills emphasized in Christianity and other religions could be acquired by all the learners. This might help to create a mass of Zambian citizens with shared consciousness toward holistic development.

10

RELIGION, WITCHCRAFT, AND POLITICS

Bernhard Udelhoven

INTRODUCTION

The disconcerting presence of witchcraft preoccupies much space in Zambia's private and public domains. Also, Africa's political imagination is saturated with references to the occult. These concepts have to be grasped and taken seriously, Stephen Ellis and Gerrie ter Haar suggest, if we want to understand political action.[1] But, since witchcraft is employed in secret, how are we to evaluate its role and power in politics?

I answer the question by analyzing how they legitimize or delegitimize political authority and ideology. Witchcraft beliefs and practices can do both, back and forth. Take the following conversation that I had in preparation for this chapter with a group of headmen and women in our rural area (which I will describe later): I asked them about the relationship of authority/political office with God and with witchcraft. At first, everybody was adamant that nobody can hold a political office unless God has given it. In their discussion, even voting seemed like an exercise that merely draws out what God has already decided, since "God has appointed the one he wants, before you vote." When I asked about vote rigging, the conversation changed: "Then, it is the devil who makes you win elections! Politicians frequent witchdoctors to buy charms to win votes. They buy body parts from the *bakamnyama* [people who kidnap or kill for the purpose of extracting human body parts as ingredients for charms]; that is why we have so many ritual killings before elections." Political authority, earlier proclaimed to be vested in God, was now seen to be the playground for witches. This, however, was not yet the end of our conversation, which

1 Stephen Ellis and Gerrie ter Haar, *Worlds of Power: Religious Thought and Political Practice in Africa* (Oxford: Oxford University Press, 2004).

was turning to mundane reasoning: "Politicians are like men who want to marry a girl," one person explained. "Before marriage, they promise the girl all that she wants to hear. Politicians do the same in their campaigns. Once in power, another reality sets in." People then commented on local issues that caused grievances and that could cause their politicians to be voted out.

I understood from the conversation that religion and witchcraft play a great role in the process of (de-)legitimizing authority, a government, or even the state. But the fire enkindled by reference to witchcraft may quickly change directions. At the same time, neither God nor the devil allows anybody to forego ordinary political maneuvers to make their life a success.[2]

Direct ways of framing the political opponent through association with witchcraft have always been part of political antagonism in Zambia. The editor of the government controlled *Daily Mail*, for example, repeatedly equated disrespect for the president, put in power by God, with witchcraft; in contrast, Chishimba Kambwiri, expelled from the ruling party, called the president a wizard in the more critically positioned *Mast*.[3] Johanneke Kamp analyzed the high frequency with which readers of an online opposition news magazine linked Satanism and road accidents (understood as human sacrifices) to the ruling party or to Zambia's political and moral situation.[4] The dynamics of framing are, of course, not always coherent. For example, in response to the murder of an albino in Lusaka's Zanimuone compound, one reader blamed the leader of the opposition, while others the ruling party for commissioning the murder to buy body parts for their charms. Most online comments, however, simply expressed sadness and shock.[5] Yes, witchcraft is very present in Zambian political language. But how does this, together with people's ways of dealing with witchcraft, make up or change political action?

In the first part, I build on insights of anthropologists and historians who have studied the legitimizing or the delegitimizing aspects of

---

2 Being a priest, I could not fail to see that a similar ambivalence is present already in the New Testament, where some passages regard the political order to be upheld by God, others by a hostile world or even the devil. Compare, for example, Romans 13 with John 15: 18–25 or Revelation 13. Neither passage however downplays a person's own responsibilities in an ambiguous and uncertain world.

3 *Daily Mail*, August 5, 2016, and August 23, 2017; *The Mast*, April 23, 2018.

4 Johanneke Kroesbergen-Kamps, "Accusations of Satanism in the Public Sphere," in *Christian Identity and Justice in a Globalized World from a Southern African Perspective*, ed. H. Kroesbergen (Wellington, SA: Christian Literature Fund, 2014), 148–162.

5 Tumfweko, "Albino Killed, Arm Chopped," accessed June 20, 2019, http://tumfweko.com/2015/12/24/albino-killed-arm-chopped-in-lusaka/#comments.

witchcraft discourse—on the scale of the state. In the second part, I want to bring the discussion down to a rural setup and see how people repositioned themselves to the state in response to different occult threats. I close with an epilogue on consequences for discussions on the Zambian Witchcraft Act.

Delegitimizing Processes of Witchcraft Discourses

Appeals to the occult with evocative images may affect and mobilize people with a greater impact than neat intellectual discourse. Several authors have aired their dissatisfaction with political studies that reduce the religious world—including that of witchcraft—to psychological categories that obscure their political potential, and called for an analysis that makes sense in the political actors' own terms.[6]

Where popular imagination associates the state with witchcraft, the state suffers from a legitimization problem. In Zambian history, we are reminded of the appeal of Millennial Watchtower revivals during colonial times, and later Jehovah Witnesses, who linked white rule, taxation, the prevailing economic and religious powers together with witchcraft to Lucifer, who now rules on earth but would soon be overcome in the battle of Armageddon.[7] The colonial regime needed extraordinary steps to keep the Watchtower threat at bay. A postcolonial example would be Kenneth Kaunda, whom rumor depicted as enmeshed in occult practices prior to his fall from power in the 1991 elections. David Gordon saw this representation as epitomizing the spiritual decay of Kaunda's humanism over and against the rising spiritual discourse of born-again Pentecostalism that accompanied the road to multi-party democracy.[8]

But, there is also a less direct way through which the occult delegitimizes a government or the state to its people: Where a state cannot control evil spiritual powers (like witchcraft), it may prove itself before its people

6 Examples for Zambia are Edith Turner, Karen Fields, Louise White, and David Gordon, though they pursued very different paths.

7 Note, however, van Binsbergen's observation, that "the specific Watchtower message, including its anti-colonial overtones, got lost behind the peasants' perception of the preachers as predominantly engaged in the eradication of sorcery." Peasants absorbed the "proletarian preachers" into a "strictly local scale." Wim M.J. van Binsbergen, *Religious Change in Zambia: Exploratory Studies* (London: Kegan Paul International, 1981), 115; see David Gordon, *Invisible Agents: Spirits in a Central African History* (Athens, OH: Ohio University Press, 2012), chapter 3, for the urban threat of Jehovah Witnesses to the colonial regime.

8 David Gordon, *Invisible Agents,* chapter 8. The political impact, however, is not easily assessed. Kaunda may have lost the 1991 elections also without his depiction as an occultist, and whether the pentecostal Christian discourse was crucial to the shift to multi-party democracy or rather accidental is open to debate.

as spiritually impotent. "Out-of-control witchcraft" delegitimizes authority that is expected to deal with it yet fails to do so. It needs to make room for a new power that is up to the job. When early Watchtower offspring dealt with witchcraft and gained popularity (for example, the infamous Tomo Nyirenda in Mkushi area and Katanga), the authority of the colonial chiefs was at stake. Nyirenda tried to gather people into their own *kitawala* villages—no longer subordinate to chiefs or to the colonial regime. Here, they could deal with witches (Nyirenda drowned them during his notorious "dippings"), which was once the privilege and duty of the chiefs.

When the *mchape/bamucapi* movements, starting with the 1930s, swept over Northern Rhodesia and village by village lined up so that diviners could identify the witches and cleanse them of their witchcraft, the colonial government saw itself forced to suspend the application of the Witchcraft Act. It was aware of its own inability to enforce the unpopular law (headmen and chiefs made sure not to inform the *Boma* when they invited a *mucapi*). As Karen Fields shows, some officials clearly saw that chiefs and headmen, crucial to indirect rule, were regarded by their subjects as accomplices of the witches when they prevented their prosecution. The colonial government allowed the witch-cleansing activities of the *bamucapi* (tolerated or even invited by the chiefs), on the same grounds that they had denied those of the early Watchtowers (directed against the chiefs): to uphold local authority and its own precarious legitimacy.

Fields remarks that the colonial government could rule but not turn people and rulers into a common "moral community."

> The renowned idea of Europe's "civilizing mission" expressed no such thing. As ideology, the "civilizing mission" was the very antithesis of moral community between rulers and ruled. As practice, it did not build on institutions by which rulers and ruled ordered a common life. There was none. And its declared purpose was the dissolution of ordered society, as Africans understood it.[9]

What did Fields understand by a common life in a "moral community"? Emile Durkheim (whose works she translated), used the term in his definition of religion: Religion unites people through a structure of common beliefs and practices.[10] In a moral community, an elaborate religious system integrates people who share the same values into a common life. The diverse outlook on witchcraft constituted for Fields the most

---

9 Karen Fields, "Political Contingencies of Witchcraft in Colonial Central Africa: Culture and the State in Marxist Theory," *Canadian Journal of African Studies* 16, No. 3 (1982), 574.

10 Emile Durkheim, *The Elementary Forms of Religious Life*, trans. Karen E. Fields (New York: Free Press, [1912] 1995), 44.

visible sign of a failed moral community between rulers and ruled in colonial times.

Another example of the delegitimizing effects of an "out-of-control spiritual world," now postcolonial, concerns the healing ministry of Archbishop Milingo at the time of Zambia's one-party state. Opposition was not allowed for fear it would erode the project of national identity, security, and modernization. Milingo exorcized evil spirits, in whose ontological reality he firmly believed. While the sick and afflicted, not politics, stood in the center of this ministry, Milingo also became a national political figure with his growing cross-cutting appeal. He himself linked the ever-growing numbers of people with demons and spiritual afflictions to the increasing levels of poverty and marginalization of the poor, which constituted an indirect but open criticism of the government. The multitudes of "out-of-control demons" were easily associated with the spiritual bankruptcy of the government, following the economic bankruptcy of the country. Kaunda supported Milingo in the early years but remained quiet during the events that culminated in his removal from Zambia. Many people saw in his silence the implicit agreement with exiling a critical voice; dealing with spiritual afflictions had become a loaded political issue.[11]

"Out-of-control witchcraft" and "out-of-control spirits" may reveal the absence of a moral community: The political system is flawed and incapable to address people's moral concerns, because ruler and the ruled are not united under the same values. But let us look now at the other side of the coin: the much evoked "moral community" is a very unstable and exploitable notion where it constitutes itself in the common fight against the witch.

Legitimizing Processes of Witchcraft

If a state fears losing its legitimacy because of out-of-control spirits or witchcraft, it will try to ensure the control of this unseen world. The postcolonial state represents itself as upholding people's system of values and as addressing common moral concerns. It postulates a moral community between rulers and ruled. In a pluralistic society, however, an important question arises: Who speaks on behalf of the moral community? Who are its representatives? And who will be excluded? Here a thought of

11 See Gerrie ter Haar, *Spirit of Africa: The Healing Ministry of Archbishop Milingo of Zambia* (Africa World Press, 1992); Marja Hinfelaar, "Legitimizing Powers: The Political Role of the Roman Catholic Church, 1972–1991," in *One Zambia, Many Histories: Towards a History of Post-colonial Zambia*, ed. Jan-Bart Gewalt, Marja Hinfelaar, and Giacomo Macola (Leiden: Brill, 2008), 129–43. Note, of course, that many other issues (including administrative and financial concerns) played into the "Milingo affair" apart from the divergent ideas about the spirit world.

Jean and John Comaroff about criminality is important: They argue that "Criminality has, in *this* Age of Global Capitalism, become *the* constitutive fact of contemporary life, *the* vernacular in terms of which politics is conducted, moral panics are voiced, and populations are ruled."[12]

If we substitute the word *criminality* with *witchcraft*, or at least recognize in witchcraft one of the main expressions of felt attacks on the moral order, we sense its legitimizing political potential. Also, the Comaroffs quote Emile Durkheim, who famously suggested that a society free of lawlessness "would fall into chaos, since it would be bereft of the signs of its own existence as an authoritative order."[13] In Durkheim's footsteps, Monica Wilson sees in the image of the witch the "standardized nightmare of a group":[14] it provides the wanted counter-image for a moral discourse about the ideals and values of a society; at the same time, it legitimizes rightful authority that can deal with witchcraft.

Going back to the Comaroffs and to contemporary imageries of criminality, a general impression of lawlessness legitimizes a stronger state with greater possibilities of policing. Lawlessness becomes easily associated with specific segments of society or minority groups. Often, this proceeds in a climate where "the relationship between fear and danger is starkly disproportionate": where the occurrence of the danger is statistically much lower than what is imagined or portrayed. The members of such groups or segments easily stand pre-accused before they have committed any crime. One of their examples is the high number of incidences of gunning down unarmed black youths in the United States by white police officers. "Policing, in the name of order, frequently makes felons before-the-fact, punishing them prior to their breaches being legally established. Or even committed."[15]

Let me apply this argument to witchcraft: People seek divination as an independent means of verification. But certain members of the population are more prone to be seen as witches than others. In Zambia, these are often old and isolated people as well as fast-rising and fast-falling business people, but the groups and patterns of accusations often changed with economic circumstances, as Elisabeth Colson showed in a compelling

---

12 Jean Comaroff and John Comaroff, *The Truth about Crime: Sovereignty, Knowledge, Social Order* (Chicago: University of Chicago Press, 2016), 119. Italics in the original.

13 Comaroff and Comaroff, *Truth about Crime*, 101.

14 Monica Wilson, "Witch Beliefs and Social Structure," *American Journal of Sociology* 56 (1952): 307–313.

15 Comaroff and Comaroff, *Truth about Crime*, 49.

long-time case study.[16] Diviners who fail to satisfy the expectations of the community that employs their services become quickly redundant.

Prior to Milingo's healing ministry, and prior to the pentecostal explosion in Zambia, Christianity was not widely recognized as a viable answer to witchcraft. People dealt with witchcraft away from the church. This has changed. In the "Christian nation," Christianity not only legitimizes the state but is also recognized as a spiritual power able to deal with the occult. This new constellation brings in new dynamics. "Out-of-control witchcraft" can become a call for a stronger state and better ways of policing, legitimized by the Christian faith, in order to fight the world of witchcraft. The question about the nature of the enemy who is associated with this world becomes pertinent.

For example, as part of the debate on a national moral discourse, witchcraft and Satanists (Satanism being *the* counter discourse of the Christian nation) have consistently been associated with homosexuality. Articles of the *Times of Zambia* in its series on gay rights referred to homosexuality, witchcraft, Satanism, Freemasonry, child-defilement, incest, and human sacrifices basically as interchangeable terms.[17] Subsuming a human condition different from that of those speaking for the moral community into a witchcraft discourse tends toward the extermination of difference. Common imagination has linked Satanism and witchcraft also to minority faiths and foreigners (particularly Rwandese businesspeople, as the looting of over 60 shops in 2016 showed in response to Lusaka's ritual killings). Christian exorcists have provided their audiences with lists of clear signs of witchcraft in the behavior patterns of people that can guide the Christians in their quest to identify the hidden powers of the devil. Such witchcraft discourses have also legitimized the expulsion of difficult children who do not respond to exorcisms.[18] The much idealized vision of a common moral community between rulers and ruled can become the engine that defines the *other*, a threat to the integrity of the privileged population, and give implicit rise to what Michel Foucault calls state racism and that—in the extreme—can lead to genocides.[19]

---

16 Elisabeth Colson, "The Father as Witch," *Africa: Journal of the International African Institute* 70, no. 3 (2000): 333–58.

17 See, for example, the contributions in the *Times of Zambia*, February 3, 2014, March 10, 2014, August 9 and 13, 2015, and others.

18 I write this from my own experiences with children who were brought to me as "possessed." See Felix Riedel, "Children in African Witch-Hunts: An Introduction for Scientists and Social Workers" (Witchcraft and Human Rights Information Network, 2012), accessed June 12, 2019, http://www.whrin.org/wp-content/uploads/2012/12/childreninafricanwitchhuntsfinalversion-1-Felix-Riedel-2.pdf

19 Michel Foucault, *The History of Sexuality, Volume I*, trans. Robert Hurley (New York: Vintage Books, 1978), 137.

So far, I have presented two different scenarios, in which "witchcraft out of control" can be used to delegitimize authority or in which it can bind rulers and ruled together in a fight against a perceived threat. Statecraft is either unable to address witchcraft concerns (absence of a moral community), or it takes part in identifying (or producing) the witch-other, less than human, for whom there is no space in society.

But does witchcraft always need to be of relevance to statecraft? Can witchcraft not be dealt with in interstitial spaces with outcomes that are irrelevant to the relationship between citizens and their state? Again, I want to pursue this question on the example of two contrasting anthropological views.

The Morphology of Witchcraft and Its Effect on Political System

Ever since Evans-Pritchard suggested a correlation between the morphology of magic/witchcraft and a political system,[20] many anthropologists saw witchcraft beliefs and practices as being dependent on but also constitutive of the social and political structure of many African societies. In Zambia's precolonial time, as we have seen, the authority of many chiefs was connected to their ability to control witchcraft and punish the witches.

One of the first examples to include the postcolonial African nation state in the economy of witchcraft came from Rowlands and Warnier, who claim that "Sorcery is not only a mode of popular action but lies at the center of state-building processes both in the present and in the past."[21] They exemplify their thesis on the concept of *evu*, found in various parts of Cameroon and translated in English as witchcraft. People describe *evu* as a substance in the human body that becomes destructive witchcraft when the selfish owner fails to integrate their powers into society, but it can also be a positive substance when fully socialized, allowing for successful social and economic power. This gives rise to complex strategies that successful people use to appease their kin (through redistribution of wealth and signs of generosity) *together* with their forces of *evu*. This double-sided meaning of *evu* (positive when socialized but destructive when not) locks economic and political success into the same discourse as witchcraft as two sides of the same coin. For the authors, the fact that many people accused of witchcraft easily confess under pressure from public opinion reinforces their argument that through confession "the

20 Edward Evan Evans-Pritchard, "The Morphology and Function of Magic," *American Anthropologist* 31, no. 4 (1929): 619–649.

21 Michael Rowlands and Jean-Pierre Warnier, "Sorcery, Power and the Modern State in Cameroon," *Man* 23, no. 1 (1988): 121.

strength of the witch's *evu* gained public recognition and was socialized to the owner's best advantage." A confessed witch (be it the outcome of false or true accusations) can gather more social capital and influence than a person with no *evu* or weak *evu* who will be unsuccessful and toothless while walking through life. The state and its officials portray themselves as embodying the common good, security, peace, and prosperity for the nation; any weakening of the state (through opposition or lack of order) will lead to violence and economic crisis. Implicitly, state officials try to present themselves in positive *evu*. The dynamics of legitimization, which extend state-building processes into rural areas, also make them subject to the *evu* discourses, resulting in a system of redistribution of resources among one's own clientele (the sign of positive socialized *evu*) at the expense of enhancing the processes of rationalization of the state machinery. The activities that enhance state formation in Africa, so the authors claim, also enhance nepotism and corruption. The analysis locks state and citizens into one single economy of witchcraft.

An engaging point of this analysis is the insight that the morality of *evu's* relationship to power and wealth is determined not in reference to some intrinsic evil—neither power nor wealth are bad (though the absence of both is); it is about being socialized or not, about the common good and common progress. This makes witchcraft a relational and a political term. Also, in Zambia, we know about socialized spiritual powers of people who wield authority over others, even if we usually distinguish them from witchcraft.[22] At the same time, as Max Marwick and James Ferguson show, the fear of witchcraft was/is used by many families to enforce customary expectations of generosity on its richer members.[23]

But there are also limits to an analysis of politics subsumed under the logic of witchcraft. One danger lies in presenting witchcraft, boiled down from the analysis of various anthropological writings, as pre-given, *quasi a priori* realities that are seen to determine people's lines of thought, a view associated with culturalism. Rowlands' and Warnier's analysis may be too neat. They present the mystery of witchcraft as quite understandable to the anthropologist. It is mostly Western observers who express

22 Legitimate spiritual power associated with rightful authority included often royal relics for the protection of the land, a headman's knowledge of protective magic, or the power of parents to bless or curse their children. We rarely name the socialized spiritual powers as witchcraft, but ambivalent spiritual concepts can easily mutate in times of conflict. Generosity and redistribution also in Zambia are signs of a positive form of authority; selfishness of negative witchcraft.

23 Max Marwick, *Sorcery in Its Social Setting: A Study of the Northern Rhodesia Cewa* (Manchester: Manchester University Press, 1965); James Ferguson, *Expectations of Modernity: Perspectives on Southern Africa* (Los Angesles, CA: University of California Press, 1999).

amazement at the readiness with which accused witches confess.[24] The analysis neglects that experiences with witchcraft can go together with a radical questioning of religious and social certainties.

Let me contrast Rowlands' and Warnier's analysis with that of Diane Ciekawy, who also argues that statecraft discourses blend with witchcraft discourses (on Kenyan examples). However, instead of working with a common, quasi national understanding of witchcraft that anthropologists have unearthed (the starting point of Rowlands and Warnier), she puts disparities at the center of her analysis. For example, national, international, and NGO-driven development discourses, church language, and local healing practices, understand and refer to witchcraft in fundamentally different ways. Ciekawy looked at the way in which these different discourses, each supported by overlapping authority structures, interact. In Kenya, where the state licenses diviners who deal with witchcraft, they have to adapt to each other in the process of which the "witch-other" is produced and prosecuted—with outcomes often very different from what initial protagonists had hoped for.[25]

Zambia's legislation is different from that of Kenya in Ciekawy's example. Zambia does not license healers to identify witches. Though one may report suspected witchcraft to the police (the Witchcraft Act, Cap 90 of the Laws of Zambia, outlaws the practice of witchcraft in section 9 to 11), the main thrust of the act proscribes the naming and identification of witches. But Ciekawy's argument applies to Zambia in an inverted sense: Diviners have to adapt their strategies to the state discourse in order to stay "under the radar" of law-enforcement. The question arises, what do these interstitial and ambivalent spaces have to say about legitimization processes of the state? For example, the "under the radar" scenario in Zambia can open up interstitial spaces in which people deal with witchcraft in ways that may be quite irrelevant to and independent of their relationship with the state. And the state machinery can also decide (especially in rural

24 Rowlands and Warnier, "Sorcery, Power and the Modern State," 124.

25 Diane Ciekawy, "Containing Witchcraft: Conflicting Scenarios in Postcolonial Africa," *African Studies Review* 41, no. 3 (1998): 1–14; Diane Ciekawy, "Witchcraft in Statecraft: Five Technologies of Power in Colonial and Postcolonial Coastal Kenya," *African Studies Review* 41, no. 3 (1998): 119–141; Diane Ciekawy, "Utsai as Ethical Discourse: A Critique of Power from Mijikenda in Coastal Kenya," in *Witchcraft Dialogues: Anthropological and Philosophical Exchanges*, ed. G. C. Bond and D. M. Ciekawy (Athens, OH: Ohio University Press, 2001), 158–189. See, however, the different interpretation of James Smith, that comes closer to the case studies I am presenting. James Smith, "Buying a Better Witch Doctor: Witch-Finding, Neoliberalism, and the Development Imagination in the Taita Hills, Kenya," *American Ethnologist* 32, no. 1 (2005): 141–158.

areas) to close its eyes to witch-hunts, just like the colonial regime did, in its attempt to avoid an unpopular stance with the voting population.

On the ground, witchcraft comes in many forms and with different ritual authorities and solutions, and therefore also with multiple ways of repositioning oneself over and against the state. I will look now at some recent actions that people took against witchcraft in the rural area where I work as a Catholic priest, and try to draw out what they say, or don't say, about a moral community between the state and its citizens.

Dealing with Witchcraft in Lumimba

The Lumimba parish stretches 150 km along the Luangwa valley and comprises the area of four chieftaincies (Mwanya, Chitungulu, Kazembe, and Chifunda), with a total population of around 50,000 people. Proximity to wildlife and the valley's isolation mark people's lives—most areas are cut off during the rainy season. Wildlife brings jobs and development opportunities to some members of the local population, but also many perils, since the animals feed on people's fields. Many activities (unlicensed hunting, fishing, and mining activities for gold and precious stones) proceed in the realm of the illegal; many families suffer as their most productive members are handed heavy prison sentences. This places people in a precarious relationship with the law. Yet, people clearly want to overcome their national isolation and look forward to more government involvement and taking more visible part in national development opportunities.

People in our parish speak different languages (Chiwiza, Chisenga, and Chinyanja), but understand each other. In most parts, social life is organized through the clan system (known as *mikowa*) that structures the various families who live together in the same clusters outside the areas designated as parks and forests. The shared history in the valley and the need for mutual support gives a special sense of cultural identity that people seek to guard during ritual events, like funerals or initiation rites. At the same time, rivalry over the few resources and a spy system that rewards people for denouncing their neighbors for wildlife offences tends toward eroding mutual trust and a sense of community. The state is both near and far: Schools and clinics are greatly valued but not always well supervised—the next district administrative center (*Boma*) is far outside the valley. Chiefs, with the help of group-headmen (and women) and councilors, handle many local disputes and control access to the land and even to the labor market in the tourism industry, but their lines of authority are renegotiated in many events and disputes.

Christianity, through the presence of various churches, marks the official religious discourse at most funerals, even of people who die non-aligned to any church. Muslims make up a significant presence. Basically, all people in Lumimba, Christian, Muslim, or non-aligned, take witchcraft for granted as an evil force that some access in secret to advance themselves by betraying others. Yet, witchcraft (*bulozi, umfiti, ufwiti*) is not one single phenomenon that people can easily define, but an evasive force to which people refer or that imposes itself on them through its various signs and codes. The four chiefs in our parish have different policies toward handling witchcraft: one has outlawed any witch-finding activities in his chiefdom, following the Zambian law and also the advice of his church (Catholic). Two chiefs moderately tolerate witch-finding and often close their eyes when headmen call in witch-finders. The fourth chief has taken at times a more active part by summoning suspected witches to his palace to be cleansed by approved witch-finders. Our parish also hosts a number of well-known traditional healers who deal with witchcraft in various ways. Our own pastoral activities in the Catholic Church, and more so that of the pentecostal and Zion churches, are marked by issues of witchcraft on a daily basis.

Case 1: A Popular Witch-cleansing

In June 2017, a large group of small villages, stretching along 15 km, called a known diviner to cleanse all their households from witchcraft. Each household had to pay 50 Kwacha for the fees and transport of the diviner and her team. Headmen, headwomen, and the local vigilantes' group (the "neighborhood watch") enforced the fee on everybody, and in some cases collected it by force. We priests asked the Catholic community (a minority in that group of villages) not to pay up and not to attend the cleansing. Those who followed our advice (a portion of the Catholic community) became labelled as witches long before the diviner arrived. As a result, one family was evicted from its vicinity, forced to abandon their house and gardens. Others slept outside their houses for weeks, for fear, after repeated threats, that their homes would be torched at night. The chief of that area was silent during the affair—he did not stop the cleansing, but upon our inquiry let us know that he was not informed. The cleansing rituals proceeded in a rather calm atmosphere. Spectators, especially women, were wearing their Sunday best clothes. There was local beer available. The diviner put a long pole with a red flag before each house, signifying "danger"; some were quickly cleared, in others it took a longer time. The diviner knew very well the Zambian Witchcraft Act that outlaws the identification of witches. When I went to see and challenge her during the cleansing, she used the terminology of "bad medicines" and said she accused nobody of witchcraft, "people accuse themselves." Indeed, some people whom she found with such bad medicines admitted their offence to her, in my presence, though the same people had denied it when I had asked them on my own. The diviner showed me and others a whole range of certificates (invalid in Zambia) to project the image not only of legality but even of being commissioned by the state. She maneuvered perfectly under the radar of law-enforcement—in no way did she want to be seen in confrontation with the state or the law. Nor did the headmen.

Culprits found with bad medicines had to pay a fee of 1,500 Kwacha, which the diviner's team, when people could not pay up, collected in the form of bags of maize, bicycles, solar panels, and radios. Some were small-scale business people with tiny shops, not very successful, which they had to close after the cleansing because of bankruptcy and looting. Others were elderly men and women whose children lived in other villages; most of them failed to raise the required money to become cleansed, even when they agreed to the charges. Their homes were raided of any remaining chicken or item of any value.

The diviner and the group-headman were not at ease with my presence, knowing that I could report the case to the police (110 km away). When the cleansing persisted, I did approach the police. The police summoned the diviner, "to be taught about the law," but she ignored the order. Subsequently, she did not show up in other parts of our parish where she had also been invited. A group-headman then wrote me a letter, in which he expressed his disappointment that I "wanted to stop the community to find a way of bringing peace, unity, and development to our area." Witchcraft was blamed not only for the lack of peace but also of development. So far, many regarded the Catholic Church as trying to prevent a local community to find their own solution to witchcraft. A few people, however, came regularly to the parish to update us and seek protection. Factions now had been established that revealed a divided community.

I tried to understand the need of the community for the diviner. I found an answer in the ambivalent link of witchcraft with the widespread use of traditional medicines, as the diviner herself had expressed it. Medicines can cure, but they can also kill. Many people use medicines to harvest protective and life-giving forces beyond the cure of known biological sicknesses. In Lumimba, medicines have connecting capacities and are used not only to work on the self but also on others. Examples are herbs and footprints used by men "that make the co-wives love each other and be like sisters," medicines that prevent a hunter from getting caught by game guards, that make a thief become mad, or that protect breastfeeding babies from disease at the expense of other babies. Several people who at one time had a case to answer admitted that they had sought medicines "to tie the judge" to obtain a favorable judgment. When somebody tries to channel mysterious energies into more sinister types of manipulation or activates them through outrageous acts (like murder or incest), everybody agrees that we have entered the heart of witchcraft (whose forces can, however, also be inherited). The borderline between helpful medicine and harmful witchcraft can be relative: A woman secretly places a small amount of powder that she obtained from a healer into her husband's food and burns some roots over their common bed to prevent him from infidelity. For her, this is legitimate medicine, allowing her to determine her marriage destiny instead of leaving this to other women. Her husband, however, regards it as witchcraft, and a diviner may point it out as being responsible for the bad dreams of her neighbors. Using manipulative medicines is rarely accompanied by an account of how these medicines work or which powers or energies they invoke; these unknown factors make others very uncomfortable—hence the need for secrecy. The widespread but secret use of many types of medicines, I believe, contributed to the felt need for a communitarian cleansing from witchcraft or harmful medicines.

Did the cleansing bring about the desired results? In its aftermath, many headmen and headwomen took part in a workshop about medicines, witchcraft, and witch-finding that I conducted together with members of other churches present. Several people, angry about the loss of their property, narrated that they felt cheated. They thought the diviner herself hid some medicines in their gardens or roofs and wondered how the all-knowing diviner misinterpreted some family relationships. Ill-feelings against the Catholic Church were forgotten. Unfolding events showed that those who spoke and acted on behalf of the community and who controlled the "neighborhood watch" vigilantes comprised a vocal fraction but did not speak on behalf of all. The diviner went away with a considerable amount of money and two (small) lorry loads of maize, chicken, and other goods, but she had not spoken the final word on witchcraft—issues were still messy and far from being sorted out. Soon after the event, a pastor from Lusaka set himself up in the same area to pray for people's spiritual problems and anoint them with holy oils, also at a fee. After an enthusiastic welcome, others named him a charlatan; he had to leave. I have little doubt that another diviner will again find fertile ground in the same villages when new rumors, fears, jealousies, and accusations arise. Obviously, I hope that my church will become more relevant for the spiritual problems of the area.

How did people position themselves toward the state in this episode? They suspended the Zambian law *temporarily* to have everybody cleansed of bad medicines and start afresh on new terms. But they showed no protest against the state. Pressure was rather put on the local headmen and headwomen to cooperate, and on non-cooperating Catholics. The

Witchcraft Act was suspended in the same way as people easily suspend laws on taxation or illegal hunting, fishing, and gold mining activities: they dislike many laws, yet demand a stronger presence of the state and its services. People's identification with the state depends on a whole range of other factors besides a common sense of justice on the question of witchcraft, which gives some perspective to our discussion on a common moral community. A second lesson for our argument is that later events (dissatisfaction with the outcome of the cleansing, reactions to our workshop, and the arrival of a new pastor) proved the "local idiom," "local worldview," and "local moral logic" to be very adaptive, and even pluralistic. Opinions about the best way of dealing with witchcraft were situational and easily adapted to new discourses, as long as these promised to offer a solution.

Case 2: Witch-killings

In early 2018, a middle-aged man (very poor) was killed in our parish in an act of great terror. His arms and legs were broken prior to being thrown into a shallow grave, onto a bed of thorns, and buried alive. His crime was bewitching a youth, who fell ill during an illegal gold-digging trip. The evidence was that the young man had dreamt of his neighbor as causing his sickness. His family challenged, beat, and threatened the said man, in the course of which he was said "to have confessed." It is not clear whether also a divination was involved. Maybe the family hoped the "witch" would reverse the witchcraft attack, but the young man died. During his funeral, women were sent away. Only a chosen group of men (family members) was allowed to proceed to the grave; they took along the said man and buried him alive next to the youth. A year earlier, two others had been killed as witches in the same village.

This killing did not find any public support. People understood it as an act of terror through which one family asserted its power over others. When one of them was bewitched, as they perceived it, the brutal killing of the "witch" sent out a strong message to others: "Don't cross us!" Many people blamed the absence of the *Boma* and of law-enforcement for such violence; the event provoked a call for stronger law-enforcement. The police (140 km away on terrible roads) moved in a few days after the event (other witch-killings in our parish did not provoke such a visit), and made people to exhume the body to enable a more appropriate burial. The police gave a beating (according to the narrative of people) to several persons who had nothing to do with the event, asked some questions to the distressed family, and disappeared again for good.

In the last ten years, this chieftaincy hosted the largest number of witchcraft-related mob killings, which many see as related not only to the isolation (inaccessible by vehicles during the rainy season) but also to the unclear authority structures on the ground. Chewa and Bisa royal families have been fighting for decades over the chieftaincy. The area then had no chief—the former chief had died; a new chief was not yet installed. Some scholars blame the Witchcraft Act for mob justice, arguing that people take the law into their own hands to deal with their witches, because they cannot do so through the courts. Here, however, the families who took the law into their own hands showed little willingness to submit the evaluation about witchcraft to any outside form of mediation. They knew who the witch was and how a witch is to be dealt with. They were not ready to be challenged in their opinion. And they could count on the absence of law-enforcement. When a new chief was installed, she asked the government for a police officer post as one of the most urgent needs of her country.

Violent witch-killings in our parish are not rare. The case that I have described outraged the community. Other cases, however, remained unreported because they happened in response to intra-family accusations. Others even found significant public support. In 2019, a young worker of a company that built communication towers in the area of our parish started to distribute traditional medicines, free of charge. "I am touched by the way people suffer, and just want to help." In every village, crowds of people (mostly women) frequented him. He teamed up with a local healer and slowly started to charge for his services. He also started now to discern witchcraft as the cause of people's affliction—always witchcraft of elderly family members. To remove charms in the homes of the elderly, he charged 1,500 Kwacha. In many houses, he found (or hid?) a charm and a snake. He seemed to have the support of the chief of that area, since some people were summoned to the palace for cleansing; he was hosted by the chief's niece, who reportedly also found him a young wife from the school children. Toward the end of the year, he killed three accused witches (all of them elderly men) at their homes by making them pass through a poison ordeal and drink "*mwavi*" (others called it, more appropriately, acid) that he administered before a mob who were cheering him on to use a larger cup; it took each person a whole week to die; at their burials, nobody was allowed to cry. I knew all three personally. One was Catholic. When I asked the Catholic community why nobody helped or intervened, I was told, "*Kabili banja*!"—"It was a family affair." People are afraid to get involved in other families' affairs, and the Catholic Church in our parish has not managed to develop a sense of community that dares to cross such family boundaries. Furthermore, the diviner found a lot of vocal support in the respective villages. "Now the witches will be afraid!" People who did not support the killings remained quiet or simply went to work in their fields. After some time, however, many expressed their shock and disagreement.

There is no police post (yet) in our large parish. If people want to call the police, they need to make a long and expensive trip to the *Boma*, unsure of the outcome. In the wake of the first two killings, the police came and summoned the diviner, but did not arrest him. I was told that he was merely obliged to buy a valid licence! After killing the third person, he boasted publicly that the police are on his side. The case (while I am writing) has yet not been concluded—many facts have not come out yet into the open. I am still hoping for a stronger response of the police. In the meantime, many other elderly men and women have paid large sums of money to the diviner (each 1,000 Kwacha) for not being forced to drink the "*mwavi.*"

What lesson can I draw from these gruesome cases? People find ways to open up interstitial spaces to deal with witchcraft, away from the law. The state (or its law-enforcing agents), in turn, can close its eyes and keep these interstitial spaces open to avoid confrontation on the issue of witchcraft, even in the face of massive violence. The police rightly cite the lack of transport, personnel, and other logistics as their main obstacle for law-enforcement. This, however, is a political issue. Law-enforcement against poaching does not know any such restrictions; people are taken to the book even for minor poaching offences—also in our most remote areas and even during the rainy season. Wildlife is an important economic resource for Zambia and its protection is supported by large international donor communities. Marginalized "witches" are not.

Case 3: Riots against a *kamnyama*

In March 2019, we experienced a riot: The shop of an upcoming businessman was looted by an enraged crowd and then burnt down together with his house. The rioting and looting occurred when an albino proclaimed that he had escaped an abduction by the said businessman, alleging that he is a *kamnyama* who wanted to sell him to be sacrificed in Nakonde (2,000 km away by road, on the border with Tanzania). Prior to this, rumors were going around that "boys in Lundazi" (the nearest town), when washing his car, discovered in it the ghost of his late brother. "He must have sacrificed his own brother to get a car!" Some disliked the businessman because he refused to give lifts in his car. Also, some quarrels with other business people had preceded the looting.

The narrative about the alleged abduction had many gaps. In other circumstances, the testimony of the man affected by albinism would not have had much weight; he was infamous for his continuous search for beer and no longer able to work, which made him vulnerable and dependent.

But during the riot, the whole community seemed to rally in support of *their* albino against the businessman. In our area, close to Malawi, the threat to albinos is real. A year earlier, an albino girl in secondary school north of our parish (in Chikwa, 120 km away) had escaped a cruel death in an attack in which her arm was cut off. A teacher was involved. A short time later, in a secondary school in our parish, a riot broke out against two other teachers involved in business: they were called *bakamnyama* and had to be transferred to another school under police protection; the school was downgraded because of a lack of teachers willing to come to the area.

But it was not the Chikwa incident that brought the talk about ritual killings to our parish. Already before, the shocking ritual killings in Lusaka (for example in Zingalume and George compounds) and elsewhere in Zambia were widely discussed. Excited women proclaimed many times, "Don't think the *kamnyamas* are far in Lusaka. They are right here among us!" In 2017, we had to intervene when another businessman was accused to be "the director of the *kamnyamas*" in local gossip in which Catholics were involved; the incident ended in a public apology at church, which the businessman accepted, and which calmed the situation. People almost *wanted to believe* in the imminent threat of *kamnyamas*. Was the concept (known since colonial times) "good to think with," as Claude Lévi-Strauss might have said? Good to think about what? When Louise White wrote about *banyama* stories of colonial times, she wanted to give back people's historical experiences through these stories.[26] She looked at them in relation to people's experiences with extracting wage labor, commodification, and money—defying somehow her own premise of taking them serious as descriptions, in the mind of the storytellers, of actual and not of symbolic happenings. Yet where "the real and the unreal become indistinguishable of each other" (according to Gilles Deleuze's apt understanding of the imagination), certain elements of a narrative gain self-evidence in certain life-situations but may be dismissed in others.

Many motives play into rioting: the thrill of excitement, jealousy about successful business people, the need to find scapegoats for personal and common frustrations, fear of foreign powers, and also greed for looting. I believe people representing "the community" wanted to assert their power over that of the upcoming businessman and also the established business community. The story had to be true; people almost wanted it to be true. The chief lived just 500 meters away but was powerless to intervene. The new narrative of a *kamnyama* in the community almost gave the mob permission to loot: Society was out of order. In Durkheim's

26 Luise White, *Speaking with Vampires* (Los Angeles, CA: University of California Press, 2000).

sense, the act of lawlessness provoked the re-establishment of order with new sensitivities. The *kamnyama* story confirmed the hidden existence of witchcraft in their midst but also opened up a way of dealing with it. Our area was graced by a visit of the police in response to the riot—a rare event; the businessman was held for some time in police custody but was then released. He cannot return to his home. Rumors about him have not come to an end. "He works with other *bakamnyama* and is planning to abduct children from this area." Various "neighborhood watch groups" organized trips of men with machetes, axes, and even guns to look for unknown *kamnyamas* who may be hiding somewhere in the bush—a vain search that nevertheless clothed the vigilante groups with a new sense of authority and legitimacy to police the community.

Having our own *kamnyamas* makes our isolated area of Lumimba part of a national discourse and outcry in response to ritual killings. *Kamnyama* stories deal with people who went missing on specific properties, dumped bodies with missing breasts, genitals, hearts, lips, possibly extracted while the victims were alive—gruesome acts that, when they happen, leave behind an empirical trail that can be investigated. The political dimension had the potential to undermine trust and destabilize the nation if left to themselves.

Apart from the cruelty that cries out for a public reaction, I see also another reason for the enormous political potential of the *kamnyama* murders, compared to other murders in Zambia: As much as people believe in witchcraft and know that witchcraft is present in their midst, they also long for strong means of corroboration. Witchcraft is ever evasive and cannot be tackled through the official courts. Ritual killings can. If witchcraft is there, the *kamnyamas* cannot be far. The police's ability to bring the culprits of ritual crime to book and people's beliefs in the presence of witchcraft meet in the *kamnyama* stories. Riots therefore have often been directed against the police, when people feared that the culprits could buy their way out.

Our local riot would not have taken place without the national awareness and panic about *bakamnyama*. The dynamics, however, showed an assertion of "community power," not against the state, but against the said businessman, and as a warning to the business community and local authorities that "we will not tolerate *bakamnyama* here!"

Case 4: Satanism

In Lumimba, people had heard for a long time about Satanism elsewhere in the country, and there was quite some excitement when it also reached our rural set-up through the schools. Satanism did not arrive out of nowhere. Spiritual perils have always plagued our local boarding school, both boys and girls, also prior to the new world of Satanism: every year some students experienced witchcraft attacks (sometimes related to events at home) but also attacks and "abductions" by various spirits. From time to time, a student was found in the bush in a confused state, while others went through psychotic states or exhibited other strong signs of being controlled by other forces. They were usually prayed over in our or in another nearby church, or they visited traditional healers, often urged on by their families. Sometimes such attacks ceased, while at other times students did not come back to school. When a large group of Catholic Charismatics from Chipata made an evangelization campaign in our area, in the course of which "many demons manifested," one student revealed that she had been initiated into Satanism in our school. The prayers of the Charismatics were praised by many beyond the Catholic community, maybe because they revealed that witchcraft and spirits were evidently plaguing the community, which people found acknowledged and addressed in the prayers. But we also heard critical voices. Some alleged that the Charismatics had come with their own demons ("We did not have these demons before!") and the chief asked me—not without a sense of irony—if some of them were not Satanists themselves.

The next step toward the arrival of Satanism came through testimonies of delivered Satanists recorded elsewhere in Zambia that students shared with each other on their phones. Some students urged others to pray vigorously, especially during specific times of the night, to battle these dangers. In 2017, a girl who had been expelled as a Satanist from another school arrived in our local school. It did not take long for her to be feared by many girls in the dormitory, also for her habit of sleep-walking during which she sometimes dressed up strangely. Students in the dormitory prayed over her, but she did not respond to the prayers. She had no friends and looked out of place. Soon she was evicted from the dorm; later she also left the school. During this episode, some girls in the dorm had weird dreams and felt being strangled at night by unseen people. Nights now became marked by extensive prayers, during which Satan was bound, rejected, and "trampled upon," which the school authorities (advised also by us) eventually stopped. The nights had become controlled by the prayer warriors. I blessed the dormitory and addressed the students several times in my efforts to diffuse the situation, but my blessings did not stop the issue of Satanism from simmering underneath daily life of the school.

In early 2019, some charismatic students of the school, unsupervised, prayed over a number of pupils during the Sunday evening prayers of Scripture Union. Two girls collapsed into a trance, crawled like snakes, "manifested Satanism," and, when being questioned, insisted that people did well to fear them: "We kill!" They reviled the prayers of the prayer warriors, boasting they were aided and controlled by several unseen companions from the underworld. Both girls then stopped talking and did not respond any longer to questions. For a week, they remained quasi dumb and refused prayers with the other girls. When these girls challenged them, one mentioned she had already sacrificed a boy by pointing at him with her finger, "in which I have five demons. He will be dead tomorrow!" The girls in the dorm wanted them expelled; the school administration wanted to send them home to be sorted out by their families. Their mothers, however, approached us priests for help and blamed the school: "In our families, there are no *mizimu* (spirits). Such manifestations have never happened at home. The problem is not with us, but with the school!"

I leave aside here the outcome of my talks with the girls. Important for my argument is the question of who was seen capable of dealing with Satanism. Satanism evolved parallel to the establishment of prayer warriors among the students whom many saw as empowered by God to deal with this new threat. When I asked the respective girls how we could help them, both asked for prayers for which they requested also that of the "prayer warriors." Satanism in Lumimba is rooted in a Christian discourse and linked to specific charisma to handle it. After our common prayers, the issue cooled down.

Interestingly, Satanism did not subsume all other spiritual perils of students in the school. Soon after the event, a boy started to see snakes around him and for days could only stutter. The school authorities brought him to us priests for prayers, which, we hope, were helpful to him. He and his friends in school did not associate his condition with Satanism but with witchcraft in his family. Satanism did not gain a monopoly over spiritual afflictions, not even in the school.

Satanism (like *kamnyama*) can mean many things; here, I am not looking at secret societies that are labelled satanic or at satanic churches from the Western world. I look at how Satanism became known in Zambia through testimonies of delivered and self-confessed Satanists in church or during prayers, most of them from youths and young adults, but also from children. In Lumimba school, Christian prayer warriors appropriated the images of these recorded testimonies. Testifying Satanists portrayed themselves as revealing the real reasons, spiritual reasons, for Zambia's calamities (accidents, deaths, unproportioned wealth) beyond those that can be perceived with ordinary eyes; in doing so, they met the expectations of the audiences. They testified to having committed horrible atrocities as part of a widespan line of command: killing ("sacrificing") family members, causing deadly accidents, drinking blood, or using aborted fetuses to produce satanic items "under the ocean" to initiate others. Christian audiences sought evidence for the truth of these narratives not from corroboration with independent investigations but from the behavior of the girls and boys during the process of deliverance, which in many cases can only be described as stunning and stirring performances ("performance" not in the sense of faking something, but in the dramaturgical sense of revealing or portraying). Sometimes, girls and boys who had long been "delivered" could fall back into trance while testifying, as if to give additional proof of the truth of their testimony.[27]

Satanism provides a powerful contrast to the *kamnyama* stories. Both are part of a national moral discourse and provide graphical details of the evasive world of witchcraft. But there is a fundamental difference: Unlike *kamnyama* events, powerful Christian pastors deal with Satanism and its victims, not the police. I have witnessed elsewhere testimonies of "delivered Satanists" before church audiences of more than a thousand people that included also police officers and lawyers, but nobody ever prosecuted the "delivered Satanists" for the "human sacrifices" that they confessed to in graphic detail; the testimonies were clearly recognized as belonging to a spiritual realm of concern with which certain pastors and Christian churches can deal, but not the police or the courts, and not even traditional healers.[28]

In Lumimba, Satanism is a problem in secondary school, which is a state institution (and in our case also a church institution) seen to equip children for the wider world, at a high financial cost for the parents. Satanism itself is a force that is seen as foreign and global. But is Satanism also an implicit critique of the state or the government, as scholars ascertained for the healing ministry of Archbishop Milingo in the early 1980s? For sure, many people in Zambia across class and gender associate Satanism with national moral decline. However, blame does not evidently go in the direction of the government or the state. Some pastors who deliver Satanists clearly support the present government as the God-given authority to rule Zambia.[29] In Lumimba, people associated Satanism with

[27] See Johanneke Kamps, *Speaking of Satan in Zambia: The Persuasiveness of Contemporary Narratives about Satanism* (PhD diss., Utrecht, *Quaestiones Infinitae*, Volume CVIII, 2018) about the interplay of testimonies with the delivering pastors.

[28] Where cases of Satanism went to court, it was often about "defamation of character." They had, in their testimonies, implicated other known people: pastors, politicians, business people, or teachers, who wanted their names to be cleared.

[29] I have looked elsewhere at the question how Schoffeleers' contested notion of political acquiescence of ritual healing in Africa applies to many deliverance ministries. Bernhard Udelhoven, "Health & Abundant Life: Catholic Healing Amidst a Plurality of Healing Paradigms in Africa," in *Handbook of the Catholic Church in Africa*, ed. Elizabeth A. Foster (Chicago: Notre-Dame Press, forthcoming).

the approaching "end times," for which one can hardly blame the government. The "end times" metaphor in Lumimba does not give rise to millennialism with a call for a new society and a reversed power structure as historians described it for the early Watchtowers in colonial times. The end times explain present-day spiritual confusions and moral decline, but otherwise people in Lumimba live and order their lives in the same way as before. Satanism is a new spiritual affliction, but one with a solution: Christian prayer, which is also seen as supporting the Zambian state.

Discussion: Witchcraft and the (de-)Legitimization of Authority in a Rural Community

Each case study came with its own symbolic world in which the crisis was felt and addressed. State and church were temporarily eclipsed from that world (case 1 and 2) or they were seen as part of the solution (the state in case 3 and the church in case 4).

In the first two case studies, people carved out for themselves an interstitial space in which they sought to address their problem away from the state; they dealt with local notions of witchcraft with which they felt familiar and for which they had their own solutions (cleansing or killing). The state was seen as irrelevant and distant from these problems. But witchcraft in their midst did not constitute a crisis with the state but with each other. Instead of welding people together into a "moral community" of shared beliefs and values ("witchcraft needs to be prosecuted"), the outcome divided the community and did not bring any end to witchcraft. With Wilson, we may say that the witch is the common nightmare of people in Lumimba parish—nearly everybody believes in the existence, presence, and threat of the witch as long as it is the "witch-in-general." Once it comes to a concrete person, the community is no longer united (unless the person has completely fallen out with their family or makes too many credible allusions to their sinister abilities). Factions, temporal coalitions, and power struggles appear with outcomes that are difficult to predict.

The last two case studies need to be understood in a more direct link to people's national awareness. They regard both *bakamnyama* and Satanism as indices for the moral erosion of Zambian society. In many churches, also in Lumimba, these notions stimulated prayers asking for God's direct intervention in the nation. They provide an interesting contrast, if I am here allowed to eclipse the fact that all notions of the occult partly overlap. *Kamnyama* events often provoked a crisis to official law-enforcement (especially to the police if seen as failing to act) but Satanism did the same to specific expressions of the Christian faith. The state stands to some degree beyond de-legitimization in Lumimba since people long for an end to their national isolation—other areas in Zambia may show very different dynamics. But the cases demonstrate that legitimization of the state is not a static state of mind but a process that is negotiated through many different events in the grey zones.

Determining the right authorities in each case was a product of internal struggles, among different options. Whether the church or state were active poles of reference in people's symbolic world or whether they were simply eclipsed depended on the notions of witchcraft that were discerned and on people's previous experiences. It is also obvious that the state and church do not merge in Lumimba to give with the Christian nation discourse a compelling Christian answer to witchcraft. In other areas in Zambia, Christianity may have a stronger impact than in Lumimba, but nowhere does it have a monopoly on the understanding of the occult. I want to close this reflection by drawing out consequences for discussions on the Zambian "Witchcraft Act."

Epilogue: Revisiting the Witchcraft Act?

The view that an African government that cannot deal with witchcraft becomes delegitimized to its people who believe in witchcraft has fueled a campaign to legalize the dealing with witchcraft and hence with witches. Rowlands and Warnier considered the move by courts in Eastern Cameroon to allow diviners as expert witnesses in the magistrate courts as "politically ... the right move since the state is more and more clearly perceived as siding (however clumsily) with the people against sorcery instead of the reverse."[30] John Hund, from a South African perspective, regarded the denial of witchcraft in the colonial and postcolonial Witchcraft Acts as a Western ethnocentric phenomenon that still suppresses the African sense of justice; he calls for acknowledged healers (in his case Sangomas) to be recognized and employed as experts in the fight against witchcraft, the only way, for him, to make courts compatible with people's own morality.[31] In Zambia, some traditional healers have claimed they could deal with witchcraft in a satisfactory way if they were but allowed by the law.[32] Zambia's postcolonial governments, through several revisions, have basically upheld the colonial Witchcraft Act.

Owen Sichone argued for witchcraft cases to be dealt with in the local courts under customary law and for denying the higher courts to intervene with the Witchcraft Act. Appeals to witchcraft elevate an existential

30 Rowlands and Warnier, "Sorcery, Power and the Modern State," 129.

31 John Hund, "Witchcraft and Accusations of Witchcraft in South Africa: Ontological Denial and the Suppression of African Justice," *The Comparative and International Law Journal of Southern Africa* 33, no. 3 (2000): 366–389.

32 Interview with Rodrick Vongo, Chairperson of the Traditional Health Practitioners' Association of Zambia (THPAZ).

private concern to the public level, forcing a public recognition, a public debate, and a response. "A common belief in the occult as antisocial behavior and the use of witchcraft accusations to bring matters into the open operates in all spheres of Zambian life."[33] In customary law, a response that recognizes the forces of witchcraft often aims at solving a tension. Within the context of the specific tension, the witchcraft accusations and also witchcraft confessions make sense and gather their momentum. Once the tension is resolved, witchcraft accusations may fade away. Otherwise, the divided parties move away from each other, which is another way of restoring peace. Sichone presents a view in which the magistrate courts and police, in league with the historical mission churches (specifically the Catholic Church), by denying the existence of witchcraft, stifle local solutions to people's social problems. He argues that this has robbed the poor, who believe in witchcraft, of possibilities and solutions to address their concerns together with the social tensions they find themselves in.

However, some cures and solutions have devastating consequences on others. Sichone is correct to stress that the denial of witchcraft by the state and the historical mission churches (nearly always!) went hand in hand with brushing over the calamity of social conflict and existential religious crisis, robbing people of a chance to "shake up" and reorder social relationships. I agree with Sichone that no person should be harassed by the law because they experience witchcraft attacks or speak about them. But where the witch is identified through rumor, a dream, an inner experience, or confirmed through divination, we should have crossed the red line of the law. Divination and spectral evidence cannot prove guilt in a pluralistic society. I believe that churches and traditional healers should be able to offer help to people afflicted by witchcraft without blaming third parties for the afflicted persons' misfortunes.[34] And, (this is the more difficult part of any "deliverance ministry") they should not neglect the challenge of dealing with the social tensions and crisis that accompany witchcraft experiences. If both aspects are addressed, I believe we have done justice to Sichone's concerns.

I want to disagree, however, with Sichone's view that the enforcement of the Witchcraft Act supports the rich and marginalizes the poor in rural areas. The poor are as often accused and convicted of witchcraft as the rich. They are often also poorly connected. The better integrated people, as well as those of a strong, united family, more easily find their way out

[33] Owen Sichone, "Discourses of the Occult in Local Power Struggles in Rural Zambia," in *The Power of the Occult in Modern Africa: Continuity and Innovation in the Renewal of African Cosmologies*, ed. James Kiernan (Berlin: Lit-Verlag, 2006), 115.

[34] I have tried to formulate such a way in *Unseen Worlds.*

of the labyrinth of local gossip and also of the diviners' discourses, which themselves are not always stable but prone to change with ongoing events and manipulations. They are more able to influence public opinion.

But I want to engage with Sichone's argument on another level. He analyzes the effects of witchcraft (its practice and its cure) under the idiom of *kupanda wanga* (the making of a charm), which is its specialized, instrumental, and ingenious aspect. His analysis links up well with the classical study of Evans Pritchard about witchcraft among the Azande,[35] and also with Claude Lévi-Strauss' notion of bricolage: Witchcraft (in its practices and counter-practices) is not the subject of a theoretical discourse but is part of a problem-solving strategy.

> The knowledge that is involved in both projecting harm and in the reversing of such misfortune is not occult in the mysterious sense of the term but comprises specialised knowledge available to those who seek it. The method by which wild honey, words of wisdom, and the power of the occult (*wanga*) are obtained is referred to as *kupanda*, which can be summed up as seek and find.[36]

I believe this view needs to be supplemented with another set of dynamics inherent in witchcraft discourses, that create boundaries of exclusion. As Sichone says, a person may produce a charm in order to instrumentalize occult powers (*kupanda ubwanga* in Chibemba), but when used against people, we speak of *kulowa* (bewitching) and of a witch (*indoshi*): People see an intimate connection between the force of witchcraft and the employer of the harmful charm as well as the victim. Diviners do not just defuse charms; they also cleanse the witch and often also the victim. "Crash-landed witches" in Zambia are beaten or killed, but they are not questioned about the technological/instrumental aspect of this widely acknowledged means of transport. The presence of witchcraft makes *kupanda ubwanga* a moral discourse, different from *kupanda ubuchi* (the ingenious art of extracting of honey guarded by vicious bees) or *kupanda amano* (the art of advising, helping a person to find a solution to their problem) with which Sichone compares the notion of witchcraft. The identification of witchcraft creates boundaries between those who are acknowledged "to see" (diviners, healers, Christian prophets, the institutions through which they work), and those who don't and who are relegated to the outside of the discernment process. But, even rural areas host pluralistic beliefs about witchcraft (including disbelief!) and about the right (and wrong!) ritual authorities to deal with it (traditional healer? Christian pastor? And will the latter also judge Muslims?) The state, the

[35] Edward Evan Evans-Pritchard, *Witchcraft, Oracles, and Magic Among the Azande* (Oxford: The Clarendon Press, 1937).

[36] Sichone, "Discourses of the Occult," 124.

law, or the local community will always have an unbalancing and intrusive effect if they privilege one way of divination over others.

The Zambian Witchcraft Act is very clumsy and defines witchcraft in a circular way. It could surely be formulated in a clearer and less ambiguous way. The application of the law becomes also ambivalent because, in Christian Zambia, prophets, pastors, and prayer groups have often taken the place of traditional diviners in identifying witchcraft, witches, and Satanism. This new situation is hardly envisaged by the Witchcraft Act that still looks at divination in the form of "throwing bones" and "boiling water tests." But arguments that build on the idea that witchcraft beliefs are at the basis of a common moral code and a common sense of justice (Hund) gloss over the different alliances that form themselves in witchcraft disputes, each seeking support also from powers outside the "community." Many diviners and healers themselves have to struggle not to be identified with witchcraft: knowing much about witchcraft makes a person liable to become a witch oneself. The resulting contradictions in principles of law and the consequences of law pluralism on governance have been forcefully drawn out by Erdmude Alber.[37] In other countries, the licensing of diviners to identify witchcraft and witches or allowing them as expert witnesses in court, has not always brought the magistrate courts closer to people's sense of justice: Cases continued to be contested or gave rise to new accusations, licensed diviners were seen to be corrupt (as much as the licensing government or the local chief), convictions were regarded as politically motivated or could fail to link up with local sentiments because witchcraft meant different things to different people.[38]

There is no need for the law to deny the forces of witchcraft, nor to affirm them. Like other religious truths, they permeate into all areas of life but cannot be proven or disproven. Since witchcraft is never a purely mystical force but always also needs one foot in the empirical world that is accessible in principle to all (as the "ritual killings" show), the law can concentrate on that aspect. The Catholic Church knows of a very useful distinction between "inner and outer forum," which separates confidential

37 Erdmute Alber, "Hexerei, Selbstjustiz Und Rechtspluralismus in Benin (Wichcraft, Self-Justice, and Pluralism of Law in Benin)," *Africa Spectrum* 36, no. 2 (2001): 145–167.

38 For Cameroon, see Cyprian F. Fisiy and Peter Geschiere, "Judges and Witches, or How Is the State to Deal with Witchcraft? Examples from Southeast Cameroon," *Cahiers D'Études Africaines* 30, no. 118 (1990): 135–56; For Sierra Leone, see Rosalinde Shaw, "The Production of Witchcraft/Witchcraft as Production: Memory, Modernity, and the Slave Trade in Sierra Leone," *American Ethnologist* 24, no. 4 (1997): 856–76; For Tanzania, see Maia Green, "Witchcraft Suppression Practices and Movements: Public Politics and the Logic of Purification," *Comparative Studies in Society and History* 39, no. 2 (1997): 319–45.

issues of pastoral counselling (where witchcraft experiences can be acknowledged) from tensions or injustices that need to be addressed publicly, and this distinction can be employed fruitfully in interventions in witchcraft disputes. Outlawing all attempts in the public sphere of linking witchcraft to a concrete person (be it by traditional healers or Christian prophets) is still the path that promises justice to all—even to those outside the "privileged population" (Foucault) of those speaking on behalf of the "moral community." At the same time, the law does well also to outlaw the practice of harmful witchcraft, even if it has to acknowledge its inability to prove and prosecute its practice. It is able, however, to focus on and prosecute those empirical elements that people associate with witchcraft and that disturb their religious and moral sensitivities, like verbal or dramaturgical threats of witchcraft and of course "ritual crime." And that is what the present Witchcraft Act, in all its clumsiness, does.

11

RELIGION, SATANIC ACCUSATIONS, AND POLITICS

Johanneke Kroesbergen-Kamps

Introduction

In contemporary Zambia, the threat of Satan and Satanism is everywhere in schools, in hospitals, on the roads, in the markets, and even in churches. Satanists are said to cause illness and death, to sell blood and organs, to cause road accidents, and to try to get one in their thrall by selling them seemingly innocent satanic products. Satanism is portrayed as an organization of evil in which people can be initiated knowingly and unknowingly, willingly, and unwillingly. This organization is believed to operate in an underground world, which can be accessed during the nights through dreams. Once initiated, the Satanists are assigned to cause chaos and slay people. Satanists operate through road accidents, fatal diseases like AIDS, and unexplained deaths in hospitals. Sacrificing people allegedly brings rewards like money, success in business, a house, a car, and an advancement in the ranks of evil.

Satanism is not a phenomenon that has a long history in Africa. The first narratives about Satanism surfaced in the 1980s, and by the 1990s, it was a known phenomenon in Zambia, too. The history of Satanism in Zambia is closely intertwined with that of Christianity. Early missionaries introduced the concept of the devil or Satan in African worldviews, and linked the African spiritual world to its evil kingdom. For the classical mission churches, Satan's evil was mostly an internal affair of doubts and transgressing desires. In the African worldview, however, harm and misfortune come from outside, the spiritual world. Churches like the classical African Initiated churches and newer neo-pentecostal churches, who acknowledged the existence of these forces and could offer protection and deliverance have, historically, done well. Within the neo-pentecostal churches' spiritual warfare theology, the struggle that rages between God and Satan in the world and in history is emphasized. Narratives about Satanism, and especially the testimonies that ex-Satanists give in Zambian churches, cannot be understood without this framework of neo-pentecostal theology.[1]

Some people, mostly adolescent women, confess in churches about their past as Satanists. In rumors and gossip shared through *radio trottoir*, others are evaluated: Could that businessman's success depend on his involvement in Satanism? Was this politician elected because he sacrificed the life of an innocent? A famous aphorism in sociology holds that "if men define situations as real, they are real in their consequences."[2] Rumor can be defined as an expression of belief, passed along from person to person, about an event that is supposed to have happened or is about to happen.[3] Rumors are described as "beliefs" or as "unsubstantiated," meaning that they lack secure standards of evidence. A defining feature of rumors is that the truth claims they bring forward are uncertain—if there were no doubt about their veracity, we would not label a statement or a narrative as "rumor."[4] It may be unclear what the origin is of a rumor,

1 For a more extensive overview of the historical roots of the phenomenon of Satanism in Zambia, see Johanneke Kamps, "Speaking of Satan in Zambia: The Persuasiveness of Contemporary Narratives about Satanism," PhD diss., Utrecht University, 2018.

2 See Thomas, William I. & Dorothy Swain Thomas, *The Child in America. Behavior Problems and Programs* (New York: Alfred A. Knopf, 1928), 572.

3 For a discussion of definitions of rumor, see, for example, Patricia A. Turner, *I Heard It Through the Grapevine. Rumor in African-American Culture* (Berkeley: University of California Press, 1993), 1; Gary Alan Fine & Patricia Turner, *Whispers on the Color Line. Rumor and Race in America* (Berkeley, CA: University of California Press, 2004), 4.

4 Rumor, legend, gossip, and accusation are categories that blend into each other. Both rumors and legends are narratives that repeat or presuppose traditional themes, like well-known stereotypes and other forms of cultural knowledge, as well as addressing contemporary issues. They are often shared from one person to another by word of mouth, and they lack secure standards of evidence. Gossip is another concept closely related to, but subtly distinct from, rumor. Like rumors and legends, gossip entails sharing information among people in networks or groups. This information may be speculative, although gossip can be based on known facts as well. Gossip can have a malicious character, if the person about whom the gossipers are talking is evaluated negatively. While the person who others gossip about is generally not present during an exchange of gossip, they are known to the participants in the conversation. In general, rumors are shared in wider, often transnational, networks than gossip, and the subjects referred to in a rumor are not personal acquaintances of those who share the rumor. Accusationsclaims that someone has committed a fault or a crime—may be part

and its truthfulness may be doubted, but if rumors are believed, they are likely to inspire action. This action can vary from spreading the rumor further to perpetrating violence against persons or property.[5] In fact, riots and violence are almost always "preceded by rumor, fueled by rumor, and then interpreted by rumor."[6] In this sense, some rumors have real and momentous consequences. Rumors are often seen as indicators of latent conflict in a community—they "constitute a powerful warning of impending trouble."[7]

Sometimes, accusations of involvement in Satanism, for example, made against new churches or local businessmen, lead to violence.[8] Although most rumors do not lead to violence, they can disturb everyday life. A growing body of academic literature describes the unwillingness of Zambians to take part in medical trials because they fear that their blood will be used in rituals and they will be initiated into Satanism by participating.[9] Since a Member of Parliament in 2011 during a church service confessed to having been a Satanist,[10] he was sacked. Shortly after that, rumors about satanic politicians have become common. Both the ruling party, the Patriotic Front (PF), and the most vocal opposition leader,

---

of all three of the discussed categories. Because the categories of rumor, legends, and gossip overlap and merge into each other, I use rumor as an overarching term.

5 See Gary Alan Fine and Bill Ellis, *The Global Grapevine. Why Rumors of Terrorism, Immigration, and Trade Matter* (Oxford: Oxford University Press, 2010), 6.

6 Fine and Turner, *Whispers on the Color Line*, 24.

7 Turner, *I Heard It*, 46.

8 Johanneke Kroesbergen-Kamps, "Accusations of Satanism in the Public Sphere," in *Christian Identity and Justice in a Globalized World from a Southern African Perspective*, ed. Hermen Kroesbergen (Wellington, SA: CLF, 2014), 148–162.

9 See P.W. Geisler & R. Pool, "Popular Concerns about Medical Research Projects in Sub-Saharan Africa—A Critical Voice in Debates about Medical Research Ethics," *Tropical Medicine and International Health* 11, no. 7 (2006): 975–982; Lynette Louise Schumaker & Virginia Bond, "Antiretroviral Therapy in Zambia. Colours, 'Spoiling', 'Talk' and the Meaning of Antiretrovirals," *Social Science and Medicine* 67 (2008): 2126–2134; Maurice Musheke, Virginia Bond & Sonja Merten, "Individual and Contextual Factors Influencing Patient Attrition from Antiretroviral Therapy Care in an Urban Community of Lusaka, Zambia," *Journal of the International AIDS Society* 15, no. 1 (2012); https://onlinelibrary.wiley.com/doi/full/10.7448/IAS.15.3.17366; Koen Peeters Grietens, Joan Muela Ribera, Annette Erhart, Sarah Hoibak, Raffaella M. Ravinetto, Charlotte Gryseels, Susan Dierickx, Sarah O'Neill, Susanna Hausmann Muela, and Umberto D'Alessandro, "Doctors and Vampires in Sub-Saharan Africa. Ethical Challenges in Clinical Trial Research," *American Journal of Tropical Medicine and Hygiene* 91, no. 2 (2014): 213–215.

10 *Zambia Watchdog*, "Southern Province Minister Confesses to Practising Satanism," accessed September 12, 2019, https://www.zambiawatchdog.com/southern-province-minister-confesses-to-practising-satanism/.

Hakainde Hichilema, from the United Party for National Development (UPND), have been associated with Satanism in the press by adherents of the opposing party. Rumors of Satanism also often spread in schools, sometimes leading to suspension of classes and dismissal or relocation of teachers.[11]

Methodology

Some of the rumors about Satanism make it to the newspapers. To assess the extent and role of accusations of Satanism in the Zambian media, I have conducted a survey of articles about Satanism. According to this survey of accusations of Satanism in the media between 2011 and 2016, politicians, teachers, businessmen, pastors, and government officials are the most accused. Of course, such a survey is subjective. Newspaper articles about rumors are not representative of all rumors about Satanism shared in Zambia. In general, only rumors with newsworthy effects, such as court cases or riots, or about persons who are themselves newsworthy such as politicians or musicians are mentioned in the media. This media filter leads to a disproportionate attention toward the most dramatic cases, and gives no indication about how often accusations are really made.[12] However, the survey of accusations of Satanism in Zambian newspapers gives an idea of the rumors that are, because of the attention they receive, the most influential, or the most severe in their consequences.

In eighty news articles, published between 2011—when I arrived in Zambia—and August 2016, the word Satanism or its cognates Satanist and satanic are found. This sample does not include articles that express the opinion of the author, like editorials, columns, or letters to the editor. I have selected only articles containing an explicit or implicit accusation of Satanism. This means that articles in which, for example, a bishop warns against Satanism in general, or about a witch-finder who can recognize Satanists, were also omitted from the sample. If the same article appeared in multiple news media, I have selected only one. The footnotes in this article give the corresponding links. Since the completion of this analysis, one of the main newspapers in Zambia, *The Post*, has been banned. Its online archive is no longer accessible, and the links therefore do not work anymore.

In these eighty articles, the accused can be divided into five categories: politicians (28 percent); businessmen and teachers (25 percent); pastors and churches (23 percent); development projects (10 percent); and others

[11] See Bernhard Udelhoven, *Unseen Worlds. Dealing with Spirits, Witchcraft, and Satanism* (Lusaka: FENZA Publications, 2015), 319–336.

[12] See Julien Bonhomme, *The Sex Thieves. The Anthropology of a Rumor* (Chicago: Hau Books, 2016), 6.

(14 percent).[13] In this chapter, my focus is on the politicians, who make up the biggest share of the accusations in the sample. The first part of the chapter takes a close look at the accusations and discusses their role in the political climate surrounding the death of President Michael Sata. In the second part, I place the accusations of Satanism against politicians in contemporary Zambia in a historical perspective, and discuss to what extent current accusations are different from rumors.

Accusations of Satanism against Politicians in Zambia

Of the eighty articles in which Satanism is mentioned, 28 percent are related to politicians. These accusations are rarely related to specific events but are made in a political context, by fellow politicians or by newspapers with a vested interest in a particular political party. Because the accusations do not refer to actual circumstances, they cannot be linked to either rural or urban contexts. In twenty of the twenty-two newspaper articles, a specific politician or political party is accused of being involved with Satanism.[14] Both the current ruling party, Patriotic Front (PF), and the main opposition party, United Party for National Development (UPND) and its leader Hakainde Hichilema, are linked to Satanism: eight articles refer to the PF, twelve to the UPND or Hakainde Hichilema. Since 1991, Zambia has been governed as a multi-party democracy. In the first multi-party elections, the Movement for Multiparty Democracy (MMD) won a landslide victory, and the party stayed in power until 2011. The below table gives an overview of the elections since 1991.

Year of election	Winner
1991	Movement for Multi-Party Democracy (MMD), Frederick Chiluba
1996	MMD, Frederick Chiluba
2001	MMD, Levy Mwanawasa
2006	MMD, Levy Mwanawasa
2008, presidential by-election	MMD, Rupiah Banda
2011	Patriotic Front (PF), Michael Sata
2015, presidential by-election	PF, Edgar Lungu
2016	PF, Edgar Lungu

13 Kamps, "Speaking of Satan in Zambia."

14 The remaining two articles are about the National Day of Prayer and Fasting held in 2015. Rumors linked the date of this day, October 18, to the number of the Beast mentioned in Revelations: 18 = 6+6+6 → 666. Implicitly, these accuse the president or his party, because he instated such a day.

The elections in August 2011 brought victory for the PF and its leader Michael Sata. In October 2014, only four days after Zambia celebrated 50 years of independence, Michael Sata died, an event that set-in motion a struggle for power within the PF. Edgar Lungu secured the leadership position and won the presidential by-elections in January 2015 with a small margin over UPND's Hakainde Hichilema. The elections in August 2016 were hotly contested, but again showed a narrow victory for Edgar Lungu and the PF. Accusations of Satanism toward politicians should be read in the light of this political context. In the following, I will discuss accusations made against Hakainde Hichilema and the UPND, and then accusations against the ruling party PF.

The most widely published accusations were against Hakainde Hichilema. In December 2014, after the death of Michael Sata and before the presidential by-elections in January 2015, Edward Chomba, a former bishop in the Holy Christian Orthodox Church, accused Hichilema of being a Freemason and therefore a Satanist who would devour babies after his election. The accusation was made at a PF rally in Kitwe. Acting President Guy Scott of the PF immediately apologized for this statement, saying (in his characteristic off-hand way),

> Allow me to wholeheartedly and unqualifiedly offer the apology of the PF leadership to Hakainde Hichilema and anybody else who by implication was accused of eating babies and drinking blood and so on and for forth [*sic*] by a certain bogus Bishop who forced himself on stage [...] Like I said, we apologise wholeheartedly, we don't want a campaign based on taking advantage of people's ignorance and superstitions, we want a campaign based on development, education, and health and democracy. So please take that as one hundred percent position of the PF.[15]

Hichilema sued Chomba and the PF for defamation. All main newspapers reported about these events, although none seemed to have followed the defamation case to its end. Despite Guy Scott's plea for a campaign that is based on issues rather than accusations, the connection between Hichilema and Satanism was heard over and over. During the campaigns for the elections in 2016, the association between Hichilema, the UPND, and Satanism was brought up again, especially in rumors on the streets and in comments on newspaper articles and Facebook posts. Newspapers in 2016 mainly published repudiations of the claim,[16] in which the UPND

---

15 Quote from *Lusaka Times*, December 23, 2014, accessed September 12, 2019, https://www.lusakatimes.com/2014/12/23/dr-scott-disowns-bishop-chomba-apologies-hh-satanism-remark/.

16 See *The Post*, June 12, 2016, accessed September 12, 2019, http://www.postzambia.com/news.php?id=18667; and *The Daily Nation*, April 1, 2016,

advised voters not to accuse others of Satanism,[17] and protested against banners used at a PF rally that read "Reject HH the Satanist."[18]

In these accusations against Hakainde Hichilema, Satanism is mentioned because of Hichilema's alleged membership in the Freemasons. In Europe, lodges of operative masons or builders, are known from the twelfth century onward.[19] In the first centuries, these groups of craftsmen operated as guilds, providing training, and preserving the knowledge of their craft. It was in the eighteenth century that these groups developed into gentlemen's circles devoted to an esoteric knowledge hidden in symbols, which could bring about a spiritual transformation. Freemasonry, as a closed system within larger society without an overt allegiance to Christianity, has attracted suspicions of Satanism since the French Revolution.[20] The false belief that Satan controls the Freemasons has been influential in Europe and beyond ever since.[21] Conspiracy theories warning against a wealthy elite intending to overthrow governments can generally be traced back to nineteenth century anti-Masonic literature.[22]

According to Ellis and Ter Haar, secret societies such as Freemasonry are popular in Africa, especially among the ruling elites, because they fit with indigenous traditions of closed associations.[23] However, they note that such secret societies are also distrusted: "Rumors drawing on the idea that great power is exclusive, and that initiation into elite networks requires ritual act that may involve blood sacrifice, lead people in many countries to associate national elections, when power is open to competition, with the abduction of children."[24] In several African countries, Freemasonry is suspected of such rituals aimed at acquiring power. When Kenyan fears about Satanism peaked in the 1990s, a Presidential

accessed September 12, 2019, http://zambiadailynation.com/2016/04/01/im-not-a -satanistsays-hh/.

17 See *Lusaka Times*, January 18, 2016, accessed September 12, 2019, https://www.lusakatimes.com/2016/01/18/111094/.

18 See *The Post*, July 22, 2016, accessed September 12, 2019, http://www.postzambia.com/news.php?id=19294; *Lusaka Times* July 22, 2016, accessed September 12, 2019, https://www.lusakatimes.com/2016/07/22/upnd-complains -ecz-pf-continued-harass-party-supporters/.

19 Roger Daches, "Freemasonry," in *Dictionary of Gnosis and Western Esotericism*, ed. Wouter Hanegraaff (Leiden: Brill, 2006), 382–388.

20 Wouter J. Hanegraaff, *Western Esotericism: A Guide for the Perplexed* (London: Bloomsbury, 2013), 35.

21 Massimo Introvigne, *Satanism. A Social History* (Leiden: Brill, 2016), 12.

22 Ruben Van Luijk, *Children of Lucifer. The Origins of Modern Religious Satanism* (New York: Oxford University Press, 2016), 280.

23 Stephen Ellis and Gerrie Ter Haar, *Worlds of Power: Religious Thought and Political Practice in Africa* (New York: Oxford University Press, 2004), 78.

24 Ellis and Ter Haar, *Worlds of Power*, 80.

Commission into Devil Worship was established. According to the report of this commission, Satanists had infiltrated Freemasonry (among other non-indigenous groups), and several efforts to proscribe Freemasonry were deployed.[25] In Zambia, Freemasonry and Satanism are seen as equals. Although factually, Satanism and Freemasonry, in their original Western forms, have nothing to do with each other, the notion that Freemasons are Satanists is not challenged by either the public or the media.

Ellis and Ter Haar's statement that politics and blood sacrifices are connected in the minds of many people is also relevant in the second major group of accusations against politicians in Zambian newspapers. Thus far, accusations against the opposition party, UPND, and its leader have been discussed. The ruling party, PF, is not immune to accusations of Satanism either. According to Ellis and Ter Haar, the abduction of children is linked to illicit rituals for the acquisition of power. In 2013, a Zambian online newspaper, the *Zambian Watchdog*, consequently linked not abductions but road accidents to sacrifice and to the ruling party. The first article that mentions Satanism, sacrifice, and the PF, published on February 2, 2013, reads:

> The Patriotic Front has been accused by residents of Mpongwe and Livingstone of practicing Satanism. In Mpongwe, some residents said Gabriel Namulambe sacrificed five PF cadres who died before and after Namulambe filed in his nomination papers. [...] In Livingstone, 200 PF supporters defected at Victoria Hall alleging that PF candidate Lawrence Evans is a Satanist. There has been an increase in road accidents after PF ascended to power. Most people suspect human sacrifice after disgraced Catholic priest Father Frank Bwalya slaughtered a chicken at a rally.[26]

The incident with the chicken happened at a rally in Luanshya in the Copperbelt Province in September 2011, and was meant to symbolize the end of the MMD in that area.[27] Although the *Zambian Watchdog* relates accusations of Satanism in 2013 to this incident, in 2011, the connection to Satanism does not seem to have been made. However, the quoted article is the first in a long line of articles connecting the PF to sacrifices, especially through road accidents. On February 3, a *Zambian Watchdog*

25 Rosalind I.J. Hackett, "Discourses of Demonization in Africa and Beyond," *Diogenes* 50, no. 3 (2003): 64.

26 See *Zambian Watchdog*, February 2, 2013), accessed September 12, 2019, http://www.zambiawatchdog.com/pf-continue-blood-sacrifices-on-zambians-this-time-killing-mwalitetas-brother-in-law/.

27 See "Father Frank Bwalya condemned for beheading a live chicken at PF rally," *Lusaka Times*, September 1, 2011, accessed September 12, 2019, https://www.lusakatimes.com/2011/09/01/father-frank-bwalya-condemned-beheading-live-chicken-pf-rally/.

headline reads: "More PF sacrifices? Masumba's baby drowns in Taima's swimming pool,"[28] and on February 5, another headline is "Satanic PF refuses to commit itself to blood-free by-elections."[29] In this article, the *Watchdog* states,

> The PF regime which many people now believe is involved in cultism and blood sacrifices has refused to sign a commitment to denounce violence in the Mpongwe and Livingstone parliamentary by-elections. [...] Many people in Zambia are now questioning the strange deaths that have been occurring from the time the PF took over power in 2011.

These articles set a baseline for a narrative that is repeated in the following months: every road accident is called a sacrifice by the *Zambian Watchdog*. In February 2013 alone, the following headlines appear:

- More sacrifices—two people perish in Kapiri accident[30]
- Sacrifices: chopper carrying PF journalists in emergency landing[31]
- Passengers survive being sacrificed as Mazhandu bus burns to ashes[32]
- Now even foreigners sacrificed in Muchinga bus accident[33]

Between February and August 2013, thirty-five articles about human sacrifice appeared in the *Zambian Watchdog*—a weekly average of five. Except three articles about actual murders, all of these refer to accidents. Often the word *sacrifice* and its cognates are only mentioned in the headline, and references to Satanism and the PF are not explicitly made. However, the narrative linking accidents, Satanism, sacrifice, and PF that was established in February 2013 is implicitly evoked in each of these

28 See "More PF sacrifices? Masumba's baby drowns in Taima' swimming pool," accessed September 12, 2019, http://www.zambiawatchdog.com/more-pf-sacrifices-masumbas-baby-drowns-in-taima-swimming-pool/.

29 See "Satanic PF refuses to commit itself to blood-free by-elections," accessed September 12, 2019, http://www.zambiawatchdog.com/satanic-pf-refuses-to-commit-itself-to-blood-free-by-elections/.

30 See "More Sacrifices—Two people perish in Kapiri accident," accessed September 12, 2019, http://www.zambiawatchdog.com/more-sacrifices-two-people-perish-in-kapiri-accident/.

31 See "Sacrifices: Chopper carrying PF journalists in emergency landing," accessed September 12, 2019, http://www.zambiawatchdog.com/sacrifices-chopper-carrying-pf-journalists-in-emergency-landing/.

32 See "Passengers survive being sacrificed as Mazhandu burns to ashes," accessed September 12, 2019, http://www.zambiawatchdog.com/passengers-survive-being-sacrificed-as-mazhandu-burns-to-ashes/.

33 See "Now even foreigners sacrificed in Muchinga bus road accident," accessed September 12, 2019, http://www.zambiawatchdog.com/now-even-foreigners-sacrificed-in-muchinga-bus-road-accident/.

headlines, and—as is obvious from the comments on the articles—is recognized by the readers.

To understand this spate of accusations, a closer look at Zambia's media landscape is needed. The Zambian Constitution grants freedom of the media. However, in practice, the government controls many media outlets.[34] Freedom also does not necessarily mean neutrality. Independent media are often connected to specific political parties or factions within these parties. The now defunct *The Post* newspaper, for example, generally reported favorably about Michael Sata's government. In the struggle for leadership after Sata passed away, *The Post* belonged to the camp that campaigned against Edgar Lungu. Not long after Lungu came into power, the headquarters of *The Post* were raided, and the newspaper ceased to exist. Another media outlet, the online *Zambian Watchdog*, presents itself as a platform for uncensored news, without fear or favor. The *Watchdog* may not favor anyone, but they are very clear about their dislike of the ruling party. In 2013, the year in which the *Zambian Watchdog* published the articles linking the PF with Satanism, Freedom House an American NGO conducting research and advocacy on democracy, political freedom, and human rights—changed Zambia's rating for freedom of the press from "partly free" to "not free." According to their motivation, "press freedom in Zambia experienced a series of setbacks in 2013. President Michael Sata and his ruling Patriotic Front (PF) government arrested and harassed independent journalists and news outlets, [and] blocked critical websites . . .. Meanwhile, the government and the PF continued to dominate the broadcast and print outlets that reach a majority of Zambians."[35] One of the affected news outlets was the *Zambian Watchdog*, whose journalists had their homes raided and whose website was blocked by internet service providers in Zambia in June 2013.

By consistently linking Satanism with the PF, the *Zambian Watchdog* is reframing this party. George Lakoff says about framing: "Frames are mental structures that shape the way we see the world . . .. When you hear a word, its frame (or collection of frames) is activated in your brain."[36] When readers of the *Watchdog* hear PF, they are bound to think about human sacrifices and Satanism. Thereby, the PF is effectively framed as a party that is evil and detrimental to the country. It is hard not to connect the blocking of the *Zambian Watchdog*'s website in 2013 to their political

34 Nelly Mwale & Joseph Chita, "Religion and the Media. The Portrayal of Prophecy in the Zambian Media," *Prophecy Today. Reflections from a Southern African Context*, ed. Hermen Kroesbergen (Wellington: CLF, 2016), 42.

35 Freedom House, "Freedom of the Press—Zambia," (2014), accessed August 17, 2016, https://freedomhouse.org/report/freedom-press/2014/zambia.

36 George Lakoff, *Don't Think of an Elephant: Know Your Values and Frame the Debate* (White River Junction: Chelsea Green, 2004), xv.

campaign to discredit the PF. In August 2013—by this time, the website of the *Zambian Watchdog* was briefly inaccessible, for Zambians as well as those outside the country—the campaign stopped, and in 2013, no more accidents were framed as sacrifice. From September 2013 to August 2016, eight more articles calling accidents sacrifice have appeared, but the popularity of this frame had clearly waned in comparison to the period from February to August 2013. This does not, however, mean that the *Zambian Watchdog* has ceased to be critical about the ruling party. Instead of bringing up references to Satanism, the *Watchdog* started in 2014 to consistently refer to Michael Sata as an "ailing president." After the hotly contested elections of 2016, President Edgar Lungu was given the label "forged president." This shows that the frames used to undermine political leadership are not necessarily of an occult nature; and the popularity of certain frames changes over time.

Accusations of Satanism against politicians are political acts, consciously done in the public sphere to influence the opinions of voters. This is particularly clear in the example of the *Zambian Watchdog* accusing the ruling party, PF. In the case of the accusations of the opposition party UPND, and its leader Hakainde Hichilema, the same process is at work, although the role of the press is different. In Hichilema's case, political opponents make the accusations at public campaign rallies. The press merely reports about the accusations, the denials of the accusations, and the ensuing court cases. In both cases, those who make the accusations are looking to reap political benefits. At the same time, these accusations fit well with an enchanted worldview that connects success, and particularly success in politics, to the sometimes-illicit support of spiritual forces.

Extraordinary Success through Extraordinary Powers

As we have seen in the previous section, success in politics is often regarded with suspicion in Africa. This suspicion is not because of the secrecy and plots for world domination that conspiracy theorists in the West accuse Freemasons of. Secrecy in Africa is not necessarily seen as a bad thing. One could say that an African society is an initiatory society, just as secret brotherhoods like the Freemasons. In traditional African societies, the distribution of power and knowledge between the generations is unequal, and both the position in the social structure and the authority this gives over those younger or of a lower rank are related to the power of knowing what is hidden from others. According to William Murphy, secrecy supports the elders' political and economic control of the youth.[37] Murphy's research is on the Kpelle of Liberia and Guinea, but the same

37 William P. Murphy, "Secret Knowledge as Property and Power in Kpelle Society. Elders Versus Youth," *Africa* 50, no. 2 (1980): 193–207.

can be said for secret societies like the Nyau in Zambia and Malawi. Initiation for boys in a society like the Nyau, or for girls in the secrets of womanhood, is a first step on the way to an adult existence. Without being initiated and being taught the secrets of adulthood, a boy cannot become a man and a girl cannot become a woman.

Secrecy has an important social function in Africa and is therefore not inherently evil. What then makes politicians suspicious? To understand this, we must look at an African worldview. The connection between politics and spiritual forces is well-known all over Africa. For example, Nimi Wariboko, writing about Nigerian Pentecostalism, gives several examples of politicians who are said to use invisible powers to become powerful.[38] Stephen Ellis and Gerrie Ter Haar give a whole list of politicians in Africa who have various religious specialists in their entourage, because they "believe that real power has its roots in the invisible world and that therefore the cultivation of spiritual power is vital for their continued political existence."[39]

Both in traditional and contemporary Africa, the spirit world forms an integral part of reality. On the other hand, Western thought, since the Enlightenment, has been shaped by a dualism that divides the cosmos into two realities: the supernatural world of God and other spiritual forces, and the natural material world of humans, animals, plants, and matter. In the past centuries, in Western Europe, the boundaries between these two realities have become more and more impenetrable. This means that humans have few direct experiences of the supernatural world in their daily lives, and also that God and the spiritual forces are not expected to intervene directly in the natural world. In the African worldview, the inhabitants of the spirit world involve themselves in human affairs. In an article about religion and the secular, Birgit Meyer uses a Ghanaian case to show that from an African point of view the spiritual and the physical are completely intertwined, and cannot be seen as distinct spheres. Rather, invisible forces are "powers that generate power. Talk about spirits offers a statement about what 'powers' the world."[40] Similarly, religion and politics in Nigeria share a common worldview or imaginary. Wariboko writes, "I name this imaginaire the *logic of invisibility*: that is, the texture of control over human flourishing, political power, and human or national destiny is

---

38 Nimi Wariboko, *Nigerian Pentecostalism* (Rochester: University of Rochester Press, 2014), 278–297.

39 Stephen Ellis and Gerrie Ter Haar, "Religion and Politics in sub-Saharan Africa," *The Journal of Modern African Studies* 36, no. 2 (1998): 190.

40 Birgit Meyer, "Religious and Secular, 'Spiritual' and 'Physical' in Ghana," in *What Matters? Ethnographies of Value in a Not So Secular Age*, eds. Courtney Bender & Ann Taves (New York: Columbia University, 2012), 107.

constituted by an invisible world."[41] According to this imaginaire, the way the world works—the logic behind it all—is a combination of the visible or physical world and the invisible or spiritual world. This spiritual world is inhabited by different kinds of spiritual beings. These spiritual forces are in a relationship with human beings. Relatives, friends, and neighbors in the physical world form a community together with ancestors, spirits, and God in the spiritual world. The quality of this relationship determines the quality of human life.

Politics and the spirit world are closely related. In an ideal traditional African community, the chief forms a link between the spiritual and the physical world through his embodiment of the mystical powers of the ancestors.[42] Though different precolonial African societies had different political systems, there are some communalities in chieftaincies. Chiefs are the leaders of local communities, and they play an important role in the distribution of assets.[43] These assets can be visible and physical; for example, chiefs manage the use of land and organize cooperative action. The chief is also connected to assets that are more spiritual in nature, such as the coming of the rains and the flow of blessings from the ancestors to the community in general.[44] Finally, the chief has the spiritual power to protect his community from the threat of witchcraft and other spiritual dangers. Good things trickle down from the spiritual world through the chief to the larger community. To be able to act as an intermediary between the spiritual and the physical world, the chief must have some control over spiritual forces. Ann Swindler writes about chiefs in Malawi: "A chief who does not accumulate control over material and spiritual resources becomes less 'sacred,' less prestigious, and thus less able to provide collective goods for his community, both in the material and spiritual realms."[45] In African societies, spiritual forces and the chief—or religion and politics—are closely linked.[46]

41 Wariboko, *Nigerian Pentecostalism,* 279.

42 Chammah J. Kaunda, "'The Altars are Holding the Nation in Captivity': Zambian Pentecostalism, Nationality, and African Religio-Political Heritage," *Religions* 9, no. 5 (2018): 145.

43 Ann Swindler, "2009 Paul Hanly Furfey Lecture: The Return of the Sacred: What African Chiefs Teach Us about Secularization," *Sociology of Religion* 71, no. 2 (2010): 159.

44 See William Watson, *Tribal Cohesion in a Money Economy: A Study of the Mambwe People* (Manchester: Manchester University Press, 1958), 168.

45 Swindler, "Return of the Sacred," 164.

46 See Ellis and Ter Haar, "Religion and Politics," 188; and David M. Gordon, *Invisible Agents: Spirits in a Central African History* (Athens, OH: Ohio University Press, 2012).

There is some academic debate about the nature of precolonial African societies. Some describe them as egalitarian "hybrid democracies"[47] in which decisions were made through consensus and in accordance with the general good. In Zambia, the Tonga have often been labelled as egalitarian.[48] But more autocratic systems did exist as well. The Bemba, for example, were at a late stage ruled as a kingdom by one clan,[49] and the Ngoni came to Zambia as a roving band of warriors.[50] The colonial governments unified this diversity by establishing what has been called an administrative chieftaincy, in which chief became a salaried position in the colonial administration.[51] This means that while chiefs are often referred to as traditional authorities, in fact not all African chiefs have precolonial roots.[52]

However egalitarian or authoritarian the political system may have been, for commoners an important principle of life was and is equivalence. Thornton defines this principle as "the value that all members of the community are, in principle, *equivalent* as human beings and as brothers and sisters."[53] Legitimate is to have what others have, namely the assets and blessings that trickle down through the chief as intermediary. This equality is safeguarded by the principle of jealousy: having more power, wealth, or luck than another comes with suspicions of witchcraft. The support of the invisible spiritual world, achieved through legitimate or illegitimate means, is vital for any form of success in the material world. Wim van Binsbergen, in his classic study on religious change in western Zambia, names four traditional professions in which a high status is acquired through individual merit rather than through community life, namely the hunter, the doctor/diviner, the trader, and the chief.[54]

47 Oita Etyang and Tengetile Nhlengethwa, "The Attrition of Democratic Gains in Africa: An Appraisal," *Journal of Language, Technology and Entrepreneurship in Africa* 8, no. 1 (2017): 54.

48 See for example, Elizabeth Colson, "Modern Political Organization of the Plateau Tonga," *African Studies* 7, no. 2–3 (1948): 85–98.

49 David Gordon, *Invisible Agents: Spirits in a Central African History* (Athens, OH: Ohio University Press, 2012).

50 J.A. Barnes, *Politics in a Changing Society: A Political History of the Fort Jameson Ngoni* (Cape Town: Oxford University Press, 1954).

51 Trutz Von Trotha, "From Administrative to Civil Chieftaincy: Some Problems and Prospects of African Chieftaincy," *The Journal of Legal Pluralism and Unofficial Law* 28, no. 37–38 (1996): 79–107.

52 Janine Ubink, *Traditional Authorities in Africa. Resurgence in an Era of Democratisation* (Leiden: Leiden University Press, 2018), 9.

53 Robert J. Thornton, *Healing the Exposed Being: A South African Ngoma Tradition* (Johannesburg: Wits University Press, 2017), 138.

54 Turrell, in his overview of *muti* murder in South Africa, gives a similar list: "The murderer was a chief in search of power, a doctor procuring powerful medicine or a businessman in search of a competitive edge over his rivals." See Rob Turrell, "*Muti* Ritual Murder in Natal: From Chiefs to Commoners (1900–1930)," *South*

Their success is ascribed to powerful medicine and sorcery. It is highly significant that medicine prepared out of human remains, so central in impersonal sorcery, is considered to be essential for the attainment and maintaining of precisely the few elevated statuses existing in the society of central western Zambia: the hunter, the doctor (*nganga*), the commercial entrepreneur, and especially the chief.[55] Why is the chief part of this list of professions that need support from the spiritual world? We have already seen that the chief functions as an intermediary between the spiritual and the physical world. Part of the chief's job is to maintain good relations with the ancestors, and to control dangerous spiritual forces in order to protect the community. Added to that comes the fact that becoming a chief is not simply hereditary. Although most chieftaincies are linked to a specific clan or lineage, birth is not the main criterion. There is usually a group of candidates for the succession of a chief. To be elected, some individual merits or support from invisible forces are needed.

Practices that are said to help obtain this support are known from different southern African contexts. Arne Steinforth describes the Malawian (Chewa) concept of *kukhwima*, which he locates in a grey zone between accepted beneficial magic and rejected witchcraft. *Kukhwima* is the name for "achieving a personal advantage at the cost of some form of compensation."[56] The personal advantages that one can receive through this practice are protection, and the accumulation of material wealth and political power. The cost of this is usually the sacrifice of a close family member, such as a parent or a child. Steinforth notes that notions of *kukhwima* have not been investigated in detail, and give no indication of how long these beliefs have been in existence. Rijk van Dijk's discussion of the same concept points to its existence before the 1990s.[57] Van Binsbergen mentions that the medicine used by hunters, diviners, traders, and chiefs is so powerful because it contains human ingredients. The killing of human beings to use their body parts in medicine to become rich is known as *muti* murder across South Africa—after the vernacular for traditional medicine—and as *dipheko* in Botswana.[58] Rob Turrell, in an overview

African Historical Journal 44, no. 1 (2001): 22.

55 Wim Van Binsbergen, *Religious Change in Zambia. Exploratory Studies* (London: Kegan Paul International, 1981), 142.

56 Arne S. Steinforth, *Troubled Minds. On the Cultural Construction of Mental Disorder and Normality in Southern Malawi* (Frankfurt am Main: Peter Lang, 2009), 181.

57 Rijk Van Dijk, "Fundamentalism and its Moral Geography in Malawi. The Representation of the Diasporic and the Diabolical," *Critique of Anthropology* 15, no. 2 (1995): 180.

58 There may be a shift in the meaning of *dipheko*. Isak Niehaus, in an article about ritual murder in the South African Lowveld defines *dipheko* as "anything prescribed by the ancestors."Isak Niehaus, "Coins for Blood and Blood for Coins:

of killings for *muti* between 1900 and 1930 writes: "The ritual killing of a human was required for the acquisition of extraordinary power. And extraordinary power was required to win competitive advantages in chiefly rivalries over people and land. This was why *muti* murders were closely associated with chiefly politics."[59]

The legitimacy of this measure to attract support from invisible forces is contested. According to Wim van Binsbergen, rumors about ritual killings tainted the position of chief: "Chieftainship took on a connotation of sorcery that the chief could not shake off even if he went so far as to attempt to monopolize the right to identify and prosecute sorcerers (e.g., by means of the poison ordeal)."[60] A similar sentiment is reflected in the Tswana proverb "A king is like a knife; he might cut his sharpener"—the sharpeners being the commoners.[61] But more positive interpretations are possible too. Arne Steinforth refers to *kukhwima* as a grey area, and other authors go even further. Wiebe de Jong writes: "Since the well-being of the entire community was in the chief's hands, it was important to strengthen him. Ritual murders, consequently, were desired, meaningful, and everyone knew that once in a while they had to be committed in order to keep or restore harmony in the community."[62] These legitimate killings were framed as human sacrifices for the good of the community, not for the individual gain of the chief.

There seems to have been a shift in this practice in the twentieth century, in which medicine murder became available for a larger public. According to Turrell, by the 1920s ritual murders were mainly executed on behalf of ambitious commoners like businessmen.[63] The traditional healers who provided *muti* containing human parts were no longer working for the collective good of the chiefdom, but for individuals who only have their own gain in mind.[64] Where the good of the community is

From Sacrifice to Ritual Murder in the South African Lowveld, 1930–2000," *Etnofoor* 13, no. 2 (2000): 36. Charlanne Burke, writing about rumors about the killing of youths in Botswana consistently translates *dipheko* as ritual murder; see Charlanne Burke, "They Cut Segametsi into Parts: Ritual Murder, Youth, and the Politics of Knowledge in Botswana," *Anthropological Quarterly* 73, no. 4 (2000): 204–214.

59 Turrell, "*Muti* Ritual Murder," 22.

60 Wim Van Binsbergen, "The Dynamics of Religious Change in Western Zambia," *Ufahamu: A Journal of African Studies* 6, no. 3 (1976): 80.

61 Ornulf Gulbrandsen, "'The Discourse of 'Ritual Murder.' Popular Reaction to Political Leaders in Botswana," *Social Analysis* 46, no. 3 (2002): 223.

62 Wiebe De Jong, "'Makhosi a via' (Chiefs Commit Ritual Murder)—Why Ritual Murders in Southern Africa Should be Seen as Meaningful Violence (and Not Senseless)," *Africa Focus* 28, no. 2 (2015): 13.

63 Turrell, "*Muti* Ritual Murder," 38.

64 Gulbrandsen, "Discourse of 'Ritual Murder," 225.

concerned, sacrifices may be accepted, but the success acquired through murder for individual gain is illegitimate. Isak Niehaus writes that from the 1960s, "all forms of sacrifice [...] became illicit."[65]

Certain practices to obtain the help of spiritual forces have become illicit when the political power shifted from chiefs to politicians. There is another difference between the discourse about chiefs and the discourse about contemporary politicians. The four traditional professions that especially need the support of spiritual forces for their success—hunters, doctors/diviners, traders, and chiefs—at first glance show a startling similarity to some of the professions that are accused of Satanism in contemporary Zambian newspapers—namely, politicians, businessmen, and pastors. Like the traditional healers and diviners, today's pastors claim insight in the workings of the spiritual world, which gives them the ability to speak blessings into the lives of their congregants and deliver them from oppression by evil spirits. Like the traders of old, contemporary businessmen may acquire wealth that makes them stand out from their community. And like the traditional chiefs, politicians hold political power in modern, large-scale African societies. But where the acquisition of spiritual powers by chiefs was taken as a fact of life and related to the beneficial ancestors, politicians are regarded with suspicion because their powers benefit only themselves and not the community. The powers that politicians acquire are, in the public imagination, related to witchcraft and Satanism. These rumors about contemporary politicians show a profound sense of betrayal by those in government.[66]

Both politicians and chiefs need the support of spiritual forces. But while politicians are accused of Satanism, in the Zambian newspapers contemporary chiefs are not—even though the ancestral source of their power is understood as demonic by some neo-pentecostal Christians. This does not mean that chiefs have fallen out of the categories of professions that need spiritual assistance. That chiefs require spiritual powers is still taken for granted. However, in the case of chiefs this is not labelled as "Satanism." What is the difference between chiefs on the one hand, and politicians, businessmen, pastors, and teachers on the other? That chiefs are supposed to act on behalf of the community, while politicians are not trusted to do so is a difference that is already mentioned. Another important difference is that they belong to different moral universes. Chiefs and headmen belong to a rural world, while the categories of people accused of Satanism are all related to urban settings. As Deborah Kaspin shows in her analysis of traditional Nyau-dancers in Malawi, national politics

65 Niehaus, "Coins for Blood," 41.

66 Gulbrandsen, "Discourse of 'Ritual Murder,'" 229.

and village politics belong to parallel universes of meaning.[67] Chiefs and village headmen are associated with tribal identity and traditional rituals through which they access spiritual powers. State officials, politicians, teachers, and Christians in general are defined as outsiders in this traditional milieu. They belong to an urban universe of meaning that has its own locus of power. In the world of the chief, spiritual powers that grant extraordinary status are morally neutral tools. In the Christian urban world these powers are rejected, and Satanism is the name for the locus of illicit spiritual power needed to be successful in this urban milieu.

Accusations of Satanism happen in the rural as well as in urban areas. In the village, teachers and government officials coming to implement development projects may be accused of involvement in Satanism. Even though these accusations play out in a rural context, the categories of those accused are linked to the urban. In the democratic nation state, politicians and the government have taken up much of the power that used to be in the hands of chiefs. For villagers, politicians and government officials are outsiders, signifying a structure of power alternative to village politics. Teachers are educated in the city, and then randomly placed in schools by the government. Because they are new in the community, they were educated in towns, and in many rural areas, the teacher is one of the few persons receiving a salary, teachers are viewed as people who belong to the urban world. The commercial farmer has connections to towns as well. His relative wealth and his trade links with customers beyond the village alienate him from village life. Accusations of pastors and churches are generally an urban phenomenon, and those accused are often of a neo-pentecostal slant. Neo-pentecostal churches—often with names ending with "International"—offer their members access to a global urban network of like-minded believers.

Politicians, businessmen, teachers, pastors, and government officials, then, all belong to the urban world. This urban world is constructed in contrast to the village world. To Zambians, "urban" signifies development, modernity, and Christianity.[68] In this urban world, extraordinary success still requires support from extra-ordinary powers. According to Nimi Wariboko, pentecostalism forms a legitimate way of controlling spiritual powers through the Christian rituals of prayer, fasting, and

---

67 Deborah Kaspin, "Chewa Visions and Revisions of Power. Transformations of the Nyau Dance in Central Malawi," in *Modernity and its Malcontents: Ritual and Power in Postcolonial Africa*, eds. Jean Comaroff & John L. Comaroff (Chicago: University of Chicago Press, 1993), 34–57.

68 Johanneke Kroesbergen-Kamps, "Dreams and Nightmares of Modernity. Accusations and Testimonies of Satanism in Zambia," in *Search of Health and Wealth: The Prosperity Gospel in African, Reformed Perspective*, ed. Hermen Kroesbergen (Wellington: CLF, 2013), 100–112.

offering.[69] Satanism, on the other hand, is the name—obviously given from a Christian perspective—for unapproved, illicit ways of accessing spiritual powers in an urban, rather than a rural world.

Conclusion

Success in politics or business in Africa is often associated with ritual killings. In her comparative perspective on witchcraft and Satanism, Jean La Fontaine discusses the label "ritual killing" at length.[70] She distinguishes three actions that may be referred to as ritual killing: human sacrifice, killing for body parts, and ritual murder. The first, *human sacrifice*, is a public, religiously sanctioned ritual that took place in many different societies, although it is no longer practiced today. Although human sacrifice involves taking the life of another human being, it should not be called murder, because murder implies illegitimate killing, which human sacrifice is not. The second, *killing for body parts* that are used in "medicines" to enhance health, wealth, or success in life, is currently happening in several African countries—South African *muti* murders are an example. According to La Fontaine, "these medicines are concoctions whose purposes are purely secular and individual; they are put together by 'specialists' who charge for their services."[71] In contrast to human sacrifice, killing for body parts does not deserve the adjective "ritual," because the act has no religious meaning and is done in secret for individual ends, rather than publicly and for the benefits of the community.[72] Lastly, *ritual murder* involves an underground organization devoted to the killing of human beings as an act of worship or to acquire illicit spiritual powers. The idea of ritual murder has a long history in Western, European society, with very similar accusations made against Christians, Jews, Cathars, and witches. Through colonialism, this "myth of ritual murder" with its European roots has reached Africa. Ritual murder, this third category of ritual killing, exists only in the mind: "Independent or material evidence such as would be demanded in a prosecution today has never existed. Yet, the idea persists because it represents in a dramatic form what is the ultimate human evil and, by contrast, emphasizes what it means to be human."[73]

In the discourse of ritual killings associated with chiefs and contemporary politicians, La Fontaine's differentiation of the three types does not work very well. Ritual killings that increase the power of the chief and

---

69 Wariboko, *Nigerian Pentecostalism.*

70 Jean La Fontaine, *Witches and Demons. A Comparative Perspective on Witchcraft and Satanism* (New York: Berghahn Books, 2016).

71 La Fontaine, *Witches and Demons*, 51.

72 See Bonhomme, *Sex Thieves*, 23.

73 La Fontaine, *Witches and Demons*, 55.

benefit the community could be called legitimate human sacrifices. The literature, however, does not make a distinction between these killings and murders for body parts. And although murders for body parts are happening in contemporary Africa, the accusations of Satanism made against politicians in Zambia cannot be linked to actual cases of murder, and seem to be examples of La Fontaine's third category of imagined ritual murder perpetrated by an evil Other. The categories shade into each other, and trying to distinguish them does not seem very fruitful. Rather than asking precisely what type of ritual killing contemporary politicians are accused of, in this chapter, I have followed the narratives about the use of spiritual forces to acquire extraordinary success to their historical roots.

In contemporary Zambia, politicians are among the professions that are most accused of involvement in Satanism. These accusations are made in a political context, to discredit either the ruling party or the opposition. In this chapter, I have argued that these accusations can be understood not only from their direct impact on the political landscape in Zambia, but also from a historical perspective. The traditional political figure of the chief has long been associated with extraordinary spiritual powers. However, there are two major differences between the rumors about chiefs and the rumors about contemporary politicians. First, chiefs were expected to act on behalf of the community, and their means of acquiring spiritual powers were accepted as a fact of life. Contemporary politicians, however, are perceived as representatives of a state that eats its own children. Their power and success do not trickle down to the members of society, but are used for their personal gain. In a society in which the principle of equivalence is important, individual gain without redistribution is rejected. Whether or not politicians use illicit means of acquiring spiritual power for their own gain, rumors of sorcery and *muti* murders are never far away. Accusations of Satanism show that members of the public have lost their faith in the ability of politicians to act on their behalf, and thereby speak to a profound disappointment in political affairs. The second difference between rumors about chiefs and rumors about politicians is that the chief belongs to a rural world of meaning. If a chief is accused of illicit accumulation, this accusation would probably be framed in terms of witchcraft. Politicians, on the other hand, belong to the urban world. In this urban world of meaning, the more globalizing discourse of Satanism is applied to suspicions of the illicit accumulation of power, wealth, and other forms of success.

PART III: THE PUBLIC CHURCH AND POLITICS

12

RELIGION, IDENTITY POLITICS, AND NATIONAL POLITICS

Chammah J. Kaunda
Marja Hinfelaar

Introduction

The declaration of Zambia as a Christian nation (hereafter, the Declaration) has brought identity politics to the fore and increased religious competition and polarization of engagement in Zambian politics, as witnessed in the 2016 elections. It has inspired political debates and pentecostal political mobilization and the struggle to redefinition the relationship between the church and the state. Under Kenneth Kaunda's regime, the institutional interests of the Roman Catholic Church (hereafter, Catholic) and mainline Protestantism had the upper hand in Zambian politics. It has been argued that, historically, the mainline churches that had middle class members were more politically engaged during Kaunda's twenty-seven-year rule.[1] Pentecostalism[2] emerged as religious groups of

1 Rachel B. Riedl, "Transforming Politics, Dynamic Religion: Religion's Political Impact in Contemporary Africa," *African Conflict and Peace building Review* 2, no. 2 (2012): 29–50.

2 Pentecostalism describes a variety of Christian communities with pneumatological orientations expressing or articulating their faith within the sociohistorical and cultural contexts of African societies. In this chapter, the term is used principally in reference to classical pentecostal churches and neo-pentecostal/independent charismatic churches (especially, the new urban-centered and prosperity-oriented churches). See Nimi Wariboko, "Pentecostalism in Africa," in *Oxford Research Encyclopedia of African History* (2017), accessed July 24, 2018, http://africanhistory.oxfordre.com/view/10.1093/acrefore/9780190277734.001.0001/acrefore-9780190277734-e-120; see also, J. Kwabena Asamoah-Gyadu, "'From Every Nation under Heaven': Africa in World Pentecostalism," in *Global Renewal*

the marginalized sectors of Zambian population. At one time, Kaunda's government opposed and imposed an embargo on the registration of Pentecostalism as a way to stem "unprecedented establishment of breakaway churches."[3] It was only during Frederick Chiluba's presidency, who claimed to have been "born-again before his ascension into power,"[4] that the mobilization shifted religious political hegemony from the mainline churches to Pentecostalism. Chiluba was quick to appropriate the language of Pentecostalism into politics. The Pentecostals responded by politicizing their religion as a response to historical religious marginalization and political suppression. The increasing politicization of Christianity in Zambian public spheres is part of the evolution and intensification in competitive identity politics in the ongoing religious battle for representation and power.[5] This especially came to the fore during the 2016 presidential election, which we use as a case study to demonstrate how the public spheres are religious contested.

The public visibility of Pentecostalism and its pursuit to convert the public sphere promotes unitary religious monopolization of national politics. In other words, the entrance of Pentecostalism in politics has caused the decline in Catholic political hegemony, provoking identity politics (perhaps even religious identity crisis) in which public spheres are increasingly perceived as spaces of religious contestation for power and legitimacy. Whereas the Catholic (often in conjunction with mainline Protestant churches) uses pastoral letters to engage politics, Pentecostalism utilizes public visibility and numbers of their congregants in the quest to endorse Christian nationalism as the foundational aspect of Zambian society. Employing identity politics theory, this study argues that both Catholic and pentecostal communities have utilized religious identity politics to seek to delegitimize each other in the public spheres. They engage in internal construction of homogeneous identities at the expense of mutual collaboration for the common good. The result is conflictive and self-interest centered political engagements that are distorting the mission of the

Christianity, vol. 3, Spirit Empowered Movements: Past, Present, and Future, eds. Vinson Synan, Amos Yong, and J. Kwabena Asamoah-Gyadu (Lake Mary, FL: Charisma House, 2016), xxxi.

3 R. Drew Smith, "Missionaries, Church Movements, and Shifting Religious Significance in the State of Zambia," *Journal of Church and State* 41, no. 3 (1999): 526. Elsewhere, Chammah J. Kaunda has detailed persecution of Zambian Pentecostalism by both the mainline churches and Kaunda's regime. See also Chammah J. Kaunda, "The Making of Pentecostal Zambia: A Brief History of Pneumatic Spirituality," *Oral History Journal of South Africa* 4, no. 1 (2016): 15–45.

4 Ogbu U. Kalu, *Power, Poverty and Prayer: The Challenges of Poverty and Pluralism in African Christianity, 1960–1996* (Trenton, NJ: Africa World Press, 2006), 145.

5 Riedl, "Transforming Politics," 39.

churches in their public role. The study concludes that identity politics have become a hindrance to progressive religious and prophetic collaborative engagements among churches in Zambian politics.

Church and Identity Politics in (Southern) Africa

The Roman Catholic Church's presence in Zambia dates to the late nineteenth century. Having set up many mission stations, churches, hospitals, and schools across Zambia, the Catholic Church has a strong national presence. In terms of identity, the Roman Catholic Church was not always as united as it appears to be. This is a result of the fact that the Catholic Church did not enter Northern Rhodesia as one missionary movement, but came from various congregations and nationalities, the White Fathers (Missionaries of Africa) came predominantly from France, Netherlands, and French-speaking Canada. The Jesuits, an elite denomination within the Church, came from England and France, the Capuchins/Franciscans from Ireland, and so on. Moreover, they settled in different parts of the country and were hardly connected at the national level. [6] A Christian theocracy was the model the White Fathers had adhered to while evangelizing the Northern Province, where they successfully created a large number of Roman Catholic enclaves.[7] These patterns of settlement created particular "spheres of influence" and strong local/ethnic affinities (like the White Fathers and the Bemba-speaking North), which reinforced regional and ethnic divisions that had a long lasting impact.[8] The opening of a teacher training college at the Jesuit Mission of Chikuni in the Southern Province at the behest of government in 1953 played an important role in the establishment of a national Catholic identity: It helped to give their students a sense of being Zambian Catholics rather than Bemba or Lozi Catholics, thus paving the way to national consciousness.[9] The establishment of a Catholic Secretariat and Zambia Episcopal Conference (ZEC) in Lusaka in 1965, also contributed to the creation of a national character of the Catholic Church in Zambia. This shift was accompanied by changes in the Church following the Second Vatican Council (1962–1965). It marked an era in which the post-war generation of missionaries lost confidence in the superiority of Western culture and started to have doubts about their evangelical mission.[10] This confusion of mission can be seen

6 Hugo Hinfelaar, *History of the Catholic Church in Zambia, 1895—1995* (Lusaka: Bookworld Publishers, 2004).

7 Robert I. Rotberg, *Christian Missionaries and the Creation of Northern-Rhodesia 1880—1924* (Princeton, NJ: Princeton University Press, 1965), 33.

8 Leroy Vail, ed., *The Creation of Tribalism in Southern Africa* (London: Currey University of California Press, 1989).

9 Carmody, *Education in Zambia*, 88.

10 Hinfelaar, *History of the Catholic Church*.

as the start of what some have called the trend of NGO-ization, or the transition from a Christian to a secular eschatology.[11] It influenced the direction of Catholic education and media, namely from confessional to professional and from denominational to ecumenical. A paradoxical situation arose in which Catholic missionaries at Catholic schools taught a secular curriculum, while being challenged by their evangelically oriented students who openly resisted secular teachings.[12]

African Pentecostalism is now variously described as a "coherent African religion"[13] or as "another phase of the quest for power and identity in Africa,"[14] or as "Africanization from below."[15] There is a sense in which African Pentecostalism is increasingly perceived as fulfilling the quest for an African spirituality that not only appeals to but also satisfies Africans' socioreligious and political aspirations.[16] The movement is regarded as having a distinctive spiritual structural integrity within

11 S. Plant, "Freedom as Development: Christian Mission and the Definition of Well-being," Seminar Paper Henry Martyn Centre, October 24, 2002, accessed September 11, 2008, http://www.martynmission.cam.ac.uk/CPlant.html.

12 This is described in full detail in T. Simpson, "'Half-London' *in Zambia: Contested Identities in a Catholic Mission School* (Edinburgh: Edinburgh University Press, 2003)

13 Tinyiko S. Maluleke, "African Christianity as African Religion: Beyond the Contextualization Paradigm," in *The Quest for Liberation and Reconciliation: Essays in Honor of J. Deotis Roberts*, ed. M. Battle (Westminster: John Knox Press, 2005), 124; see also Wariboko, "Pentecostalism in Africa." where Wariboke argues that African "Pentecostalism has helped make Christianity an African religion."

14 Ogbu Kalu, *African Pentecostalism: An Introduction* (Oxford: Oxford University Press, 2008), 4.

15 Birgit Meyer, "'If You are a Devil You are a Witch and if You are a Witch, You are a Devil': The Integration of 'Pagan' Ideas into the Conceptual Universe of Ewe Christians in Southeastern Ghana," *Journal of Religion in Africa* 22, no. 2 (1992): 98–132; Birgit Meyer, "'Delivered from the Powers of Darkness': Confessions of Satanic Riches in Christian Ghana," *Africa: Journal of the International African Institute* 65, no. 2 (1995): 236–55; "'Make a Complete Break with the Past': Memory and Postcolonial Modernity in Ghanaian Pentecostalist Discourse," *Journal of Religion in Africa* 28, no. 2 (1998): 316–49; "The Power of Money: Politics, Occult Forces and Pentecostalism in Ghana," *Africa Studies Review* 41, no. 3 (1998): 15–37; *Translating the Devil: Religion and Modernity Among the Ewe in Ghana* (Edinburgh: Edinburgh University Press, 1999).

16 Joseph Quayesi-Amakye, "A Yeast in the Flour: Pentecostalism as the African Realisation of the Gospel," *Studia Historiae Ecclesiasticae* 42, no. 3 (2016): 71-84; Kwabena Asamoah-Gyadu, "Pentecostalism and the Influence of Primal Realities in Africa," in *The Many Faces of Global Pentecostalism*, eds. Harold D. Hunter and Neil Ormerod (Cleveland, TN: CPT Press, 2013): 139–61; Emmanuel K. Larbi, "The Nature of Continuity and Discontinuity of Ghanaian Pentecostal Concept of Salvation in African Cosmology," *Asian Journal of Pentecostal Studies* 5, no. 1 (2002): 87–106; Ogbu U. Kalu, "Preserving a Worldview: Pentecostalism in the African Maps of the Universe," *Pneuma*, 24 no. 2 (2002): 110–137.

African religious landscape by virtue of its cultural sensibilities and approach to both African spirit world and sociopolitical issues. Increased demography of membership has given social privilege and popularity to most of its leaders. In this way, the movement has made its presence felt in the public life of many African countries.[17] However, the existence of church associations/councils in many African countries has not promoted a single narrative of the movement's approach to sociopolitical issues as each movement seeks to be relevant and influence the public spheres with its own distinctive practices and convictions. Scholars argue that African pentecostal criterion of belonging is based on born-again ethos.[18] This ethos emphasizes belonging while othering those perceived as not born-again.[19] This keeps Pentecostalism in constant struggle as to what it means to belong to wider religious associations. This constant contestation of belonging means that most Pentecostals create their identities in exclusion of other religious identities. Their multiple and often exclusive identities present a challenge to collective religious engagement in politics. This remains one of the greatest threats to religious effective contribution to public life in Africa. Scholars also note that an ever increase in pentecostal political identities are an attempt not only to monopolize the public spheres but to colonize national politics with "born-again" beliefs and practices.[20] This process is described as pentecostalization of society and national politics.[21] Pentecostalization is the combination of demo-

17 Paul Gifford, *Christianity and Politics in Doe's Liberia* (Cambridge: Cambridge University Press, 1993); Paul Gifford, *African Christianity: Its Public Role* (London: Hurst, 1998); Paul Gifford, *Christianity, Politics and Public Life in Kenya* (London: Hurst, 2009); Paul Freston, *Evangelicals and Politics in Asia, Africa and Latin America* (Cambridge: Cambridge University Press, 2001); J. Kwabena Asamoah-Gyadu, "The Church in the African State: The Pentecostal/Charismatic Experience in Ghana," *Journal of African Christian Thought* 1, no. 2 (1998): 51–57; David Maxwell, *African Gifts of the Spirit: Pentecostalism and the Rise of a Zimbabwean Transnational Religious Movement* (Oxford: James Currey, 2006); Marshall Ruth, *Political Spiritualities: The Pentecostal Revolution in Nigeria* (Chicago: University of Chicago Press, 2009); Vinson Synan, Amos Yong, and Kwabena Asamoah-Gyadu, eds., *Global Renewal Christianity: Spirit-Empowered Movements Past, Present, and Future, vol. III: Africa and Diaspora* (Lake Mary, FL: Charisma House Publishers, 2016).

18 Abimbola O. Adesoji, "The New Pentecostal Movement in Nigeria and the Politics of Belonging," *Journal of Asian and African Studies* 52, no. 8 (2017): 1159–1173.

19 James S. Bielo, "Walking in the Spirit of Blood: Moral Identity among Born-again Christians," *Ethnology* (2004): 271–289.

20 Ruth Marshall-Fratani, "Mediating the Global and Local in Nigerian Pentecostalism," *Journal of Religion in Africa* 28, no. Fasc. 3 (1998): 282.

21 Marshall, *Political Spiritualities*.

graphic expansion, influence on other religions, and impact on society and politics.[22]

It started with increased competition for membership that forced Catholic and mainstream Protestantism to adopt some pentecostal beliefs and practices.[23] Having situated itself as a massive and vibrant religious presence in Africa, Pentecostalism seeks to influence the public spheres.[24] This conviction is based on the quest for Pentecostalism to permeate all aspects of life. Pentecostal politics calls for all decisions, actions, and explanation of sociopolitical and economic life to be done through Christianity. In this way, the born-again ethos perceived as a model of practice that will solve Africa's political problems is not only a source of pentecostal identity, but also an ideological system.[25] In fact, some scholars are concerned that the born-again approach has a potential to be religiously intolerant as it promotes narrow exclusionary notions, nationalism based on single-religious discourse, and reproduction of its dogmatism in public spheres. In addition, the born-again motif also tends to spiritualize sociopolitical and economic problems, which too often is blamed on either an "individual sin" or "demons" rather than on political institutions or corruption.[26] The search to exorcise demonic forces out of political spheres has given rise to radical identity politics of exclusion as this pentecostal-type political knowledge is not public knowledge but

22 Henri Gooren, "The Pentecostalization of Religion and Society in Latin America," *Exchange* 39 (2010): 356.

23 Various scholars in different parts of Africa have noted how African Pentecostalism forced mainline churches to alter their theologies and practices in radical ways in order to accommodate its worldview. See for example, Akoko Robert Mbe, "'You Must Be Born-Again': The Pentecostalisation of the Presbyterian Church in Cameroon," *Journal of Contemporary African Studies* 25, no. 2 (2007): 299–315; Damaris S. Parsitau, "From the Periphery to the Centre: The Pentecostalisation of Mainline Christianity in Kenya," *Missionalia* 35, no. 3 (2007): 83–111; Cephas N. Omenyo, *Pentecost Outside Pentecostalism: A Study of the Development of Charismatic Renewal Mainline Churches in Ghana* (Zoetermeer: Boekencentrum, 2006); Jonathan Kangwa, "Pentecostalisation of Mainline Churches in Africa: The Case of the United Church of Zambia," *The Expository Times* 127, no. 12 (2016): 573–584.

24 David M. Gordon, *Invisible Agents: Spirits in a Central African History* (Athens, OH: Ohio University Press, 2012); Adriaan van Klinken, "Homosexuality, Politics and Pentecostal Nationalism in Zambia," *Studies in World Christianity* 20, no. 3 (2014): 259–281; Adriaan van Klinken, "Pentecostalism, Political Masculinity and Citizenship: The Born-again Male Subject as Key to Zambia's National Redemption," *Journal of Religion in Africa* 46, nos. 2, 3 (2016): 129–57; Adeshina Afolayan, Olajumoke Yacob-Haliso, and Toyin Falola, eds., *Pentecostalism and Political Philosophy in Africa* (Durham: Carolina Academic Press, 2018).

25 Afolayan, Yacob-Haliso, and Falola, *Pentecostalism;* Marshall-Fratani, "Mediating the Global and Local"; Marshall, *Political Spiritualities.*

26 Marshall, *Political Spiritualities.*

masked in spiritual mysteries that only Pentecostals understand.[27] This makes such knowledge inaccessible to other religions and critical secular political actors. This itself promotes religion-based conflict of interests that arises from competitive identity politics based on the quest to monopolize the public spheres. In what follows, we concisely investigate the history of religion and politics in Zambia.

History of Religion and Politics in Pre-declaration

The Catholic Church's public engagement started with the production of the first pastoral letter in 1953, which was informed by the long-established Social Teachings of the Church (STC). The STC holds that "the essence of Christianity is a call to active involvement in the affairs of this world. Christians live a unitary life. Christians are the same people that face political, economic, and cultural realities of everyday life. They cannot afford then to be aloof to the realities that affect their daily life. This is why the church recognizes that it has a mission to be involved in promoting the welfare of the human person in all the spheres of life."[28] While the Catholic Church was the largest denomination in Northern Rhodesia at Independence, many of the political elite were trained in the protestant schools, most notably Lubwa Mission.[29] The establishment of large lay movements translated into a tangible influence at the grassroots level. At a public level, the pastoral statements, often in conjunction with the other main-stream churches, as well as their well-funded influential media (Icengelo, Yatsani, etc.) made the Catholic Church highly visible in the public sphere.

Pentecostalism entered Zambia from the 1940s and did not seek to contextualize and maintained a hostile attitude toward African cultures. As a result, Pentecostalism did not make serious impact in Zambia. The movement remained largely a shadow of mainline Protestantism and Catholic. The Pentecostals defined themselves as a soul-winning movement and believed that Catholics were not saved, and that mainline Protestantism was dead spirituality.[30] The local expressions of Pentecostalism, especially with the rise of new Pentecostal-charismatics were political from the beginning in as much as it took a resistance

27 Nimi Wariboko, *Nigerian Pentecostalism* (Rochester: University of Rochester Press, 2014).

28 Joe Komakoma, ed., *The Social Teaching of the Catholic Bishops and other Christian Leaders in Zambia. Major Pastoral Letters and Statements. 1953–2001* (Ndola: Mission Press, 2003), 2.

29 At Ipenburg, *All Good Men: The Development of Lubwa Mission, Chinsali, Zambia 1905–1967* (New York: Peter Lang, 1992).

30 Chammah J. Kaunda, "The Making of Pentecostal Zambia: A Brief History of Pneumatic Spirituality," *Oral History Journal of South Africa* 4, no. 1 (2016):15–45.

posture through radical identification with the marginalized populations. However, the Zambian Pentecostalism became visible in formal politics only after the Declaration of Zambia as a Christian nation (hereafter, the Declaration) by the second republic president, Frederick J.T. Chiluba. The claim by Chiluba to have been born-again meant that Pentecostalism had an upper hand in Zambian politics.[31] Since then, Pentecostalism has established schools, orphanages, and clinics in many parts of Zambia, especially in urban areas.[32] But, a sudden pentecostal entry into formal politics has brought its own challenge. The pentecostal ideology of competing for followers with the Catholic and the mainline churches has taken a new direction based on competition for state privileges. In the context in which Pentecostals were marginalized, entry into formal political spheres is perceived not only as a way of mobilization of followers but also converting the nation to Christ as Nevers Mumba insistently argues, "Zambia shall be saved."[33]

Religion and Politics in Post-declaration

From Independence until the mid-2000s, the Catholic Church upheld its unity and spoke with one voice, mostly in the forms of pastoral statements. In its public role, the Catholic Church frequently cooperated with the other mainstream church bodies, Christian Council of Zambia (CCZ) and Evangelic Fellowship of Zambia (EFZ), as well as with civil society, like the Oasis Forum, which was an alliance of mainstream churches, the women's movement, the Non-Governmental Organizations Coordinating Council (NGOCC), and the Law Association of Zambia. The Oasis Forum played a particularly important role to prevent President Chiluba's desire to run for an unconstitutional third term. Cracks in this unity began to appear when in the late 2000s, the Catholic Church became increasingly critical of the MMD regime and part of its hierarchy, both priests and nuns, openly backed Patriotic Front (PF), the opposition party that was led by Michael Sata, a Bemba-speaking Catholic. This resulted in conflict

31 Austin Cheyeka, Marja Hinfelaar, and Bernhard Udelhoven, "The Changing Face of Zambia's Christianity and its Implications for the Public Sphere: A Case Study of Bauleni Township, Lusaka," *Journal of Southern African Studies* 40, no. 5 (2014): 1031–1045.

32 Adriano Chalwe, "An Evaluation of the Mission History of Pentecostal Assemblies of God in Zambia" (PhD diss.,, North-West University, Potchefstroom, 2008); Naar M'fundisi, "Pentecostal and Charismatic Spiritualities and Civic Engagement in Zambia (1964–2012)," (PhD diss., University of Birmingham, 2014).

33 Austin Cheyeka, "Towards a History of the Charismatic Churches in Postcolonial Zambia," in *One Zambia, Many Histories: Towards a History of Postcolonial Zambia*, ed. Jan-Bart Gewald, Marja Hinfelaar, and Giacomo Macola (Boston, MA: Brill, 2008), 144–63.

between the ruling MMD and the Catholic Church in Zambia, which in turn brought to the fore some of the underlying identity issues. This tension found expression, for instance, in the television series by journalist Chanda Chimba III. The series, aired on government television, was titled, "Patriots vs. Troublemakers," and accused the Catholic Church and some of her priests for siding with the opposition PF and, according to the title of the program, of unpatriotic behavior and inciting ethnic genocide (going to the extent of drawing parallels with Rwanda). The popularity of the Radio Icengelo editor, Fr. Frank Bwalya, got a lot of attention among the Bemba-speaking audience on the Copperbelt, the hotbed of Zambian politics, and furthered the perception of the strong Bemba/Catholic partisan support for PF.

Interestingly, this conflict was not taking place only between the MMD and Catholics but also between the Catholics and Pentecostals. The Pentecostals who have positioned themselves as the chief architect and guardian of the Declaration[34] have perceived the Declaration as a tool for national redemption and their framework for engaging in politics. Since the rejection of Chiluba's Declaration by the two mother bodies, Zambia Episcopal Conference (ZEC) and Christian Council of Zambia (CCZ) which is mainline Protestant, the Pentecostals have perceived the mainstream Christianity with suspicion, especially the Catholics. The Catholics have maintained that "no nation is Christian by proclamation but by deeds."[35] In addition, the ZEC has consistently argued that Zambia is a secular state.[36] ZEC's demand for a secular state is viewed by some Pentecostals as jealousy, arising from a loss of political status following the rise of Pentecostalism.[37] Zambian Pentecostals have used suspicion of the Catholics' indifference to the Declaration as a tool of exclusion. This suspicion is deeply entrenched to the extent that during the 2011 presidential campaign, many Pentecostals campaigned against Michael Sata, for fear that he would remove the Declaration from the Constitution, he being a Catholic as already indicated.[38] In Zambia, Pentecostals perceive main-

34 Chammah J. Kaunda, "'From Fools for Christ to Fools for Politicians': A Critique of Zambian Pentecostal Theopolitical Imagination," *International Bulletin of Mission Research* 41, no. 4 (2017): 296–311.

35 Joe Komakoma, ed., *The Social Teaching of the Catholic Bishops and Other Christian Leaders in Zambia: Major Pastoral Letters and Statements 1953–2001* (Ndola: Mission Press, 2003), 264.

36 Catholic Bishops of Zambia, "The Catholic Bishops Oppose the Inclusion of Christian Nation Clause in the Draft Constitution," accessed July 9, 2017, https://www.lusakatimes.com/2012/08/22/catholic-bishops-oppose-inclusion-christian-nation-clause-draft-constitution/.

37 Chammah J. Kaunda, *The Nation That Fears God Prospers: A Critique of Zambian Pentecostal Theopolitical Imaginations* (Minneapolis, MN: Fortress Press, 2018).

38 Kaunda, *Nation That Fears God Prospers*.

stream Christianity as deficient in spiritual discernment to understand the covenantal political implications of the Declaration for the nation. In other words, the political implications of the Declaration are rooted in the covenant with God, entered into in the frame of the prosperity theological principle.[39] However, some scholars such as David Gordon feel that the political theology that undergirds the Declaration is "profoundly disempowering in the sense that it advocates a rather naive faith in faith alone as the path to prosperity, but the new Christianity also does not necessarily involve a reformulation of civil society, personal morality, and consciousness (even while it claims to do so)."[40] The fact that the Declaration was framed with distinctly pentecostal political thought, means that "it subjects the nation as a whole to the discourse of being 'born-again in Christ' and to the project of combating the influence of Satan in the life of the nation."[41] Identity politics between the Catholics and Pentecostals became more evident during the 2016 presidential election.

2016 Presidential Election and Identity Politics

Because of their important role in political mobilization, many Catholic leaders were co-opted/rewarded by the PF when they came into government in 2011. Fr. Frank Bwalya left the priesthood and became the PF spokesperson, thereafter, he was appointed as the Zambian High Commissioner in Australia. Fr. Charles Chilinda, a Jesuit Priest based at St Ignatius Church and a staunch supporter of PF, became a close confidante of President Sata and was a regular visitor to the State House. Under Lungu's presidency (from 2015 onward), Fr. Chilinda was appointed to the board of 12 members of the Advisory Board, Fundraising, and Technical Committee to spearhead the construction of the National House of Prayer. This initiative was strongly opposed by the Catholic hierarchy and created some tension with priests who took part in it. Because an important segment of the Catholic Church openly supported PF, it could no longer be regarded as a non-partisan actor. It led to internal divisions, as those congregants who did not support PF felt misrepresented.

The 2015 and 2016 elections further highlighted the divisions along ethnic lines, with some clergy contributing to the ethnic hate speech. Archbishop Telesphore Mpundu, who was close to President Sata but not to his successor Edgar Lungu, became a vocal critic of PF. When opposition leader Hakinde Hichilema was arrested and detained on charges

39 Naomi Haynes, "Zambia Shall be Saved!" *Nova Religio* 19, no. 1 (2015): 13.

40 David M. Gordon, *Invisible Agents: Spirits in a Central African History* (Athens, OH: Ohio University Press, 2012), 180.

41 Adriaan Van Klinken, "Homosexuality, Politics and Pentecostal Nationalism in Zambia," *Studies in World Christianity* 20, no. 3 (2014): 265.

of treason, the bishops released a strongly worded pastoral statement in June 2017 in which the head of the Bishops Conference, then Archbishop Mpundu, stated that "Zambia eminently qualifies to be branded a dictatorship."[42] While those pastoral letters were signed by all bishops, disunity now reared its head. In the following days, Chipata Catholic Auxiliary Bishop Benjamin Phiri and Bishop Alick Banda publicly distanced themselves from the statement, undermining the authority of the pastoral letter.

While the Catholics reject the Declaration, the Pentecostals remain preoccupied with safeguarding the Declaration. This has meant siding with any presidential candidate who seems to have a soft corner for the Declaration. This also means that in the cases where mainstream Christianity challenges authoritarian tendencies among Zambian politicians, some Pentecostals tend to side with them as long as they have promised to protect the Declaration. President Lungu has followed Chiluba's footsteps by publicly re-declaring Zambia as a Christian nation and added, "Zambia set free from the dark forces of evil."[43] This was done in association with Pentecostals, who some believe have contributed in Lungu's winning the 2016 presidential election. There were a lot of accusations of "tribalism" among Pentecostals themselves. The bishops and pastors who surrounded President Lungu were mostly from his ethnic group, the Ngoni. After he won elections, Lungu appointed many pentecostal pastors in various positions. He also introduced the Ministry of National Guidance and Religious Affairs (therefore, MNGRA), which some thought was done to appreciate Pentecostals for supporting him during the campaign.

Similar to the response that was given to Chiluba's Declaration, in a joint statement, the ZCCB and CCZ rejected the introduction of MNGRA, also maintaining that it was both "unwise and unnecessary . . . in view of the various financial and economic challenges our country is currently facing."[44] They further argued that "Zambians want their country to be

42 Sishuwa Sishuwa, "The Real Reasons Zambia's Opposition Leader was Released from Jail," in *African Arguments*, September 19, 2017, accessed September 12, 2019, https://africanarguments.org/2017/09/19/the-real-reasons-zambia-opposition-leader-was-released-from-jail/.

43 Kamufisa Manchishi, "President Edgar Lungu Speaks at the Day of Prayer & Fasting," accessed October 18, 2016, https://www.youtube.com/watch?v=UDEw7zTM2rU.

44 *Vatican News*, "Catholics and Protestant Churches in Zambia Against New Ministry of Religion," accessed October 28, 2016, http://en.radiovaticana.va/news/2016/09/21/catholics_and_protestants_in_zambia_against_new_ministry/125974.

a democratic [*sic*] rather than a theocratic [*sic*]."[45] However, the creation of the ministry received uncritical support from many Pentecostals, including the Evangelical Fellowship of Zambia (EFZ).[46] Most of these Pentecostals perceived Lungu as a Christian president and also tend to distance themselves from strong prophetic messages from church mother bodies. For example, when ZCCB issued a pastoral letter over human rights abuse and repression as mentioned above,[47] some prominent pentecostal leaders dissociated themselves. They argued that they were looking for "reconciliation of the nation, for healing that is why [they did not] agree even with terms used in the circulated pastoral letter such as dictatorship and demeaning language on the head of state. That for me is not the role of the church. The church is supposed to be a reconciliator and not the one to be in the forefront igniting the fire."[48]

Critiquing Identity Politics in Zambian Christianity

The forgoing demonstrates how religious identity politics have become a hindrance to constructive religious collaborative engagement in political spheres. The rise of hyper-partisan politics now prevents the historical ecumenical cooperation between the mainstream churches and civil societies. Their watchdog function, or "mirror of the nation" function, appears to have been lost. Their identity politics have delegitimized the prophetic voice of the whole church and contributed to fomenting authoritarian and political resistance to accountability to the prophetic voice of the church. The churches in Zambia are creating exclusive and conflict identities through othering other religious systems in the political spheres. In short, Zambian church's interpretation of political engagement is overrun by exclusiveness that is contrary to the values that undergird a religious pluralistic society such as Zambia. Unfortunately, religious identities have been created by sidelining not only other religious systems but at times even

45 *Vatican News*, "Catholics and Protestant Churches in Zambia."

46 The EFZ has become very pentecostal in theology and ethos. See EFZ, "Our Executive Board Members," http://www.efzsecretariat.org (October 17, 2016); Other scholars have made this observation, too. See Paul Gifford, *African Christianity: Its Public Role* (London: Hurst, 1998); Richard Burgess, "Pentecostals and Political Culture in Sub-Saharan Africa: Nigeria, Zambia and Kenya as Case Studies," in *Global Pentecostal Movements: Migration, Mission and Public Religion*, ed. Michael Wilkinson (Leiden: Brill, 2012), 17–42.

47 *Lusaka Times.com*, "Release HH, Demands Church Mother Bodies," June 16, 2017, accessed June 18, 2017, https://www.lusakatimes.com/2017/06/16/release-hh-demands-church-mother-bodies/.

48 Peter Adamu, "PF-Aligned Journalist Narrates Experience at Church Bodies' Presser," *Zambia Reports*, June 16, 2017, accessed June 18, 2017, https://zambiareports.com/2017/06/16/pf-aligned-journalist-narrates-experience-church-bodies-presser/.

other perspectives within the same denomination as could be seen from the Catholic Church. In doing so, they have positioned themselves as the only religious system that is truly concerned with issues of justice and the need for application of strong morals in politics.

Conclusion

The chapter discussed the ways the Declaration has brought identity politics to the fore, increased religious competition, and polarization of political engagement, as witnessed in the 2016 elections. The increasing politicization of Christianity in Zambian public spheres is part of evolution and intensification in competitive identity politics in the ongoing religious battle for representation, power, and access to public resources. Interrogating this situation from identity politics theory has made it clear that both Catholic and pentecostal Christians have utilized religious identity politics in the search to delegitimize each other in the public spheres. They engage in internal construction of homogeneous identities at the expense of mutual collaboration for the common good. The result is conflictive and self-interest centered political engagements that have distorted the mission of the church and its prophetic responsibility. Thus, identity politics is hindering constructive prophetic praxis of the church in Zambian politics.

13

PENTECOSTALISM, PARTISANSHIP, AND CIVIC ENGAGEMENT[1]

Elizabeth Sheridan Sperber
Erin Hern

INTRODUCTION

The rise of born-again Christian movements across sub-Saharan African states has significant implications for democratization, ethnic politics, and civil society in the region, and Zambia is no exception.[2] Religious views can influence individuals' levels and forms of political participation, partisan identities, policy preferences, and political beliefs. Yet, despite the well-noted significance of religion for politics in other parts of the world,[3]

---

1 Elizabeth S. Sperber and Erin Hern, *Pentecostal Identity and Citizen Engagement in Sub-Saharan Africa: New Evidence from Zambia. Politics and Religion*, 1–33. © The Religion and Politics Section of the American Political Science Association, published by Cambridge University Press, reproduced with permission. Support for this publication was given by the Fulbright Foundation and New York University's McSilver Institute for Poverty Policy and Research.

2 Gwyneth McClendon and Rachel Beatty Riedl, "Individualism and Empowerment in Pentecostal Sermons: New Evidence from Nairobi, Kenya," *African Affairs* 115, no. 458 (2015): 119–144; John F. McCauley, "Africa's new Big Man Rule? Pentecostalism and Patronage in Ghana," *African Affairs* 112, no. 466 (2013): 1–21; John F. McCauley, "The Political Mobilisation of Ethnicity and Religion in Africa," *American Political Science Review* 108, no. 4 (2014): 801–816.

3 For a review of this literature, see Anna Grzymala-Busse, "Why Comparative Politics Should take Religion (More) Seriously," *Annual Review of Political Science* 15 (2012): 421–442, which underscores that "doctrinal differences often translate into distinct patterns of state institutions, economic performance, and policy preferences," and that "religious attachments affect voting and popular mobilisation," 421. In sub-Saharan Africa, we know that the older Christian churches, in particular, played major roles in facilitating some third

comparative political scientists have tended to leave questions about the political role of religion—especially African Pentecostal movements—understudied.[4] One partial explanation for this lack of attention may stem from the dearth of reliable, relevant survey data on Pentecostals' political attitudes and behavior. As we discuss below, existing surveys that include questions about politics have generally lacked large samples of Pentecostals. In contrast, surveys that focus on minority religious groups have often excluded questions about partisan politics.

This chapter advances understanding of pentecostal Christianity and Zambian politics by presenting and analyzing original survey data that allows us to address questions about pentecostal political preferences and participation. Specifically, we explore relationships between pentecostal church membership, partisan preferences, and formal political behavior, as well as Pentecostals' degree of geographic spread (concentration) (N=1,500).

In general, Zambian members of pentecostal churches were more politically inclined and engaged than all other Zambians, regardless of religion. Despite high levels of political engagement, Pentecostals in our sample were less likely to contact political officials. This finding is consistent with recent qualitative[5] and experimental findings[6] about political authority in pentecostal congregations, which we discuss in Section 2. We also find suggestive evidence that non-urban Pentecostals were geographically concentrated and reported relatively unified partisan preferences. This is an important finding, as it implies that Pentecostals may constitute meaningful voting blocs; it is also possible that Pentecostalism spreads more rapidly in close-knit communities with shared political identities.

Below, we clarify what we mean by Pentecostalism and explain its relationship to other born-again movements and Christian traditions. We then delimit the scope of "political" attitudes and behaviors addressed in

wave democratic transitions, working in coalitions with both secular and denominational partners. Monica D. Toft, Daniel Philpott, and Timothy Samuel Shah, *God's Century: Resurgent Religion and Global Politics* (New York: WW Norton, 2011.); Lastly, research increasingly demonstrates that the relationship works both ways, with political outcomes (such as elections) influencing religiosity, under certain conditions. See Michele F. Margolis, "How Politics Affects Religion: Partisanship, Socialization, and Religiosity in America," *The Journal of Politics* 80, no. 1 (2018): 30–43.

4 Exceptions include Ruth Marshall-Fratani, "Mediating the Global and Local in Nigerian Pentecostalism," *Journal of Religion in Africa* 28, no. 3 (1998): 278–315; and Ruth Marshall, *Political Spiritualities: The Pentecostal Revolution in Nigeria* (Chicago: University of Chicago Press, 2009).

5 Naomi Haynes, "Egalitarianism and Hierarchy in Copperbelt Religious Practice: On the Social Work of Pentecostal Ritual," *Religion* 45, no. 2 (2015): 273–292.

6 McCauley, "Africa's New Big Man Rule?"; McCauley, "Political Mobilisation."

this chapter—namely, formal (i.e., conventional) behaviors such as voting and attitudes such as partisan preference. In studying formal political participation, however, we do not seek to undercut the rich body of qualitative scholarship that explores the dynamic boundaries of the "political" with respect to African religion. We then describe our data and methodological approach (Section 3). In Section 4, we present key findings, both descriptive statistics and regression analysis of the original survey data, and conclude with a discussion concerning future research.

Context and Definitions

Sub-Saharan Africa has experienced a demographic explosion of Christianity in recent decades: whereas only two contemporary sub-Saharan states were majority-Christian in 1950 (South Africa and Namibia), twenty one were majority-Christian by 1970, and at least twenty five of the region's forty largest countries are majority-Christian today.[7] The growth of Christianity was spurred in part by the growth of born-again traditions, including independent, pentecostal, and charismatic Christian movements. In this chapter, we focus specifically on Pentecostalism in Zambia.

Born-again traditions often overlap, and some believers are "doubly affiliated," meaning that they regularly attend services at multiple churches.[8] Some advocate more research on diversity of beliefs and practices within pentecostal,[9] charismatic and evangelical traditions.[10] In this chapter, we follow influential scholarship[11] as well as leading theologians and demographers[12] in characterizing churches as pentecostal if they endorse and

---

7 Todd M. Johnson and Gina A. Zurlo, eds., *World Christian Database (WCD)* (Leiden: Brill, 2015), http://worldchristiandatabase.org/wcd/home.asp. This includes Angola, Botswana, Burundi, Cameroon, Central African Republic, Congo, Congo DR, Ethiopia, Gabon, Ghana, Kenya, Lesotho, Madagascar, Malawi, Mozambique, Namibia, Rwanda, South Africa, South Sudan, Swaziland, Tanzania, Togo, Uganda, Zambia, and Zimbabwe.

8 Austin Cheyeka, Marja Hinfelaar, and Bernhard Udelhoven, "The Changing Face of Zambia's Christianity and its Implications for the Public Sphere: A Case Study of Bauleni Township, Lusaka," *Journal of Southern African Studies* 40 no. 5 (2014): 1031–1045.

9 WCD data indicates that concern about the "doubly affiliated" may be overblown, as fewer than 5 percent of all Christians reported this status, on average, in sub-Saharan African countries.

10 Cheyeka, Hinfelaar, and Udelhoven, "Changing Face of Zambia's Christianity."

11 Paul Freston, *Evangelicals and Politics in Asia, Africa and Latin America* (New York: Cambridge University Press, 2004); Terence O. Ranger, ed., *Evangelical Christianity and Democracy in Africa* (New York: Oxford University Press, 2008).

12 D.W. Bebbington, "Evangelical Christianity and the Enlightenment," *Crux*, 25, no. 4 (1989): 29–36; Johnson and Zurlo, *World Christian Database*;

promote personal relationships with God, as well as members actively exercising "the gifts of the Holy Spirit" such as prophecy, faith healing, or glossolalia. Pentecostals may therefore belong to one of the older, transnational, classical Pentecostalism (e.g., Assemblies of God), either one of the megachurches, or the smaller locally initiated African pentecostal churches, many of which were established since the early 1990s.[13]

Another key characteristic of Pentecostalism widely in the African context, concerns traditional African religion and spiritual beliefs. Pentecostal leaders condemn traditional religion, spirituality, and even some traditional customs as demonic.[14] This stance positions pentecostal churches in opposition to African Independent Churches, or AICs, which are distinguished by their reverence for African traditions, such as honoring ancestor spirits. Hence, pentecostal Christianity is quite distinct from AICs, such as Zion or Apostolic churches.

Similarly, religious studies scholars and demographers distinguish Pentecostalism from Evangelical Christianity, which is typically associated with older mission traditions, such as the Baptist, Methodist, and Lutheran churches.[15] With a capital "e," Evangelicalism refers to born-again Protestants who emphasize personal relationships with God, yet, believe that gifts of the Holy Spirit were *only experienced in biblical times*. In this way, Evangelicals differ from Pentecostals, for whom experiencing the gifts of the Holy Spirit (e.g., speaking in tongues, prophesying, and engaging in faith healing) are central worship practices. Additionally, Pentecostals are distinct from charismatic Christians, i.e., members of Catholic or mainline Protestant churches (e.g., Anglican-derived), who embrace beliefs and practices associated with Pentecostalism, but do so from *within* charismatic sub-groups of these older churches.[16]

Luis Lugo and Alan Cooperman, *Tolerance and Tension: Islam and Christianity in Sub-Saharan Africa* (Washington, DC: Pew Research Center, 2010), accessed December 2016, http://www.pewforum.org/2010/04/15/executive-summary-islam-and-christianity-in-sub-saharan-africa/.

13 Lugo and Cooperman, "Tolerance and Tension"; Haynes, "Egalitarianism and Hierarchy." For a concise history of Zambian Pentecostalism, see Chammah J. Kaunda, "The Making of Pentecostal Zambia: A Brief History of Pneumatic Spirituality," *Oral History Journal of South Africa 4*, no. 1 (2016): 15–45.

14 Deji Ayegboyin and Ishola S. Ademola, *African Indigenous Churches: An Historical Perspective* (Lagos: Greater Heights Publications, 1997); Birgit Meyer, "Christianity in Africa: From African Independent to Pentecostal-Charismatic Churches," *Annual Review of Anthropology* 33 (2004): 447–474.

15 Johnson and Zurlo, *WCD*.

16 Johnson and Zurlo, *WCD*; Scholars of different nations and disciplinary backgrounds occasionally use these terms interchangeably, while others distinguish between older pentecostal churches and newer neo-charismatic ones. We forego use of the contested term *neo-charismatic* in this chapter for the sake of clarity.

Though these categorical distinctions sometimes blur in believers' lives, they are important for social science research. For instance, although the beliefs and practices of believers may overlap across Christian traditions, church members support and are exposed to widely differing *religious institutions*, which also tend to have different political affiliations and roles in public life. These traditions exhibit variation in transnational ties, hierarchical leadership structure, and training requirements for clergy in locally initiated pentecostal, older Evangelical and the Catholic Church, respectively. There is evidence that such institutional differences matter for religious communities.[17]

Additionally, embracing the ideal definitions described above enables scholars to use research methods to gain important insights into the possible relationships between religion and political behavior. While surveys alone cannot comprehensively illuminate complex religiopolitical dynamics, social scientists should nevertheless use survey research to study religion and African politics, much as we study religion and politics in other parts of the world. To date, however, few if any large-scale academic survey studies have reliably identified and examined the political interest, engagement, and partisanship of African Pentecostals.[18]

Despite the lack of survey research on the topic, however, ethnographic, historical, and recent experimental research describes some sociocultural implications of pentecostal growth in sub-Saharan Africa. This literature makes two broad points that are particularly relevant here. First, anthropologists have documented that African Pentecostals often reject the liberal distinction between the "personal" and the "political."[19] Rather, Pentecostals often view the practice of their faith, and especially their attempts to evangelize (spread) Pentecostalism to others, as their primary mode of "political" engagement. These ideas flow logically from the belief

---

17 Stathis N. Kalyvas, "Commitment Problems in Emerging Democracies: The Case of Religious Parties," *Comparative Politics* (2000): 379–398; Elizabeth Sperber, "*Deus ex Machina*? New Religious Movements in African Politics" (PhD diss., New York: Columbia University, 2016); Amy S. Patterson and Tracy Kuperus, "Mobilising the Faithful: Organisational Autonomy, Visionary Pastors, and Citizenship in South Africa and Zambia," *African Affairs* 115, no. 459 (2016): 318–341.

18 In *Christianity, Islam, and Liberal Democracy: Lessons from Sub-Saharan Africa*, (New York: Oxford University Press, 2015), Robert A. Dowd explores the impact of religious diversity on religious conflict. Although the book does not focus primarily on the politics of Pentecostalism, it explores potential variation in Pentecostals' attitudes toward religious conflict in Nigeria and Uganda. We exclude the Pew Forum's 2010 valuable report on demographic trends in African religion in this assessment, as it is not a peer-reviewed social scientific study.

19 See Barbara Bompani and Caroline Valois, eds., *Christian Citizens and the Moral Regeneration of the African State* (London: Ashgate Publishing, 2017).

that formal politics (i.e., conventional party politics and modes of political participation, like voting) is largely tainted by corruption, and can only be transformed into something morally pure after society members themselves embrace transformative religious change by becoming born-again and accepting Jesus Christ as their savior. In this sense, the personal—the way of one's life—is political insofar as it reflects moral commitments that define individuals' conduct in society. Particularly in states where governments are associated with mass corruption, violence, repression, or dysfunction, such an individualistic, pious view has had an intuitive appeal for many.

However, as Pentecostals have grown in number in some sub-Saharan states, they have become increasingly visible in conventional politics. This shift is often explained as a coordinated effort by umbrella associations of church leaders who believe that if their co-religionists are elected or appointed to powerful positions in government, they will be able to positively influence governance. As a new, interdisciplinary volume explored,[20] these Pentecostals seek to establish a new Christian citizenship in their countries—often by having elected leaders declare the country officially Christian and by placing morally upright Christians in positions of power. Pentecostals in many African states seek to promote their religious beliefs by getting fellow Pentecostals elected, not only because they believe Pentecostals will abstain from corruption, but because they also want pentecostal politicians to use the organs of the state to help promote born-again Christian values as a salve for the nation's ailments.[21]

We seek to complement these findings by exploring the possibility that pentecostal citizens express distinctive views about electoral politics and engage uniquely in politics. Specifically, we consider individuals' self-reported views about different parties and forms of government, their willingness to participate in electoral politics (i.e., by identifying with a party, voting, or contacting their representatives), and the degree to which they report feeling interested in or following news about formal political outcomes. Of course, even if Pentecostals share similar partisan preferences and patterns of participation, they may also perceive these forms of participation as less important than evangelization. Although we investigate the former kind of politics in this chapter, we do not contest the significance of the latter, nor do we suggest that more pious forms of politics are of diminished significance for Pentecostals who engage actively in formal politics.

---

20 Barbara Bompani and Caroline Valois, "Sexualising Politics: The Anti-Homosexuality Bill, Party-politics and the New Political Dispensation in Uganda," *Critical African Studies* 9 no. 1 (2017): 1–19.

21 Paul Gifford, *The Christian Churches and the Democratisation of Africa* (Leiden: Brill, 1995); Bompani and Valois, "Sexualising Politics."

Additionally, extant literature has also emphasized a dualism or ambivalence in African Pentecostals' relationship to conventionally defined political attitudes and behaviors in recent years.[22] Summarizing this literature, Haynes concludes that "Pentecostal ritual life both draws believers into democratic, open-ended, and largely egalitarian religious communities, and produces clear distinctions between individuals, resulting in differentiated, hierarchical structures."[23] Contemporary African Pentecostalism is thus seen to embody "a tension between democratic and authoritarian instantiations of the Holy Spirit."[24] Extant research, in other words, implies that Pentecostalism may simultaneously encourage both pro- and anti-democratic political influence. Far from making it politically irrelevant, this ambivalence opens up important new questions about how pentecostal movements may eventually influence the fate of liberal democratic ideals in many backsliding African electoral democracies.

Descriptive and experimental studies from Kenya are consistent with the idea that Pentecostals embrace new pairings of political attitudes. McClendon and Riedl,[25] for instance, evaluated the impact of Pentecostal messages on individuals' reported aversion to inequity and their self-efficacy. Self-efficacy is often associated with political participation and, by extension, democracy. By contrast, tolerance of inequity is often linked to tolerance for antidemocratic elite behavior. The authors found that randomly exposing individuals to pentecostal messages caused immediate boosts in self-efficacy and decreased aversion to inequity. Hence, these findings resonate with the apparent paradox of pentecostal political engagement: On the one hand, Pentecostals may develop social attitudes and behavioral tools that make them more effective individuals, and on the other hand, their religious praxis may simultaneously undermine an interest in greater equality.

A partial explanation for this paradox is found in a second strand of the literature, which focuses on top-down, seemingly quid-pro-quo relationships between some political elites and pentecostal leaders.[26] Although these studies acknowledge that instrumental reasons never fully eclipse

22 Marshall, *Political Spiritualities*.

23 Haynes, "Egalitarianism and Hierarchy," 274.

24 Haynes, "Egalitarianism and Hierarchy," 289; Marshall, *Political Spiritualities*; Ogbu Kalu, *African Pentecostalism: An Introduction* (New York: Oxford University Press, 2008); Terence O. Ranger ed., *Evangelical Christianity and Democracy in Africa* (Oxford Scholarship Online, 2008).

25 McClendon and Riedl, "Individualism and Empowerment."

26 Paul Gifford, *Christianity, Politics and Public Life in Kenya* (London: Hurst, 2009); David Maxwell, "'Catch the Cockerel Before Dawn': Pentecostalism and Politics in Post-Colonial Zimbabwe," *Africa* 70, no. 2 (2000): 249–277; Sperber, "*Deus ex Machina*?"

non-instrumental and expressive reasons for religious participation,[27] they argue that instrumental elite links nevertheless facilitate clientelism and anti-democratic political practices. In Côte D'Ivoire, pentecostal elites with ties to ruling politicians promoted electoral violence to defend the politicians' tenure in office.[28] In other African countries, favored pentecostal leaders have been tied to electoral manipulation and illiberal constitutional amendments.[29] In countries like Zambia, pentecostal leaders publicly admitted that their brethren promoted the ruling party and decried opposition leaders before elections in hopes of "political recognition," such as government appointments, cash, media access, and public promotion.[30] At other times, pentecostal and political leaders advocated illiberal reforms, such as restricted LGBTQ rights and declaring nations officially Christian, tactics that increased the popularity of elites' religious groups and political parties. Campaigns against LGBTQ rights have been so prominent in recent years that van Klinken and Chitando[31] described them as a new form of pentecostal nationalism, wherein "homosexuality is considered to be a threat to the purity of the nation and is associated with the devil."[32] While expressive motivation may be important for individual Pentecostals, they have simultaneously engaged in illiberal,

---

27 In the African context, see Mike McGovern, *Making War in Côte d'Ivoire* (Chicago: University of Chicago Press, 2011), 98.

28 Cédric Mayrargue, "The Expansion of Pentecostalism in Benin: Individual Rationales and Transnational Dynamics," in *Between Babel and Pentecost: Transnational Pentecostalism in Africa and Latin America*, eds. André Corten and Ruth Marshall-Fratani (Indianapolis, IN: Indiana University Press, 2001), 274292; McGovern, *Making War*, 67–101.

29 Daniel J. Smith, *A Culture of Corruption: Everyday Deception and Popular Discontent in Nigeria* (Princeton, NJ: Princeton University Press, 2010), 214; Austin Cheyeka, "Towards a History of the Charismatic Churches in Post-Colonial Zambia," in *One Zambia, Many Histories*, eds. Jan Bart Gewald, Marja Hinfelaar, and Giacomo Macola (Leiden: Brill, 2008), 144–163; Paul Gifford, *Ghana's New Christianity: Pentecostalism in a Globalizing African Economy* (Indianapolis, IN: Indiana University Press, 2004).

30 In an article entitled, "Sata Meets Pentecostal Pastors," November 12, 2011, *The Lusaka Times* reported that after opposition leader Michael Sata won a surprise victory in presidential elections against the incumbent MMD party, pentecostal pastors apologized to Sata, and "the clergymen further stated that it was sad that certain pastors who wanted political recognition from the MMD regime went out of the way to utter embarrassing remarks against President Sata, accessed December 5, 2017, https://www.lusakatimes.com/2011/12/01/sata-meets-pentecostal-pastors/.

31 Adriaan Van Klinken and Ezra Chitando, eds., *Public Religion and the Politics of Homosexuality in Africa* (Abingdon: Routledge, 2016).

32 Van Klinken and Chitando, *Public Religion and the Politics of Homosexuality*, 259; Bompani and Valois, "Sexualising Politics."

instrumental partnerships with African politicians. Qualitative research on Pentecostalism in Zambian politics echoes this broader view.[33]

Implications for Formal Political Participation and Partisanship

Although sub-Saharan states are characterized by low-levels of partisan attachment, research discussed above implies that Pentecostals may be more prone to partisan attachment than their peers. Yet, given significant state-level variation in party institutionalization,[34] and an apparent increase in party-level strategies to build allegiant constituencies,[35] it seems more reasonable to expect that Pentecostals will constitute voting blocs only where relatively strong parties have cultivated links to pentecostal elites.

Scholars have previously lacked the survey data to answer questions about the relationship between pentecostal church membership and partisanship. In this chapter, we present cross-sectional statistical analyses to address the extent to which Pentecostals differ from other Christians in their political participation and partisanship identities. We also explore how geographically concentrated non-urban Pentecostals are and whether they shared voting patterns.

Empirical Expectations in the Zambian Context

In this chapter, we focus on the Zambian context, which other chapters in this volume help contextualize. Until 2011, Zambian society generally

33 Austin Cheyeka, "Zambia, a 'Christian Nation' in Post Movement for Multiparty Democracy (MMD) Era, 2011–2016," *International Journal of Humanities and Social Science* 6, no.7 (2016): 159–172; Chammah J. Kaunda, "The Day of Prayer and Its Potential for Engendering Public Ecclesiology Ecumenism in Zambia," *Religions* 9, no. 12 (2018): 393; Chammah J. Kaunda and Mutale M. Kaunda, "Mobilising Religious Assets for Social Transformation: A Theology of Decolonial Reconstruction Perspective on the Ministry of National Guidance and Religious Affairs (MNGRA) in Zambia," *Religions* 9, no. 6 (2018): 176.

34 Rachel Beatty Riedl, *Authoritarian Origins of Democratic Party Systems in Africa* (Cambridge: Cambridge University Press, 2014). For a summary of this literature, see Jaimie Bleck and Nicolas Van de Walle, "Parties and Issues in Francophone West Africa: Towards a Theory of Non-mobilisation," *Democratisation* 18, no. 5 (2011): 1125–1145.

35 Michael Bratton and Mwangi S. Kimenyi, "Voting in Kenya: Putting Ethnicity in Perspective" (University of Connecticut Economics Working Papers No. 200809, 2008), accessed June 1, 2017, http://digitalcommons.uconn.edu/econ_wpapers/200809/; Nic Cheeseman and Miles Larmer, "Ethnopopulism in Africa: Opposition Mobilisation in Diverse and Unequal Societies," *Democratisation* 22, no.1 (2015): 22–50; Elena Gadjanova, "Measuring Parties' Ethnic Appeals in Democracies," *Party Politics* 21, no. 2 (2015): 309–327.

viewed Pentecostals as a loyal base of support for the ruling Movement for Multiparty Democracy (MMD) party. After two decades of extraordinary corruption and widening economic inequality, rural poverty, and youth unemployment, however, it was not obvious how religious and partisan identities would relate *after* the MMD's narrow loss in Zambia's 2011 elections. On the one hand, Pentecostals may have felt a partisan attachment to the MMD and might therefore have continued to prefer the MMD even after they lost power. On the other hand, Zambian pentecostal leaders regularly embraced the notion (during MMD rule) that God selects the nation's leaders. The role of churches, pentecostal leaders argued, was to support the government of the day. If this logic holds, then we would expect Pentecostals to embrace the PF after their win. Alternatively, Pentecostals might have chosen a third path, and disengaged from politics altogether following the MMD's loss in 2011.

We attempt to adjudicate between the three empirical possibilities above by exploring correlations between self-reported pentecostal church membership and political variables included in an original individual-level survey conducted in Zambia in 2013–14. Expanding on the question of political engagement, we consider partisanship as well as two other questions: (1) How politically active were Pentecostals during the 2011 election? (2) What types of political actions (if any) were Pentecostals most likely to engage in?

Data and Methods

Site Selection and Survey Methodology

The following section presents analysis using data of a survey conducted by Hern across four districts in Zambia, including Livingstone and Kazungula Districts in Southern Province, Kabwe District in Central Province, and Solwezi District in Northwestern Province.[36] The survey was conducted between October 2013 and February 2014 with 1,500 respondents. In each province, enumerators surveyed 500 respondents, stratified according to urban/rural residence and gender. Originally conducted as part of a larger study of political participation, the study used a stratified random sample of households across urban and rural constituencies in the three provinces, selected purposively for varying levels of economic development. In each district, the sample was stratified using the government's urban and rural constituency designations. Enumerators identified equal number of respondents from each urban and rural constituency within two and a half hours of travel time from the district's town center

36 Erin Hern, *Developing States, Shaping Citizens: Service Delivery and Political Participation in Zambia* (Ann Arbor: University of Michigan Press, 2019).

using a random walk household sampling strategy. The response rate was 83 percent.[37]

The site selection for this survey excluded Zambia's major urban areas in Lusaka and the Copperbelt. However, the sample was equally divided between urban and rural constituencies around Zambia's smaller cities of Livingstone, Kabwe, and Solwezi. In Kabwe, many residents have close ties to Lusaka and travel there frequently. In Solwezi, many respondents indicated having migrated from the Copperbelt once the Kansanshi mine re-opened. While exclusion of Lusaka and the Copperbelt results in the exclusion of strictly urban Zambian Pentecostals, we are confident that the respondents included in the sample reflect much of Zambia's diversity, particularly considering the ties between Zambia's smaller and larger cities.

Coding Religion in the Data

Respondents were first asked if they belonged to any religion. Three respondents refused to answer, 58 (less than 4 percent of the sample) reported, "not belonging to any religion," and 15 individuals reported belonging to a religion, but declined to name their religious group of affiliation. If respondents replied in the affirmative to this first question, they were then asked "what kind of church, mosque, synagogue, or temple do you go to?" Responses were recorded verbatim, and the interviewers subsequently coded these according to (1) world religion and (2) Christian tradition (e.g., Catholic, mainline Protestant, Pentecostal, Evangelical).[38]

---

37 In Kabwe and Solwezi, the districts include both urban and rural constituencies, while in Southern Province, respondents from Livingstone District are urban and Kazungula District are rural.

38 Many respondents described their churches simply as Catholic, Evangelical, or Pentecostal. Additionally, we coded Baptist, Methodist, and Lutheran churches as Evangelical. In Zambia, mainline Protestants generally belong to the United Church of Zambia, which was established at Independence when several older Protestant churches united. Anglicans and members of other churches that belong to the World Council of Churches were also coded as mainline Protestant. All Zion churches were coded as African Independent Churches, but there were very few of these. Other churches with conventional Pentecostal church names, such as "Jesus International Ministries" or "Global Ministry of the Holy Spirit" were coded as pentecostal, as were members of larger pentecostal churches, such as the Assemblies of God, BIGOCA, and the Bread of Life Church. In applying this coding scheme, Sperber drew on extensive prior research with Independent, Pentecostal, Evangelical, and other mainline churches in Zambia, as well as the membership lists of the various Zambian church "mother bodies" (umbrella organizations), which she had previously obtained. To protect the anonymity of our subjects, we do not publish a list of all the churches coded in this study. More detail is available upon request.

Our coding scheme mirrors the categories that Zambians use to describe Christian traditions in the country. This includes a distinction between older traditional evangelical churches (e.g., Baptist, Lutheran, and Methodist), and pentecostal churches (including international pentecostal churches, such as the Assemblies of God, and smaller pentecostal churches, which often have "international," "global," "Jesus," or "Holy Spirit" in their names), but no further distinction within the community of self-described pentecostal churches.[39] In Section 4 (below), we report descriptive statistics for these groups, along with other major Christian blocs in Zambia, such as the Seventh Day Adventists (SDA), Jehovah's Witnesses, and New Apostolic Church. These latter three churches represent relatively strict international Christian denominations, and their church institutions are believed to abstain from any direct political engagement.[40]

Based on this coding, we generated a binary variable equal to 1 if respondents reported attending a pentecostal church, and 0 otherwise. In robustness checks, we recode this variable to combine Pentecostals and self-described Evangelicals, and to combine Pentecostals and members of the New Apostolic Church. Results are robust to these alternative coding schemes. Yet, as we discuss below, we find evidence that pentecostal church membership correlates with distinct political characteristics, which indicates that our preferred classifications are justified by the data.

The sample included one person reporting as Hindu and two of Muslim affiliations. This is consistent with the most recently available census data, which found that only 1 percent of Zambians identified as Muslim, and that there were no other numerically prominent non-Christian groups in the country.[41]

Variables and Modelling Strategy

We examine the relationship between membership in a pentecostal church and four dependent variables: voting, contacting local officials,

---

39 Although some scholars of global Pentecostalism advocate for an additional distinction between the older, larger pentecostal churches and newer, smaller ones (sometimes referred to as neo-pentecostal or neo-charismatic), this is not a meaningful distinction to most Zambian respondents, pastors, or the leadership of their national level "mother bodies." We note that most Zambian pentecostal churches participate in joint worship activities and pastors' training, generally embrace similar doctrine and worship styles, and have similarly been accused of "singing the songs" of incumbent politicians. We therefore do not impose this distinction in our coding.

40 Pentecostals were not more likely to report *not* having a party preference.

41 *The 2010 Census of Population National Analytical Report* (Lusaka: Zambian Central Statistical Agency, 2012), accessed May 31, 2020, https://www.moh.gov.zm/docs/reports/ZDHS%202013-2014%20report.pdf.

political interest, and party preference. During the survey period (2013–2014), Zambia's presidential election for 2016 was scheduled. The sitting president subsequently died in office, triggering a special election, but that was unforeseen at the time of the survey. *Vote16* is a binary variable that takes the value of 1 if respondents reported intention to vote in the 2016 election, otherwise 0. *ContactLocal* is another binary variable that takes the value of 1 if respondents reported ever trying to contact a local government official, otherwise 0. *PoliticalInterest* is an alpha-scaled index including two ordinal variables: one that asks whether respondents ever talked about politics and another that asks whether they were interested in politics. Each variable is scaled 0-3 (never to always). Because they are highly correlated (average inter-item covariance of 0.73), we use Cronbach's alpha to generate a single scaled variable, standardized around a mean of zero with a variance of one. Finally, *PreferOpposition* is another binary variable that takes the value of 1 if respondents reported preference for an opposition party, and 0 if they preferred the incumbent PF. The 378 respondents who reported no party preference are dropped from these models. This included 20 percent of Pentecostals in our sample.[42]

In each model, the primary explanatory variable is pentecostal (described above). We model the three binary outcome variables—*Vote16*, *ContactLocal*, and *PreferOpposition*—using logistic regression. Coefficients are expressed as odds ratios for ease of interpretation. We model *PoliticalInterest*, a continuous index, using OLS. We cluster standard errors in each model by the unit of stratification, i.e., the ward (village). Standard control variables were included in each model, including dummies for urban residence, sex, formal employment, age, education, and ethnic group.[43] Province level fixed effects account for unobserved variation across the three surveyed provinces.

Results

Descriptive Differences

Table 1 presents descriptive statistics for all the major religious groups present in significant numbers in the survey data. Of the 95 percent who reported religious belonging, the largest religious groups included Pentecostals (representing 24.5 percent of our final sample), Catholics

42 Pentecostals were not significantly more likely to report *not* having a party preference.

43 Because reports of income are often unreliable in African contexts, we use a dummy variable indicating formal employment as a proxy for higher income While many Zambians work in the informal economy, and formal employment is not a perfect proxy for income, formal employment correlates with income and is a rough measure of class.

(20.3 percent), mainline Protestants (17.2 percent), and Evangelicals (e.g., Baptists and Methodists, 7.4 percent). Although Zambian Census data has not distinguished Pentecostals from mainline Protestants or Evangelicals, it generally finds that roughly 20 percent of the national population identifies as Catholic, which corresponds almost exactly to the share of Catholics in our sample, giving us greater confidence in the degree to which our sample reflects the broader Zambian population.

Table 1: Descriptive statistics by religious group

	Percentage							*Mean score*
	Of sample	*Church attendance*	*Female*	*Urban*	*Voting*	*Contact officials*	*Prefers opposition*	*Political Engagement*
Pentecostal	24.5	92.3	51.4	55.1	95.1	32	35	0.18
Evangelical	7.4	89.8	44.8	35.2	86.7	33.3	31.4	-0.02
Mainline Protestant	17.2	89.6	53.9	54.7	93.5	40.7	29	0.1
Catholic	20.3	90.7	49.7	55.9	92.1	40.7	26.6	0.04
SDA	11.4	91.8	42.6	50.0	95.1	38.3	28	-0.09
Jehovah's Witness	7	93.8	54.0	48.0	28	24	16	-0.58
New Apostolic	11.1	90.1	50.6	32.9	92.1	40	26.6	-0.1
Other	1.12	15	62.5	56.3	81.3	25	18.7	-0.29
None	-	8.2	51.3	44.7	77.6	22.4	34.2	-0.11
Sample mean		*87*	*50.3*	*50.2*	*87.9*	*36.2*	*38.7*	*-0.01*

Notes: Of the total survey sample, 5.1 percent reported that they did not actively belong to a religious group. The category "other" includes the very small number of Zion church members (African Independent churches) as well as several observations who reported ambiguous church names. We include the "nones" for descriptive comparison in this table but exclude them from samples used in regression analyses. Only three responses to our binary question concerning religious belonging were missing. Column two identifies the percentage of each religious group in our regression analyses. "Church attendance" denotes the percentage of respondents who reported attending religious services at least once per week. The usable N=1,441.

Interestingly, Pentecostals were not significantly more likely to report attendance at religious services than many other large religious groups, such as the Catholics and mainline Protestants. Similarly, both the gender and urban/rural breakdown of Pentecostals was comparable to other large religious groups as well, with roughly 50 percent of Pentecostals identifying as female, and a slightly higher rate of urban-dwellers than rural Pentecostal respondents. With more than 95 percent of Pentecostals reporting intention to vote in 2016 and receiving correspondingly high scores for political engagement (e.g., regularity of talking about politics and self-reported interest in politics), Pentecostals appear to be more politically engaged than other religious groups, with one puzzling exception: Pentecostals were significantly less likely to report having contacted a political official. They reported the highest levels of support for an opposition party.

Importantly, Pentecostals differed from members of older Evangelical churches, particularly in terms of self-reported political engagement and intention to vote. The Evangelical sample is small, however, and disproportionately rural, which makes direct comparison difficult. It is also worth noting here that, as one would expect, Jehovah's Witnesses were significantly less likely to report any type of political involvement; this corresponds with their doctrinal prohibition on participation in politics, and increases our confidence that individuals felt comfortable to report both relatively high and low levels of participation in our survey.

These descriptive statistics correspond with the main findings of the regression analyses presented below: Overall, we find that Pentecostals in our samples reported higher than average levels of political interest and were more likely to report an intention to vote in 2016 but were simultaneously less likely to have contacted political officials. They were also more likely to support opposition parties (including the MMD), and less likely to support the incumbent party (PF). We explore each of these findings in turn.

Political Engagement

Table 2 displays the results of OLS regression predicting *PoliticalInterest*. Model I was a bivariate regression without any control variables. Including individual-level control variables (Model II) leaves results virtually unchanged. Adding fixed effects for province and respondents reported, ethnic identity (Model III) does not change the direction or statistical significance of the coefficient but reduces its magnitude. These results are also robust to inclusion of the religious "nones" in the sample, and alternative coding of the variable "Pentecostal" (e.g., coding Evangelicals or New Apostolic Church members as Pentecostals). As expected, however, coding Evangelicals as Pentecostals dampens the magnitude and significance of our results, which underscores the political differences across these groups.

In order to determine whether Pentecostals' higher degree of political interest translates to a higher level of political participation, we use logistic regression to estimate the relationship between Pentecostalism and two binary outcome variables: *Vote16* and *ContactLocal.* These results, displayed as odds ratios in Table 3, indicate that Pentecostals are nearly four times as likely to express an intention to vote than non-Pentecostals, but about 30 percent less likely to report contacting local government officials. Notably, residents of Southern Province, a hotbed of opposition activity, and members of the Tonga and Luvale ethnic groups are also significantly more likely to express intent to vote. Vote intention therefore appears to correlate with publicly voiced group-level dissatisfaction with the government.

Table 2: Correlates of PoliticalInterest

	I	II	III
Pentecostal	0.238***	0.230***	0.187**
	(0.069)	(0.076)	(0.075)
Urban		0.097	0.090
		(0.062)	(0.058)
Male		0.367***	0.360***
		(0.039)	(0.038)
Age		-0.000	-0.006
		(0.029)	(0.028)
Education		0.024***	0.028***
		0.007	(0.008)
Formal Employment		0.0136	0.008
		0.014	(0.062)
Fixed effects	No	No	Yes
N	1427	1426	1426
Adj R^2	0.0128	0.0705	0.0858

Note: OLS including a constant term (not shown), with SEs clustered by ward (the unit of stratification). SEs parenthesized. Significance denoted by * if $p<0.10$, ** if $p<0.05$, *** if $p<0.01$.

Table 3: Correlates of Political Participation

	ContactLocal	*ContactLocal*	*Vote16*	*Vote16*
Pentecostal	0.742**	0.777*	3.123***	3.669***
	(0.103)	(0.115)	(0.775)	(0.966)
Urban		0.912		0.897
		(0.173)		(0.198)
Male		1.235		1.201
		(0.171)		(0.233)
Age		1.462***		1.227*
		(0.098)		(0.144)
Education		1.008		1.114*
		(0.022)		(0.070)
Formal Employment		1.714***		0.817
		(0.242)		(0.215)
Fixed effects	No	Yes	No	Yes
N	1427	1426	1427	1371
AIC	1878.3	1844.5	1006.0	976.0
BIC	1888.8	1986.6	1016.5	1111.8

*Note: Logit models including a constant term (not shown), with SEs clustered by ward (the unit of stratification) and exponentiated coefficients. SEs parenthesized. Significance denoted by *if p<0.10, **if p<0.05, ***if p<0.01.*

Party Preference

Dissatisfaction with the current government may explain, in part, why Pentecostals have higher levels of political interest and a greater likelihood of expressing intention to vote, but less likely to report contacting officials. Indeed, models presented in Table 4 reveal that Pentecostals were significantly more likely to express a preference for an opposition party, e.g., the MMD, than the PF. This relationship is robust to the addition of individual-level control variables (Model II) but loses statistical significance when we include fixed effects for province and ethnic group (Model III). As with results presented above, these findings are robust to inclusion of the religious "nones" in the sample, and alternative coding of the variable "Pentecostal."

Table 4: Correlates of Party Preference

	I	II	III
Pentecostal	1.497** (0.24)	1.544** (0.269)	1.074 (0.19)
Urban		1.048 (0.243)	1.120 (0.210)
Male		1.194 (0.167)	1.212 (0.176)
Age		0.998 (0.077)	0.910 (0.082)
Education		0.896** (0.041)	0.932 (0.043)
Formal employment		0.841 (0.156)	0.661* (0.140)
Fixed effects	No	No	Yes
N	1069	1069	1069
AIC	1418.6	1412.3	1299.744
BIC	1428.5	1447.2	1434.05

*Note: OLS including a constant term (not shown), with SEs clustered by ward (the unit of stratification). SEs are in parentheses. Significance denoted by *if p<0.10, **if p<0.05, ***if p<0.01.*

Religious belonging is concentrated along regional lines within our sample. This intriguing finding was difficult to assess empirically prior to this study, and is likely an artefact of patterns of missionary settlement in colonial Zambia, wherein missionaries from different churches and denominations often overlapped with ethnic and linguistic identities.[44] Pentecostals in our sample are largely concentrated in North-western Province, where people were four times more likely to prefer opposition over the ruling PF party. Similarly, the ethnic groups most likely to express preference for opposition were the Tonga and Toka-Leya of the Southern Province (usual suspects), alongside the Kaonde (concentrated in the North-western Province), and the Lamba (concentrated in the Copperbelt). Many Kaonde were longtime residents of North-western

[44] This is the case both because Evangelism required missionaries to master a local language, and also because missionary schools and publications iteratively incentivized the extension of local linguistic and, to a lesser extent, cultural boundaries. Daniel Posner, *Institutions and Ethnic Politics in Africa* (Cambridge: Cambridge University Press, 2005).

Province, a historically neglected outpost that has received little government attention. The Lamba are likely to be migrants from the Copperbelt and/or to have ties to Lamba in the Copperbelt.[45] While the incumbent PF originally had a base of support in the Copperbelt, declining global copper prices and the perception that the government was not adequately protecting laborers from foreign mine owners may account for the apparent turn of opinion among Lamba in our sample. The Kaonde and Lamba are concentrated in North-west Province, and each of these groups has a disproportionate number of Pentecostals, explaining why province and ethnic group fixed effects mute the significance of the relationship between Pentecostalism and opposition party support.

To be clear, this survey data does not allow us to address questions about causality: We conclude that pentecostal church membership *corresponded* with partisan preferences, but we cannot draw causal inferences about how church membership may *influence* partisanship. Yet, our analysis allows us to conclude that many Zambian Pentecostals exhibit higher rates of political interest and lower rates of contacting political officials than their Christian peers. We also present important evidence concerning the geographic concentration of Pentecostals, which points to the importance of further survey data collection to analyze the relationship between individuals' religion and party identification over time. Future research should build on this study by including more provinces and larger samples within surveyed areas to improve statistical inference.

Conclusion

Using original data collected across three provinces in Zambia, this chapter presents evidence that Pentecostals are more likely to report political interest and are *less* likely to contact political officials than their peers—virtually all of whom report membership in other Christian denominations. This chapter also documents that Pentecostals are geographically concentrated, which matters for formal politics in democracies. Evidence indicates that these findings have some bearing on the relationship between Pentecostalism and aspects of formal political participation in other African states.[46]

45 On Lamba migration history see Brian Siegel, "The 'Wild' and 'Lazy' Lamba: Ethnic Stereotypes on the Central African Copperbelt," in *The Creation of Tribalism in Southern Africa*, ed. Leroy Vail (London and Berkeley: James Currey and University of California Press, 1989), 350–71. Lamba also had a history of supporting the MMD: In 2011, Lamba chiefs endorsed the (then-incumbent) MMD candidate for president.

46 Elizabeth S. Sperber and Erin A. Hern, "Pentecostal Identity and Citizen Engagement in Sub-Saharan Africa: New Evidence from Zambia," *Politics and Religion* 11, no. 4 (2018): 830–862.

Our findings are also consistent with the stylized fact that Pentecostals were more likely to support the MMD party surrounding the 2011 election of Michael Sata. Though we cannot infer with certainty that religious identification *drives* this finding, this is important, especially in the light of recent debates over the degree to which a coherent social category of "Pentecostals" can be said to exist. Interestingly, following Sata's death in office, Pentecostals have increasingly voiced public support for the new leader of the Patriotic Front and Zambia's current president, Edgar Lungu. The electoral pressure group "Christians for Lungu," for instance, was widely associated with members of pentecostal churches and Lungu has undertaken a number of headline grabbing projects and reforms that are lauded by Pentecostals and criticized by leaders of the older mission churches.[47] This includes the declaration of a National Day of Prayer, the ongoing construction of a national "church" in Lusaka, and the establishment of a new government Ministry focused on religious affairs.[48] Under Lungu, state media has also used the term *Church Mother Bodies* to refer to clusters of pentecostal organizations in the absence of the Catholic or mainline Protestant churches, which elevates the status of pentecostal church bodies (e.g., the Independent Churches of Zambia and the Bible Gospel Church in Africa), and dilutes the status of older mission churches.[49]

Considering the continued political salience of pentecostal religious identity under a new ruling party, the evolving political correlates of Pentecostalism in Zambia merits further research. In particular, this chapter suggests that it is possible to recognize variation in some religious beliefs and practices within and across pentecostal churches, while also conducting careful analysis of survey data to gain leverage on the questions about how "Pentecostal" church membership may correspond to certain political attitudes and behaviors. Future research on related topics would also benefit from the use of experimental methods to gain leverage on the causal effects of pentecostal messaging on Zambians' formal political behavior.

---

47 Cheyeka, "Zambia, a 'Christian Nation.'"

48 Kaunda, "Day of Prayer."

49 See, for instance, "Church Mother Bodies Praise Lungu for not Interfering in HH's Case," *Lusaka Times*, April 18, 2017, accessed March 1, 2019, https://www.lusakatimes.com/2017/04/18/three-church-mother-bodies-praise-lungu-not-interfering-hhs-case/; "Church Mother Bodies Welcome Government's Move to Build the 7,500-seater House of Prayer," *Lusaka Times*, October 28, 2015, accessed March 1, 2019, https://www.lusakatimes.com/2015/10/28/church-mother-bodies-welcome-governments-move-to-build-the-7500-seater-house-of-prayer/.

14

POLITICAL ENGAGEMENT, IDENTITY, AND THE UNITED CHURCH OF ZAMBIA

Joseph Darius Simukonda
Jonathan Kangwa

Introduction

The mission statement of the United Church of Zambia (UCZ) affirms its commitment to spreading the Christian message of salvation to Zambians in order to improve their economic, social, and spiritual wellbeing.[1] The UCZ is the largest Protestant church in Zambia, which was established on January 16, 1965 at Mindolo mission in Kitwe as an amalgamation of The Church of Barotseland, established by the Paris Evangelical Missionary Society of France, the Zambia District of the Methodist Church, established by the Methodist Missionary Society of Britain, and the United Church of Central Africa in Rhodesia that incorporated the churches established by the Church of Scotland and the London Missionary Society. As a union church, the UCZ has inherited colonial or missionary theology.[2]

1 United Church of Zambia (UCZ) Strategic Plan 2016–2020 (UCZ Synod, 2016), 20.

2 Koffi Appiah-Kubi and Torres Sergio argue that "missionary theology is centered on the conversion of the infidel and making of the new elite. The essential task of the missionary is to heal, convert, and Christianise people. It is to proclaim the gospel, to be the herald of Christ's good news." To take the argument further, Chrispin Mbalazi argues that "missionary theology taught that the reign of God was an afterlife, a future hope . . . in missionary theology the reign of God had no relevance, but later when this life was no more." Jonathan Kangwa adds that "the missionaries who had come to Zambia from Europe were influenced by the Enlightenment. They emphasised a perceived dichotomy between the spiritual and the secular. . .. This suggests that, the missionaries' missiological approach was spiritually oriented to an extent where Africans were told to abandon their

This chapter analyzes the political engagement of the UCZ in Zambia and how the church seeks to create its Christian identity.[3] It employs decolonial public theology espoused by Chammah J. Kaunda as an analytical tool. Kaunda suggests that decolonial public theology is a paradigm shift from academia centered epistemology to the "epistemology of margins seeking to decolonize the publics."[4] We will return to this below. What this entails is that, decolonial public theology seeks to utilize the existential challenges of the margins in the context of oppression and exploitation perpetrated by either religious or political elites.[5] Paulo Freire appends that, the experiences of the oppressed should be the starting point of transformation.[6] Using decolonial public theology, the chapter analyzes

---

culture." He further notes that "African converts to Christianity were taught to abandon their traditional culture and concentrate on preparing their souls for life in heaven. They were made to believe that Christians are mere pilgrims on earth. Therefore, economic, social, and political matters are of little importance to them because their real home is heaven." Kangwa Mabuluki affirms thus, "Generally, the content of most UCZ Christian Education programs reflects a very strong focus on spiritual formation. There is only a scanty and ineffective civic or social transformation component. In fact, in some teaching materials, especially children and youth materials, the social and civic component is totally missing." See Koffi Appiah-Kubi and Torres Sergio, *African Theology En-route* (Maryknoll: Orbis, 1979), 24; Chrispin Mbalazi, *Theological Renewal and the Role of the Church in Social Reconstruction of Zambia* (MA Dissertation, Cape Town University, South Africa, 1999), 78; Jonathan Kangwa, "Pentecostalisation of Mainline Churches in Africa: The Case of the United Church of Zambia," *The Expository Times* 127, no. 12 (2016): 573–584; Kangwa Mabuluki, *The Role of the Churches in Educating People for the Development of Democracy: The Case of the United Church of Zambia* (PhD diss., University of KwaZulu-Natal, South Africa, 2015), 142.

3 Rowan Williams explains that Christian identity entails that we are to reveal, like the Jewish people, that God is a *God of justice, impartial, universal, and a God who is free to forgive offences.* He further explains that Christian identity is not just about relations with other human beings and our labors to shape those relationships according to justice and mercy. Christian identity is 'liturgical' in both senses, the work of a people, a community, showing God to each other and to the world around them, in daily action and in worship. . .Christian identity is to belong in a place that Jesus defines for us. By living in that place, we come in some degree to share his identity, to bear his name and to be in the same relationships he has with God and with the world. See Rowan Williams, *What We Mean by Christian Identity*, World Council of Churches Address, 2006, accessed November 22, 2018, aoc2013.brix.fatbeehive.com.

4 Chammah J. Kaunda, "Baptising Zambia's Edgar Changwa Lungu: Critiquing the Utilization of the Declaration of Zambia during the Presidential Campaign of 2016," *International Journal of Public Theology*, no. 13 (2019): 72–93.

5 Kaunda, "Baptising Zambia's Edgar Changwa Lungu," 75.

6 Paulo Freire, *Pedagogy of the Oppressed*, trans. Myra Bergman Ramos (London: Penguin Books, 1996[1970]).

selected pastoral letters and press statements of the UCZ generated from the Minutes of the Synod Executive and full Council meetings between 2012 and 2017. The theory will help in the decolonization of the UCZ's public engagement with political issues in Zambia.

This chapter utilized qualitative method in the generation and analysis of the relevant information on the topic under consideration. This involved the use of interviews from Synod high-profiled ministers. The chapter will also utilize document analysis as a method of data collection where selected pastoral letters and press statements of the UCZ will be generated from Minutes of the Synod Executive and full Council meetings between 2012 and 2017 to ascertain how the UCZ engages with politics in Zambia and how it seeks to create its Christian identity. The qualitative method is engaged with using decolonial public theology in order to demonstrate that the UCZ could create its missional Christian identity that seeks justice in the public space.

Unpacking Decolonial Public Theology

Decolonial public theology entails that the African theologians should begin to critically reflect on God's mission of justice, liberation, and decolonization of those publics.[7] Further, the praxis of a decolonial public theology seeks to analyze power relations in publics. It critiques dominant ideologies that privilege a sector of society at the expense of the masses.[8] Nico Koopman emphasizes this by inviting Christians to critically consider how they should engage in public life. He asserts that Christians' engagement in public life should be informed by the problems that surround God's people in Africa that range from lack of pure drinking water, food, healthcare and housing, education and employment, safety and security, peace and prosperity, well-being and wellness in body, soul, and spirit.[9] In the same vein, Freire points out that dehumanization is not historical but is something that we experience in the present time.[10] And this recognition enables one to begin the process of humanization that should be informed by decolonial public theology.

---

7 Kaunda, "Baptising Zambia's Edgar Changwa Lungu," 75; See also, Chammah J. Kaunda and Mutale Kaunda, "Mobilising Religious Assets for Social Transformation: A Theology of Decolonial Reconstruction Perspective on the Ministry of National Guidance and Religious Affairs (MNGRA) in Zambia," *Religions* 9, no. 176 (2018):1–13.

8 Kaunda, "Baptising Zambia's Edgar Changwa Lungu," 75.

9 Nico N. Koopman, "Some Contours for Public Theology in South Africa," *International Journal of Practical Theology* 14, no. 9 (2010): 123–138.

10 Freire, *Pedagogy of the Oppressed* 44.

To further detail on the intentionality of decolonial public theology, Kaunda remarks that it is "critical of State Theology,"[11] "that perpetuate[s] values and interests that serve the state in ways which become so taken for granted that they form the citizens' very subjective systems of values and presupposition, and hence inform their thoughts and behavior in subtle and penetrating ways."[12] The Kairos document underscores,

> Decolonial public theology does not baptise the status quo but advocates for justice in society.. . . it speaks against injustices publicly for the emancipation of the oppressed. It is knowledgeable of what is happening, analyses what is happening and then interprets what is happening in the light of the gospel.. . . this means that the starting point for decolonial public theology is our experience of the present experience of oppression, tyranny, conflicts, crisis, and struggle.[13]

Decolonial public theology demands a social analysis of the complex power relations within the public domain. It seeks to promote a political project of decolonization of the publics in the name of the common good.[14] This argument makes it evident that the emphasis of decolonial public theology on the common good is consistent with the teachings of Jesus Christ who came to serve humanity (John 10:10). Hendricks emphasizes thus:

> The example of Jesus tells us that we must be passionately and unwaveringly proactive in our struggle against practices, structures, systems, and attitudes of unjust entitlement that stand in the way of a fully inclusive and loving society. We must respond with passion and righteous anger to every barrier that excludes anyone from the fullest fruits of our nation's bounty. Jesus's example shows us that like his anger, our own anger should propel us to go to the seat of unjust power, be it the temple, the church, the state house, or the White House, and give our collective testimony against today's priests of oppression that we the people are neither unclean nor unworthy, and

---

11 Kaunda, "Baptising Zambia's Edgar Changwa Lungu," 76; State theology was defined by theologians in the apartheid regime in South Africa as simply "the theological justification of the status quo with its racism, capitalism, and totalitarianism. State theology blesses injustice, canonises the will of the powerful, and reduces the poor to passivity, obedience, and apathy." See, The Kairos Document, *A Challenge to the Church: A Theological Comment on Political Crisis in South Africa*, 1986, 37–80. Available at Ujamaa Centre for Biblical and Theological Community Development and Research, University of KwaZulu-Natal, accessed August 11, 2018, http://ujamaa.ukzn.ac.za.

12 Kaunda, "Baptising Zambia's Edgar Changwa Lungu," 76.

13 Kairos Document, "Challenge to the Church," 63.

14 Kaunda, "Baptising Zambia's Edgar Changwa Lungu," 76.

therefore we will accept neither second-class status nor second-class treatment.[15]

Hendricks would agree with Kaunda that Jesus employed decolonial public theology by challenging the privileged for the sake of the common good of everyone in society. And as Marshal observes, "supremely characteristic of Jesus was his orientation to the social margins—the destitute, the weak, social outcasts, women, children, Samaritans, the physically deformed, those in prison, the sick, and the possessed."[16] Jesus advocated for an inclusive and egalitarian community. Drawing insights from decolonial public theology, this chapter will therefore interrogate the problematic mode of public theological engagement within the UCZ that has constrained its positive contribution to politics in Zambia. The utilization of decolonial public theology is well fitted to assess the UCZ's public engagement because it seeks to "critique the religious conservatism that cooperates with political elites to maintain the status quo."[17]

UCZ's Political Engagement

The involvement of the UCZ in politics in Zambia can be seen in its pastoral letters, Royal Address to the President of the Republic of Zambia, and some statements made as a response to the political happenings in the country. In 2012, the Synod of the UCZ raised the issue of basic needs and high levels of unemployment, especially of the youth, in the Royal Address to the President.

> Your Excellency, the Synod recognized your effort in wooing investors to Zambia as one way of creating jobs. However, we are very concerned about the non-availability of sufficient job opportunities for our people in spite of the efforts. We believe that parties are elected into office to, among other things, provide job opportunities for the citizens so that they can look after themselves and their families, advance their lives and contribute to the nation. We call on your government to be in a hurry to create job opportunities for our people by ensuring that private and public investments and projects are realigned to provide for sustainable, meaningful, and long-term jobs. In addition, the processes of empowering Zambians to own businesses needs [*sic*] to be simplified. Connected to this is the fact that our people want to have their basic human needs met. As government, the inadequacy and cost of basic needs for our people is something

15 Obery M. Hendricks, *The Politics of Jesus: Rediscovering the True Revolutionary Nature of Jesus' Teachings and How They have been Corrupted* (New York: Doubleday, 2006), 166.

16 Chris Marshal, "A Prophet of God's Justice: Reclaiming the Political Jesus," *Stimulus* 14, no. 3 (2006): 35.

17 Kaunda, "Baptising Zambia's Edgar Changwa Lungu," 77.

> that should raise concern and calls for greater effort to ensure that our people have access to plentiful and affordable health care, shelter, transport, education, food, and drink.[18]

In the same letter, the UCZ Synod appealed to the president to empower the youth with employment. The Synod reminded the government that unemployment resulted in increased social evils such as street thefts, defilement, and rape of young children and women.[19]

In 2013, the UCZ Synod Executive wrote a letter to the president in which two concerns were raised.

> The UCZ is concerned with inadequate medical supplies, trained medical personnel, and the poor attitude of some of the available staff in these institutions; further, we are concerned with the food security of the nation which was being threatened by the partial drought and pest attacks experienced in the season. We appeal to you, the President, to ensure that food stocks available in the country are managed prudently.[20]

In 2014, the UCZ Synod Executive wrote a congratulatory message to the president in which it also raised its concerns regarding the depreciation of the local currency and non-adherence to the country's tax laws by some investors.

> We congratulate you, your Excellency for the massive development projects, which your government has embarked on resulting in job creation. Notably, road construction, creation of new districts, and opening of new mines. . . we are concerned about the fluctuation of the currency against the major foreign currencies, and hope that the government would do everything possible to correct the situation.. . . As a church, we have noticed from media revelations that there was evasion of tax by some foreign mine entities working in Zambia, which was sad reading. The church therefore, appeals to the government to ensure that foreign company owners are made to comply with existing tax laws.[21]

The depreciation of the currency continued in 2015. The cost of living continued to increase. The UCZ Synod continued to write letters to the government to remind them to put measures in place to address the

---

18 UCZSEM, Minutes of the 26th Full Synod Council Meeting of the UCZ, Diakonia Centre in Kabwe, June 9–15, 2012, 244.

19 UCZSEM, Minutes of the 26th Full Synod Council Meeting, 2012, 244.

20 UCZSEM, Minutes of the Synod Executive Meeting of the UCZ, Diakonia Centre, Kabwe, April 13–17, 2013, 64.

21 UCZSEM, Minutes of the Synod Executive Meeting of the UCZ, Diakonia Centre, Kabwe, 13-17, April, 2014, 243–244.

decline of the economy.[22] In 2016, the UCZ Synod made a press statement that addressed the political situation in the country.

> The Synod of the UCZ is satisfied by efforts by the Government to improve transport and infrastructure, but cautions against contracting unsustainable debt and a return to the debt trap of the past caused by a new form of structural adjustment; the Synod meeting calls on the government to protect the poorest, weakest, and most vulnerable in society; the Synod urges the government to provide an enabling environment for both employment-creators and seekers. The meeting regrets that the macroeconomic growth enjoyed by Zambia over the past decade has not been translated into increased formal employment. Therefore, the church urges the government to take further steps towards greater diversification of the economy with less dependence on the export of raw agricultural or mineral primary commodities, but to add value to them here at home.[23]

Apart from the press statement, a Royal Address to the president was also made in which the UCZ Synod thanked the government for the slight appreciation of the Kwacha, controlling of smuggling of maize and mealie-meal, and the improvement of the nation's transport, communications, and infrastructure. The letter went on to appeal to the government to reduce the gap between the rich and the poor and curb political violence that was being fueled by poverty. The government was reminded that the youth were patronizing political rallies as a way of earning a living. The letter also cautioned the government against contracting unsustainable economic debt in order to avoid a return to the debt trap of structural adjustment of the past.[24]

The same letter condemned the use of austerity as an ideology and an economic tool in the country. The UCZ Synod appealed to the government to protect the weak, the poor, and the vulnerable. The letter concluded by thanking the government for the introduction of a minimum wage of K750 and requested that it be reviewed considering that the Lusaka Basic Needs Basket then stood at almost K5,000 per month.[25]

More recently in 2017, the UCZ Synod Executive addressed the president through a Royal Letter stating that "We, as a church will stand alongside the government in care and support for the marginalized in society and to work at redistributing wealth and power to address the present

22 UCZSEM, Minutes of the Synod Executive Meeting of the UCZ, 2015, 73.

23 UCZSFCM, Minutes of the 28th Full Synod Meeting of the UCZ, 2016, 269.

24 UCZSFCM, Minutes of the 28th Full Synod Meeting of the UCZ, 2016, 269.

25 UCZSFCM, Minutes of the 28th Full Synod Meeting of the UCZ, 2016, 269.

imbalances in our nation."[26] The UCZ also brought to the attention of the president the fall in the price of maize that had hit many subsistence farmers' income and risked increasing poverty in the rural areas. The church requested that a just price of maize be set and paid to these farmers.[27] In light of this, we can see that the UCZ Synod engages with the state through pastoral letters, Royal Addresses, and media statements. A critical analysis of these pastoral letters and statements show how the UCZ engages with the public and how it seeks to create its Christian identity in the Zambian political environment.

The UCZ and its Prophetic Role in Politics

In the preceding section, we have seen how the UCZ engages with politics in Zambia through pastoral letters and press statements. Looking at these letters and press statements, one would think that the UCZ is on course with its prophetic task given that the president is engaged with various political issues from time to time. However, utilizing decolonial public theology the UCZ's mode of public engagement does not address oppressive social and political structures adequately. The approach that the UCZ uses can be referred to as prophecy accomplished from within because it fails to promote justice in the public space. As decolonial public theology emphasizes, real prophetic task must be critical of inequalities that are constructed by elites in society. Analyzing the UCZ's approach to politics in Zambia, it is evident that its position is compromised and this has made the citizenry lose confidence in it and labelled it as a church of the state. As Kaunda observes, "the church loses its authenticity when its missio-political consciousness becomes compromised and, at worse, reduced to an instrument for perpetuating the reigning political ideology."[28] Such a scenario can make the church become "no more than an extension of the government institutions."[29] The other doubt that we have on the UCZ's mode of public engagement that relies on letter writing is that there is no certainty as to whether these letters actually reach the president. One of our respondents in the UCZ Synod hierarchy stated,

> The pastoral letters are compromised and I doubt if at all they even reach the president, but if they do, the question is how many Zambians will access that information that is contained in those letters so that they can say this is what the UCZ has said on such and such a matter. Further, if the letters do reach the president, I doubt if

---

26 UCZSEM, Minutes of the Synod Executive Meeting of the UCZ, Diakonia Centre, Kabwe, November 12–13, 2017, 68.

27 UCZSEM, Minutes of the Synod Executive Meeting of the UCZ, 2017, 68.

28 Kaunda, "Baptising Zambia's Edgar Changwa Lungu," 91.

29 Kaunda, "Baptising Zambia's Edgar Changwa Lungu," 91.

> the president has ever responded to those letters. So, what I have seen in many years that I have been in ministry is that the UCZ seems not to be doing well in her prophetic ministry.[30]

The other concern regarding the UCZ's mode of political engagement of letter writing is that there is no evidence of feedback from the government and the president in particular. This was confirmed by one of our respondents in the UCZ Synod hierarchy who stated: "I am not too sure because I have not carried out a research to find out if at all those letters reach the president, all I have seen in the Synod meetings is that the meeting would request for letter writers to help and write a letter to the president but for the response from the president, I have not seen that."[31]

From the foregoing, it is obvious that the UCZ does not receive any feedback from the president on the concerns raised on political matters, thus, it can be deduced that the UCZ's prophetic political involvement is done from within the walls of the church. Its approach is ineffective and futile as it does not confront social and political structures that deny the poor masses the fullness of life. Besides, the clergy and lay leaders who work with people in communities that are poverty-stricken do not know anything about the letters written to the president. Thus, an inference can be made that the writing of pastoral letters and Royal Addresses are merely academic exercises. This kind of prophetic engagement needs to be decolonized. Just like decolonial public theology seeks justice in public space, social activists and scholars such as Chang-Hoon Kim argue that prophetic preaching should always recognize that the church is not a closed community. The church can influence or be influenced by the society of which it is a part.[32] Kim adds,

> Prophetic preaching on social issues should not remain in the realm of the church. Prophetic preaching should often proclaim God's will on current issues in the public market-place for the purpose of awakening the consciousness of the nation. For this, preachers can visit local or national governments or utilize the mass media.[33]

Kim underscores that all social and political events that happen on the earth are related to God who rules over the world.[34] Therefore, the prophetic ministry of the church should take the issues arising from the context seriously as espoused by decolonial public theology. The church should not be separated from the community and focus solely on spiritual

30 UCZSOM4, December 16, 2016, Interview, Kitwe, Zambia.

31 UCZOM2, November 15, 2016, Interview, Kalulushi, Zambia.

32 Chang-Hoon Kim, "Prophetic Preaching as Social Preaching," *Evangelical Review of Theology* 30, no 2 (2006): 146.

33 Kim, "Prophetic Preaching," 147.

34 Kim, "Prophetic Preaching," 146.

matters. Matters affecting the wellbeing of the people in the community should be engaged with seriously. In keeping with Kim's observation and decolonial public theology, the Kairos Document developed in South Africa to dismantle apartheid is compelling. The document calls for transformative prophetic engagement in a political environment. According to the Kairos Document, transformative prophetic engagement is "a call to action and not a theoretical understanding of the signs of the times."[35] It calls for the church to be "critical of the *status quo* and calls for repentance and change."[36] The document reasons that "the prophetic ministry of the church confronts the evils of the time and speaks out against them in no uncertain terms. It denounces socioeconomic injustices and announces an inclusive society."[37] This is where the UCZ is failing. There has been no sustained effort to create her public Christian identity that is able to call a demon by name. Utilizing decolonial public theology, the UCZ can make use of its presence in every part of the country to conscientize people about political machinations that deny them the fullness of life. Korten notes,

> Informed by a theory of action that identifies an inadequate mobilizing vision as the root cause of contemporary development failure . . . the focus of the fourth generation is on communication of ideas and information through the mass media, newsletters, recorded media, school curricula, major media events, study groups, and social networks of all types to energise voluntary action by people both within and outside their formal organizations in support of social transformation.[38]

Considering the above, it can be argued that true prophetic engagement should be able to communicate ideas publicly so that the oppressed can be conscientized. In this manner, the poor are empowered to engage in demonstrations that may put pressure on the government and other institutions to re-visit certain policies that disadvantage the poor. So, the UCZ should endeavor to make its position known in the public, to expose systems responsible for the oppression of the Zambian people. The UCZ can learn from Jesus who embraced transformative public engagement as espoused by decolonial public theology. As Hendricks explains, Jesus's public engagement exposed powers. He called the Roman authorities "a destructive, demonic, unclean presence."[39] Like eighth century BCE

---

35 The Kairos Document, "Challenge to the Church," 63.

36 The Kairos Document, "Challenge to the Church," 63.

37 The Kairos Document, "Challenge to the Church," 64.

38 Korten, "Getting to the 21st Century," 121.

39 Hendricks, "Politics of Jesus," 147–148.

Jewish prophets, Jesus denounces the Roman authorities for oppressing the poor people. Hendricks underscores,

> In perfect prophetic fashion, Jesus causes the demon to be known by its name. He speaks as a prophet should speak: boldly and on point, identifying the demon in no uncertain terms. He blames the people's plight not on the victimised, but on the victimisers, the Roman legions. He cuts through all excuses, obfuscation, and mealy-mouthed explanations to tell the people the unvarnished truth.[40]

Taking into consideration what decolonial public theology entails, it is evident that transformative prophetic engagement should always side with the poor. Thus, the UCZ should endeavor to confront social and political powers in public space in order to "subvert the logic of subjugation, manipulation, and exploitation."[41] Utilizing decolonial public theology, the UCZ is hereby challenged to move from its uncritical public engagement of writing pastoral letters to the president that end up buried in Synod minutes. Instead, it should try to write open letters that can be accessed by citizens in newspapers, social media like Facebook, radio, television, and other forms of communication. This will enable the UCZ to be prophetically in solidarity with the poor in a real sense. Through the process of conscientization, the poor will "begin to see themselves as subjects of their own history, as being able to take their destiny in their own hands."[42]

Decolonizing the UCZ and its Identity as a Public Religion

The position of the UCZ on church-state relations is explained in Article 17(B) of the UCZ Constitution that states, "The UCZ shall have the right to be free in all spiritual matters from the direction or interference of any civil or military government."[43] The same constitution adds that, "The UCZ reserves the right to comment on matters of national interest without necessarily consulting any other body or authority."[44] In view of these constitutional provisions, the UCZ emphasizes its autonomy and its non-partisanship with regard to political engagement in Zambia. Although the constitution provides for the UCZ to be a prophetic church,

40 Hendricks, "Politics of Jesus," 147–148.

41 Kaunda, "Baptising Zambia's Edgar Changwa Lungu," 77.

42 C. Rowland, *The Cambridge Companion to Liberation Theology*, 2nded. (New York: Cambridge University Press, 2007), 19.

43 UCZ Constitution, *The Constitution of the United Church of Zambia* (Lusaka: Synod Publication, 2014), 30.

44 UCZ Constitution, *Constitution of the United Church of Zambia*, 30.

in practice the church embraces a cooperationist[45] type of church-state relations.[46] The UCZ rarely criticizes the government. It considers itself as a partner in development with the ruling government. Further, being critical of the ruling government is seen as taking sides with the opposition political parties and therefore being partisan.

First and foremost, we note that the UCZ has always been in support of the ruling government. The cordial relationship between the state and the UCZ can be traced back to precolonial times, when the missionaries were supported by the colonial government. Consequently, some missionaries supported the colonial project because they were sponsored by the colonial government. Given this background, the UCZ has inherited much from its forerunners with regard to church-state relations. Our respondent in the UCZ Synod hierarchy remarked,

> The prophetic voice of the church is weak; because as a church, we are still shaped after what was handed over to us by missionaries. Only now we are able to speak of theology in our own context, but initially we just adopted what had been handed down to us, that is, the kind of theology that respects the government so much that it works hand in hand with the government. So, one has to be very careful each time he/she wants to say something against the government. We have inherited a theology that supports the *status quo*. When you talk about the missionary societies that came to Zambia, they were supported by their government and therefore would not want to say anything against the government.[47]

In keeping with the above, it can be argued that the UCZ has taken a non-confrontational approach to national issues. The church tends to have closed-door meetings with politicians instead of doing this in the public space. The church believes in the notion of not criticizing politicians in the media. As one respondent remarked, "'come and counsel me in the office' is the kind of ministry that the UCZ has adopted. But then,

---

45 Carl Esbeck notes that the church and state are not opposed to each other. Both are in the service of human beings. So, between them there must be dialogue, cooperation, and solidarity. The church and state have a God-given mandate to reinforce each other in a symbiotic relationship. Although this mutual dependence between church and state is inevitable, each has a distinct role and is not to invade the jurisdiction assigned to the other within the created order. See Carl H. Esbeck, "Five Views of Church-State Relations in Contemporary American Thought," *BYU Law Review* 1, no. 2 (1986): 398.

46 Raymond Kumalo refers to this as "uncritical acceptance of church-state relation" where the state and the church is one and the same thing. See Raymond S. Kumalo, "'The People Shall Govern': The Role of the Church in the Development of Participatory Democracy in South Africa," *Scriptura* 101 (2009): 246–258.

47 UCZUL1, November 22, 2016, Interview, Kitwe, Zambia.

it is high time we came out of it and make the church's prophetic voice be heard and noticed in Zambia, and work toward liberating the poor from their predicaments."[48]

Second, we note that the UCZ never sides with the opposition political party even when it is right in advocating for the rights of the poor in the country. In many cases, the UCZ has been pro-government. This is a result of the precedent of our fathers and mothers who were even co-opted in government. When Zambia gained political independence in 1964, some church leaders took up appointments in government. Marja Hinfelaar notes,

> Most church leaders at independence supported the UNIP government and as such, a number of clergies were promoted to high public offices. For example, Rev. Jalabafwa Chipeso of the United Church of Zambia (UCZ) became Lusaka Rural District Governor, Rev. Merfyn Temple also of the UCZ worked in the Land Resettlement Office, while his colleague Rev. Mwape sat on the National Commission on One-Party State in 1972.[49]

Apart from some church leaders getting jobs in government, the UCZ gets material benefits from the government. Politicians support massive building projects undertaken by the church. The church has thus been passive because it is one with the government. It is difficult to bite the finger that is feeding.

Third, the UCZ has not clearly defined its prophetic ministry with regard to church-state relations. The church has not drawn a line as to when it should support the government and when it should voice out and reject certain things that the government is doing that disadvantage the poor. Church leaders and ministers feel their responsibility is to always support the government of the day, even if it has become oppressive and its policies are not pro-poor. The UCZ should learn to "confront evils perpetrated by the government, for that is why the church is there in the first place—to be a voice for the voiceless."[50]

Another example to demonstrate how the UCZ has compromised the nonpartisan provision of its constitution is the directive from the Ministry of Religious Affairs and National Guidance contained in a letter dated October 8, 2018. In this letter, the UCZ is asked by the government to

---

48 UCZUL3, November 22, 2016, Interview, Kitwe, Zambia.

49 Marja Hinfelaar, "Legitimizing Powers: The Political Role of the Roman Catholic Church, 1991–1992," in *One Zambia, Many Histories: Towards a History of Postcolonial Zambia*, ed. Gewald Jan-Bart, Marja Hinfelaar, and Macola Giacomo (Leiden: Brill, 2008), 131.

50 UCZSOM3, December 3, 2016, Interview, Mufulira, Zambia.

spearhead national prayers for reconciliation held on October 18, 2018.[51] While it is good for the church to pray for peace and reconciliation in the country, the problem was that the prayers were organized by the ruling party to prevent the opposition party from criticizing the government for its failure to improve the economy. From the preceding, we can argue that the UCZ's prophetic position, which is well articulated in its constitution, has been underplayed as a result of the church adapting "State Theology"[52] and "Church Theology"[53] as espoused in the Kairos Document of South Africa.

In view of the above, the point we are stressing here is that the prophetic voice of the UCZ has been compromised because of some traditions received from missionaries who adopted a cooperationist model of church-state relations. The UCZ in practice seems to propose a position whereby there is no confrontation between the church and political powers. This approach has made the church to keep silent on a number of national issues affecting the majority Zambians. This passivity is an attempt for the UCZ to maintain its cordial relationship with the state. How then should the UCZ engage with national political issues? As already noted, embracing a decolonial public theology may enable the church to address political and economic issues adequately.

Contours of Decolonial Public Theology for UCZ

Decolonial public theology of the church should be rooted in a life-giving Christian theology of transformation. As liberation theologians help us understand, the starting point of a life-giving theology of transformation in the context of poverty is "the perception of scandals" in the context of

---

51 Ministry of Religious Affairs and National Guidance, Letter to the United Church of Zambia to host prayers (October 8, 2018).

52 State theology was defined by theologians in the apartheid regime in South Africa as simply "the theological justification of the status quo with its racism, capitalism, and totalitarianism. State theology blesses injustice, canonizes the will of the powerful, and reduces the poor to passivity, obedience, and apathy. See, The Kairos Document, "Challenge to the Church," 49–53.

53 Church theology is a theology that is aware of the prevailing circumstances in society but fails to engage in an in-depth analysis of the signs of the time. Although it uses ideas from Christian tradition, it uncritically applies them to the context. Church theology lacks social analysis. In the context of South Africa in the apartheid regime, church theology tended to make use of the absolute principles of reconciliation, negotiations, non-violence, and peaceful solutions and applied them indiscriminately and uncritically to all situations. Thus, church theology pays very little attention to analyzing what is actually happening in society and why it is happening. It fails to develop a social analysis that would enable it to understand the mechanics of injustice and oppression. See, The Kairos Document, "Challenge to the Church," 55–60.

poverty and discrimination where people die of hunger and disease despite being in the midst of abundant resources.[54] The theological motivation for the church to denounce injustice and any form of discrimination is found in the fact that "the biblical God is fundamentally a living God, the author and sustainer of all life."[55] Jesus Christ identified himself with the marginalized. He made a personal option for the poor and the socio-political outcasts.[56]

As a form of liberation theology, decolonial public theology is transformative and reconstructive. It engages social and political structures that perpetuate injustice and discrimination at three levels: the social, the individual, and the religious.[57] It does this to promote social reconstruction and transformation for the well-being of the citizenry as espoused by a decolonial reconstruction theology that stipulates that transformational theology should be able to engage "in the process of decolonizing, liberating, and redesigning the existing, but dysfunctional and colonial-shaped structures."[58] It is for this reason that the church should protest against social structures that contribute to "collective oppression, exclusion, and marginalization."[59] The church should hold politicians accountable for failure to deliver good social services to the people. For example, instead of merely praying for the patients of cholera, the church should challenge the government to deliver clean water, social amenities, and improved medical facilities to the citizens.[60] As Kaunda and Kaunda emphasize, religion in Zambia should be seen as national spiritual capital for social consciousness raising that will be able to challenge the dominant political thought.[61]

54 Leonardo Boff and Clodovis Boff, *Introducing Liberation Theology*, trans. Paul Burns (Maryknoll, NY: Orbis Books, 1987), 2.

55 Boff and Boff, "Introducing Liberation Theology," 44.

56 Boff and Boff, "Introducing Liberation Theology," 44.

57 See Boff and Boff, "Introducing Liberation Theology," 3.

58 Kaunda and Kaunda, "Mobilising Religious Assets," 2–3.

59 Boff and Boff, "Introducing Liberation Theology," 3.

60 Chammah J. Kaunda and Mutale M. Kaunda have argued that prayer that is "situated in the public spaces has the potential to challenge the status quo and promote the rearrangement of social norms, love-driven politics, and the religious, economic, and cultural values of a particular community." They emphasize that prayer should act as "the power of the weak" and foster "a spirituality of resistance that could bring about a new social consciousness and lead to authentic political transformation," See Chammah J. Kaunda and Mutale M. Kaunda, "An Announcement of a New Spiritual Dispensation: Pentecostalism and Nationalism of Prayer in Zambia," *Journal of Theology for Southern Africa* 161 (2018): 74–75.

61 Kaunda and Kaunda, "Mobilising Religious Assets," 2.

Decolonial public theology focuses on addressing "injustice and denial of human rights."[62] This involves the process of conscientization. The church should help people to "develop their power to perceive critically the way they exist in the world in which they find themselves."[63] In this process, individual Christians, as citizens of the country begin "to see the world not as a static reality but as a reality in the process of transformation."[64] Through conscientization, the church empowers citizens to act towards sociopolitical transformation.

Decolonial public theology demands the church to engage with injustice and oppression at a religious level. It is a tool that helps the church to recognize injustice, oppression, and all that denies people the fullness of life, are social sins. Social sin is unacceptable as it is "contrary to the plan of the creator and to the honor that is due to him [God]."[65] Dehumanization of any form is a distortion of the image of God and God's intention for humans to have life in abundance.[66] The church should not spiritualize the oppression of people. It must identify the causes of poverty and oppression in order to embark on transformative action. Where the root cause of oppression is found to be in the social political structures, the church should be bold enough to denounce them in order to make "possible the pursuit of a fuller humanity."[67]

To sum up, a decolonial public theology that can enable the UCZ to do its prophetic ministry meaningfully should be rooted in God's salvific agenda. It must identify the root causes of injustice and oppression and inspire people by the power of the Holy Spirit to make concrete steps to denounce causes, be they structural, individual, or at a religious level. The UCZ should stay away from teachings and forms of spirituality that make its members to think that oppression will disappear on its own through skin-deep prayers. The church must "struggle to change structures" that deny people the abundant life that Jesus Christ would want them to have.[68]

Conclusion

The chapter has examined how the UCZ engages in politics and how it creates its Christian identity. It has shown that the UCZ's public engagement is informed by missionary theology. Using decolonial public theology, the chapter has unmasked how the UCZ's prophetic task has

---

62 Boff and Boff, "Introducing Liberation Theology," 3.

63 Freire, "Pedagogy of the Oppressed," 12.

64 Freire, "Pedagogy of the Oppressed," 12.

65 Boff and Boff, "Introducing Liberation Theology," 3.

66 Freire, "Pedagogy of the Oppressed," 44.

67 Freire, "Pedagogy of the Oppressed," 47.

68 Freire, "Pedagogy of the Oppressed," 50.

been compromised through pastoral letters and press statements that are buried eventually in Synod minutes. In short, the UCZ is seen by the citizenry as an extension institution of the government. For the UCZ to liberate itself and become a church that struggles with the downtrodden, decolonial public theology may help to deconstruct and reconstruct its theology so that it becomes a life-giving theology.